RESTful Java Web Servi

Third Edition

A pragmatic guide to designing and building RESTful APIs
using Java

Bogunuva Mohanram Balachandar

BIRMINGHAM - MUMBAI

RESTful Java Web Services

Third Edition

First published: November 2009

Second edition: September 2015

Third edition: November 2017

Production reference: 1151117

Published by Packt Publishing Ltd.
Livery Place
35 Livery Street
Birmingham
B3 2PB, UK.
ISBN 978-1-78829-404-1

www.packtpub.com

Credits

Author
Bogunuva Mohanram Balachandar

Reviewer
Mohamed Sanaulla

Commissioning Editor
Aaron Lazar

Acquisition Editor
Denim Pinto

Content Development Editor
Vikas Tiwari

Technical Editor
Madhunikita Sunil Chindarkar
Jash Bavishi

Copy Editor
Muktikant Garimella

Project Coordinator
Ulhas Kambali

Proofreader
Safis Editing

Indexer
Tejal Daruwale Soni

Production Coordinator
Arvindkumar Gupta

Cover Work
Arvindkumar Gupta

About the Author

Bogunuva Mohanram Balachandar works as associate director for a leading American multinational corporation, listed in NASDAQ-100, that provides digital, technology, consulting, and operations services. He has extensive experience in the design and development of multiple enterprise application integration projects, using various tools and technologies such as Oracle SOA Suite, Oracle Service Bus, Oracle AIA, IBM WebSphere Process Server, web services, RESTful services, Business Process Execution Language (BPEL), IBM WebSphere MQ, TIBCO EMS, Java, JMS, and Spring Integration.

He is certified in SOA, web services, and cloud technologies and has over 16 years of IT industry experience in software design and development. Prior to joining his current employer, he worked with IBM, Accenture, and Wipro.

Balachandar, in his current role, is responsible for designing the integration landscape for a leading bank.

Balachandar currently lives in London, UK with his wife, Lakshmi, and daughters, VeenaSri and NavyaSree.

Acknowledgments

There is a famous saying in India, *Matha, Pitha, Guru, Deivam*, which sets the order in which a person must show respect, starting with *Matha* (mother), and going on to *Pitha* (father), then *Guru* (teacher), and finally, *Deivam* (God).

First and foremost, I would like to thank my parents, Mr. BN Mohanram and Mrs. S Rajeswari, for laying the foundation of the core values required to become a responsible citizen. I have no words to explain the extensive support provided by them in every stage of my life; all I can say is that I am blessed to have them as my parents.

My teachers, Dr. SM Kannan and the late Dr. Sri Krishna, from KLN College of Engineering, incubated the desire for knowledge and innovation in me. I would like to thank them for their guidance and also for giving me opportunities on several occasions to interact with the young engineers of my college, be it as a guest lecturer or during brainstorming discussions on the latest technology trends.

"A woman not only protects herself but tirelessly takes care of her husband and preserves the family reputation." I would like to thank my wife, Mrs GL Lakshmi, for taking care of me and my family without any expectations. My special thanks to my daughters for sacrificing some of their play time so as not to disturb me while I wrote this book.

I would like to thank Packt for giving me this opportunity. My special thanks to Packt team members, Mr. Anurag Ghogre, Mr. Vikas Tiwari, Mr. Ulhas Kambali, and Mr. Denim Pinto for their extensive support whenever required. My sincere thanks to the technical reviewer, Mr. Mohamed Sanaulla, for detailed feedback on all the chapters and ensuring the quality of the content. My special thanks to my colleague Mr. Raja Malleswara Rao Pattamsetti for connecting me with Packt.

My sincere thanks to my elder brother, Mr. BM Karthikeyan, my relatives, and my friends for their unconditional support and well wishes.

Finally, I strongly believe all this has been possible only with the blessings of the Almighty. My thanks to the Almighty and I hope he brings peace and prosperity to this planet.

About the Reviewer

Mohamed Sanaulla is a software developer with more than 7 years of experience in developing enterprise applications and Java-based backend solutions for e-commerce applications.

His interests include enterprise software development, refactoring and redesigning applications, designing and implementing RESTful web services, troubleshooting Java applications for performance issues, and TDD.

He has a strong expertise in Java-based application development, ADF (JSF-based JavaEE web framework), SQL, PL/SQL, JUnit, designing RESTful services, Spring, Struts, Elasticsearch, and MongoDB. He is also a Sun Certified Java Programmer for the Java 6 platform. He is a moderator for `https://javaranch.com/`. He likes to share findings on his blog (`https://sanaulla.info`).

I would like to thank everyone who has helped me in the process of reviewing this book.

www.PacktPub.com

For support files and downloads related to your book, please visit www.PacktPub.com. Did you know that Packt offers eBook versions of every book published, with PDF and ePub files available? You can upgrade to the eBook version at www.PacktPub.com and as a print book customer, you are entitled to a discount on the eBook copy. Get in touch with us at service@packtpub.com for more details. At www.PacktPub.com, you can also read a collection of free technical articles, sign up for a range of free newsletters and receive exclusive discounts and offers on Packt books and eBooks.

https://www.packtpub.com/mapt

Get the most in-demand software skills with Mapt. Mapt gives you full access to all Packt books and video courses, as well as industry-leading tools to help you plan your personal development and advance your career.

Why subscribe?

- Fully searchable across every book published by Packt
- Copy and paste, print, and bookmark content
- On demand and accessible via a web browser

Customer Feedback

Thanks for purchasing this Packt book. At Packt, quality is at the heart of our editorial process. To help us improve, please leave us an honest review on this book's Amazon page at https://www.amazon.com/dp/1788294041.

If you'd like to join our team of regular reviewers, you can email us at customerreviews@packtpub.com. We award our regular reviewers with free eBooks and videos in exchange for their valuable feedback. Help us be relentless in improving our products!

Table of Contents

Preface

The World Wide Web (also known as WWW) has been the backbone of the information age, connecting distributed systems over networks. It has become an integral part of our day-to-day life; take, for example, reading a newspaper, checking the weather, searching for information via Google, or any other search engine. It is essential to note that all the information used by the systems is dispersed across the networks and transmitted via the WWW. Given the reach of the WWW, have you ever thought what are the architecture or design principles to be considered while developing an application for internet usage? How can you improve the scalability of a web application? With the advent of emerging technologies such as cloud, social media, and the Internet of Things, what considerations must be taken while developing a web application? I believe similar questions may have been in the mind of Roy Thomas Fielding. Roy Thomas Fielding's research on *Architectural Styles and the Design of Network-Based Software Architectures* (`http://www.ics.uci.edu/ ~fielding/pubs/dissertation/top.htm`) comes up with answers to these questions, with a novel architectural style for distributed hypermedia systems, popularly known as **RE**presentational **S**tate **T**ransfer, abbreviated to REST.

This book familiarizes the reader with the concepts of REST. It serves as a practical guide for developing web applications following the REST architectural style, using Java APIs. This book is organized with plenty of real-life examples each chapter to help the reader gain hands-on experience and boost their confidence in applying what they have learned.

What this book covers

Chapter 1, *Introducing the REST Architectural Style*, covers the REST software architectural style and the core architectural elements that form a RESTful system.

Chapter 2, *Java APIs for JSON Processing*, gives an overview of the JSON messaging format and the popular tools and frameworks around JSON.

Chapter 3, *Introducing the JAX-RS API*, introduces the JAX-RS APIs. This chapter will explain how we can build RESTful web services with the JAX-RS APIs.

Chapter 4, *Advanced Features in the JAX-RS APIs*, takes a deeper look into the advanced JAX-RS APIs, with many real-life use cases.

Chapter 5, *Introducing JAX-RS Implementation Framework Extensions*, discusses some of the very useful JAX-RS implementation framework extension APIs that are not yet a part of the JAX-RS standard.

Chapter 6, *Securing RESTful Web Services*, explores how to secure RESTful web services using different authentication and authorization techniques.

Chapter 7, *Description and Discovery of RESTful Web Services*, describes the popular solutions that are available today for describing, producing, consuming, and visualizing RESTful web services.

Chapter 8, *RESTful API Design Guidelines*, discusses best practices and design guidelines that developers will find useful while building RESTful web services.

Chapter 9, *The Role of RESTful APIs in Emerging Technologies*, discusses the applicability of the RESTful API in recent technology trends such as cloud, IoT, single-page applications, and open data protocol.

Appendix, *Useful Features and Techniques*, discusses on the tools needed for building and testing JAX-RS application with various packaging or deployment models. Also covers the technique to convert JPA models into OData-enabled RESTful web services.

What you need for this book

The examples discussed in this book were built using the following software and tools:

- The Java SE Development Kit 8, or newer versions
- NetBeans IDE 8.2 (with the Java EE bundle), or newer versions
- Glassfish Server 4.1, or newer versions
- Maven 3.2.3, or newer versions
- Oracle Database Express Edition 11g Release 2, or newer versions
- The HR sample schema that comes with the Oracle database
- The Oracle database JDBC driver (ojdbc7.jar or newer versions)

Detailed instructions for setting up all the tools required to run the examples used in this book are discussed in the Appendix, *Useful Features and Techniques*.

Who this book is for

This book is for Java developers who want to design and develop scalable and robust RESTful web services with the Java APIs. Contents are structured by keeping an eye on real life use cases from the RESTful API world and their solutions. Although the JAX-RS API solves many of the common RESTful web service use cases, some solutions are yet to be standardized as JAX-RS APIs. Keeping this in mind, a chapter is dedicated in this book for discussing extension APIs, which takes you beyond JAX-RS. This book also discusses the best practices and design guidelines for your REST APIs. In a nutshell, you will find this book useful while dealing with many real life use cases, such as dynamic resource configuration, message broadcasting with the server-sent event, HATEOAS, and so on.

Conventions

In this book, you will find a number of text styles that distinguish between different kinds of information. Here are some examples of these styles and an explanation of their meaning. Code words in text, database table names, folder names, filenames, file extensions, pathnames, dummy URLs, user input, and Twitter handles are shown as follows: "The `DynamicFeature` interface is executed at deployment time for each resource method."

A block of code is set as follows:

```
[{"departmentId":10,"departmentName":"IT","manager":"John Chen"},
{"departmentId":20,"departmentName":"Marketing","manager":"Ameya
    J"},
{"departmentId":30,"departmentName":"HR","manager":"Pat Fay"}]
```

New terms and **important words** are shown in bold. Words that you see on the screen, for example, in menus or dialog boxes, appear in the text like this: "Navigate to **Configurations** | **server-config** | **Security** | **Realms** | **File**."

Warnings or important notes appear like this.

Tips and tricks appear like this.

Reader feedback

Feedback from our readers is always welcome. Let us know what you think about this book-what you liked or disliked. Reader feedback is important for us as it helps us develop titles that you will really get the most out of. To send us general feedback, simply email feedback@packtpub.com, and mention the book's title in the subject of your message. If there is a topic that you have expertise in and you are interested in either writing or contributing to a book, see our author guide at www.packtpub.com/authors.

Customer support

Now that you are the proud owner of a Packt book, we have a number of things to help you to get the most from your purchase.

Downloading the example code

You can download the example code files for this book from your account at http://www.packtpub.com. If you purchased this book elsewhere, you can visit http://www.packtpub.com/support and register to have the files emailed directly to you. You can download the code files by following these steps:

1. Log in or register to our website using your email address and password.
2. Hover the mouse pointer on the **SUPPORT** tab at the top.
3. Click on **Code Downloads & Errata**.
4. Enter the name of the book in the **Search** box.
5. Select the book for which you're looking to download the code files.
6. Choose from the drop-down menu where you purchased this book from.
7. Click on **Code Download**.

Once the file is downloaded, please make sure that you unzip or extract the folder using the latest version of:

- WinRAR / 7-Zip for Windows
- Zipeg / iZip / UnRarX for Mac
- 7-Zip / PeaZip for Linux

The code bundle for the book is also hosted on GitHub at `https://github.com/PacktPublishing/RESTful-Java-Web-Services-Third-Edition`. We also have other code bundles from our rich catalog of books and videos available at `https://github.com/PacktPublishing/`. Check them out!

Errata

Although we have taken every care to ensure the accuracy of our content, mistakes do happen. If you find a mistake in one of our books-maybe a mistake in the text or the code-we would be grateful if you could report this to us. By doing so, you can save other readers from frustration and help us improve subsequent versions of this book. If you find any errata, please report them by visiting `http://www.packtpub.com/submit-errata`, selecting your book, clicking on the **Errata Submission Form** link, and entering the details of your errata. Once your errata are verified, your submission will be accepted and the errata will be uploaded to our website or added to any list of existing errata under the Errata section of that title. To view the previously submitted errata, go to `https://www.packtpub.com/books/content/support` and enter the name of the book in the search field. The required information will appear under the **Errata** section.

Piracy

Piracy of copyrighted material on the internet is an ongoing problem across all media. At Packt, we take the protection of our copyright and licenses very seriously. If you come across any illegal copies of our works in any form on the internet, please provide us with the location address or website name immediately so that we can pursue a remedy. Please contact us at `copyright@packtpub.com` with a link to the suspected pirated material. We appreciate your help in protecting our authors and our ability to bring you valuable content.

Questions

If you have a problem with any aspect of this book, you can contact us at `questions@packtpub.com`, and we will do our best to address the problem.

1
Introducing the REST Architectural Style

In this chapter, we will cover the **Representational State Transfer (REST)** software architectural style, as described in Roy Fielding's PhD dissertation. You may find a brief discussion on HTTP before getting into the details of REST. Once the base is set, we will be ready for the next step. We will then discuss the set of constraints, the main components, and the abstractions that make a software system RESTful. Here is the list of topics covered in this chapter:

- The REST architectural style
- Introducing HTTP
- The evolution of RESTful web services
- The core architectural elements of a RESTful system
- The description and discovery of RESTful web services
- Java tools and frameworks for building RESTful web services

The REST architectural style

REST is not an architecture; rather, it is a set of constraints that creates a software architectural style, which can be used for building distributed applications. A major challenge to the distributed applications is attributed to the diversity of systems in an enterprise offering silos of business information, as depicted in the following diagram:

You can read *Architectural Styles and the Design of Network-based Software Architectures, Roy Fielding, 2000,* which talks about the REST architectural style, by visiting
`http://www.ics.uci.edu/~fielding/pubs/dissertation/top.htm.`

Often, an enterprise demands simplified access and updates to data residing in different systems. Fielding arrived at REST by evaluating all the networking resources and technologies available for creating distributed applications. He observed that without any constraints, one may end up developing applications with no rules or limits that are hard to maintain and extend. After considerable research on building a better architecture for a distributed application, he ended up with the following constraints that define a RESTful system:

- **Client-server**: This constraint keeps the client and server loosely coupled. In this case, the client does not need to know the implementation details in the server, and the server is not worried about how the data is used by the client. However, a common interface is maintained between the client and server to ease communication.
- **Stateless**: There should be no need for the service to keep user sessions. In other words, each request should be independent of the others. This improves scalability, as the server does not need to manage the state across multiple requests, with some trade-off on the network performance.
- **Cacheable**: This constraint has to support a caching system. The network infrastructure should support a cache at different levels. Caching can avoid repeated round trips between the client and the server for retrieving the same resource.
- **Uniform interface**: This constraint indicates a generic interface to manage all the interactions between the client and server in a unified way, which simplifies and decouples the architecture. This constraint indicates that each resource exposed for use by the client must have a unique address and should be accessible through a generic interface. The client can act on the resources by using a generic set of methods.
- **Layered system**: The server can have multiple layers for implementation. This layered architecture helps to improve scalability by enabling load balancing. It also improves the performance by providing shared caches at different levels. Being the door to the system, the top layer can enforce security policies as well.
- **Code on demand**: This constraint is optional. This constraint indicates that the functionality of the client applications can be extended at runtime by allowing a code download from the server and executing the code. Some examples are the applets and the JavaScript code that get transferred and executed at the client side at runtime.

The following diagram illustrates a high-level architectural view of a RESTful system:

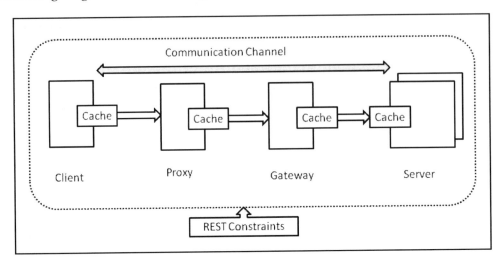

The preceding constraints do not dictate what kind of technology to use; they only define how the data is transferred between components and the benefits of the guidelines. Therefore, a RESTful system can be implemented in any available networking architecture. More importantly, there is no need for us to invent new technologies or networking protocols. We can very well use the existing networking infrastructures, such as the **World Wide Web (WWW)**, to create RESTful architectures. Consequently, a RESTful architecture is one that is maintainable, extendable, and distributed.

Before all the REST constraints were formalized, we already had a working example of a RESTful system—the web. Now, you may ask why introduce these RESTful requirements to web application development when it is agreed that the web is already RESTful.

Here is the answer, we first need to qualify what it means for the web to be RESTful. On one hand, the static web is RESTful because static websites follow Fielding's definition of a RESTful architecture. For instance, the existing web infrastructure provides caching systems, stateless connections, and unique hyperlinks to resources, where resources include all the documents available on every website, and the representation of these documents is already set by files being browser-readable (the HTML files, for example). Therefore, the static web is a system built in the REST-like architectural style. In simple words, we can say that REST leverages these amazing features of the web with some constraints.

On the other hand, traditional dynamic web applications have not always been RESTful because they typically break some of the outlined constraints. For instance, most dynamic applications are not stateless, as servers require tracking users through the container sessions or client-side cookie schemes. Therefore, we conclude that the dynamic web is not normally built in the REST-like architectural style.

 The REST architectural style is not specific to any protocol. However, as HTTP is the primary transfer protocol for the web today, REST over HTTP is the most common implementation. In this book, when we talk about REST, we refer to REST over HTTP, unless otherwise stated.

Now, you may be curious to learn more about a RESTful system. The rest of the chapter will definitely help you to know the internals. However, the topics on the RESTful system that we are going to discuss in the coming sections may need some basic knowledge of HTTP. So, let's take a crash course on HTTP to learn some basics and then proceed with our discussions thereafter. You can skip the next section if you are already familiar with HTTP.

Introducing HTTP

Hypertext Transfer Protocol (HTTP) is the foundation of data communication for WWW. To comprehend HTTP, it is essential to understand the etymology of hypertext. The major constraint of written text is its linearity, that is, not being able to easily reference other text that the user can easily access. Hypertext overcomes this constraint, with the concept of hyperlinks, which allows the user to easily navigate to the referenced section. HTTP is an application layer protocol that defines how hypertext messages are formatted, transmitted, and processed over the internet. Let's have a quick recap of HTTP in this section.

HTTP versions

HTTP has been consistently evolving over time. So far, there have been three versions. HTTP/0.9 was the first documented version, which was released in the year 1991. This was very primitive and supported only the GET method. Later, HTTP/1.0 was released in the year 1996 with more features and corrections for the shortcomings of the previous release. HTTP/1.0 supported more request methods such as GET, HEAD, and POST. The next release was HTTP/1.1 in the year 1999. This was a revision of HTTP/1.0. This version is in common use today.

HTTP/2 (originally named HTTP 2.0) was published in 2015. It is mainly focused on how the data is framed and transported between the client and server. It is currently supported by major browsers and as of May 2017, 13.7% of the top 10 million websites support HTTP/2.

To learn more about HTTP, you can refer to Wikipedia you may find the relevant page at
`http://en.wikipedia.org/wiki/Hypertext_Transfer_Protocol`.

Understanding the HTTP request-response model

HTTP works in a request-response manner. Let's take an example to understand this model better.

The following example illustrates the basic request-response model of communication between a web browser and a server over HTTP. The following sequence diagram illustrates the request and response messages sent between the client and server:

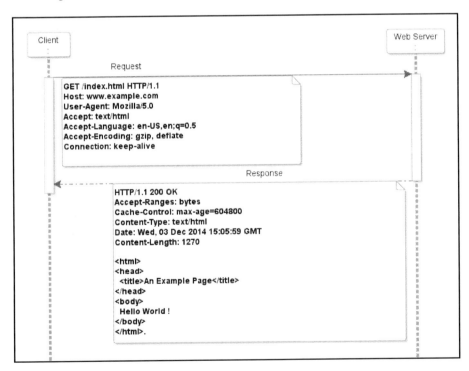

Here is the detailed explanation for the sequence of actions shown in the preceding diagram.

The user enters `http://www.example.com/index.html` in the browser and then submits the request. The browser establishes a connection with the server and sends a request to the server in the form of a request method (URI) and a protocol version, followed by a message containing the request modifiers, client information, and possible body content. The sample request looks as follows:

```
GET /index.html HTTP/1.1
Host: www.example.com
User-Agent: Mozilla/5.0
Accept: text/htmlAccept-Language: en-US,en;q=0.5
Accept-Encoding: gzip, deflate
Connection: keep-alive
```

Let's take a minute to understand the structure of the preceding message. The following code is what you see in the first lines of request in our example:

```
GET /index.html HTTP/1.1
```

The general format for the request line is an HTTP command, followed by the resource to retrieve and the HTTP version supported by the client. The client can be any application that understands HTTP, although this example refers to a web browser as the client. The request line and other header fields must end with a carriage return character followed by a line-feed character. In the preceding example, the browser instructs the server to get the `index.html` file through the `HTTP 1.1` protocol.

The rest of the information that you may see in the request message is the HTTP header values for use by the server. The header fields are colon-separated key-value pairs in the plain-text format, terminated by a carriage return and followed by a line feed character. The header fields in the request, such as the acceptable content types, languages, and connection type, are the operating parameters for an HTTP transaction. The server can use this information while preparing the response to the request. A blank line is used at the end of the header to indicate the end of the header portion in a request.

The last part of an HTTP request is the HTTP body. Typically, the body is left blank unless the client has some data to submit to the server. In our example, the body part is empty as this is a `GET` request for retrieving a page from the server.

So far, we have been discussing the HTTP request sent by the client. Now, let's take a look at what happens on the server when the message is received. Once the server receives the HTTP request, it will process the message and return a response to the client. The response is made up of the reply status code from the server, followed by the HTTP header and a response content body:

```
HTTP/1.1 200 OK
Accept-Ranges: bytes
Cache-Control: max-age=604800
Content-Type: text/html
Date: Wed, 03 Dec 2014 15:05:59 GMT
Content-Length: 1270

<html>
<head>
  <title>An Example Page</title>
</head>
<body>
  Hello World !
</body>
</html>.
```

The first line in the response is a status line. It contains the HTTP version that the server is using, followed by a numeric status code and its associated textual phrase. The status code indicates one of the following parameters: informational codes, success of the request, client error, server error, or redirection of the request. In our example, the status line is as follows:

```
HTTP/1.1 200 OK
```

The next item in the response is the HTTP response header. Similar to the request header, the response header follows the colon-separated name-value pair format terminated by a carriage return and line feed characters. The HTTP response header can contain useful information about the resource being fetched, the server hosting the resource, and some parameters controlling the client behavior while dealing with resource, such as content type, cache expiry, and refresh rate.

The last part of the response is the response body. Upon successful processing of the request, the server will add the requested resource in the HTTP response body. It can be HTML, binary data, image, video, text, XML, JSON, and so on. Once the response body has been sent to the requestor, the HTTP server will disconnect if the connection created during the request is not of the `keep-alive` type (using the `Connection: keep-alive` header).

URL = [http/ftp] + URI
　　　protocol　　　path

Uniform resource identifier

You may see the term **Uniform Resource Identifier (URI)** used very frequently in the rest of the chapter. A URI is a text that identifies any resource or name on the internet. One can further classify a URI as a **Uniform Resource Locator (URL)** if the text used for identifying the resource also holds the means for accessing the resource, such as HTTP or FTP. The following is one such example:

```
https://www.packtpub.com/application-development
```

> In general, all URLs such as `https://www.packtpub.com/application-development` are URIs.
>
> To learn more about URIs, visit
> `http://en.wikipedia.org/wiki/Uniform_resource_identifier`.

Understating the HTTP request methods

In the previous session, we discussed about the HTTP GET request method for retrieving a page from the server. More request methods similar to GET are available with HTTP, each performing specific actions on the target resource. Let's learn about these methods and their role in client-server communication over HTTP.

The set of common methods for HTTP/1.1 is listed in the following table:

Method	Description
GET	This method is used for retrieving resources from the server by using the given URI.
HEAD	This method is the same as the GET request, but it only transfers the status line and the header section without the response body.
POST	This method is used for posting data to the server. The server stores the data (entity) as a new subordinate of the resource identified by the URI. If you execute POST multiple times on a resource, it may yield different results.
PUT	This method is used for updating the resource pointed by the URI. If the URI does not point to an existing resource, the server can create the resource with that URI.
DELETE	This method deletes the resource pointed by the URI.

(Handwritten annotations: POST → insert new stuff; PUT → update (and can create))

TRACE	This method is used for echoing the contents of the received request. This is useful for the debugging purpose with which the client can see what changes (if any) have been made by the intermediate servers.
OPTIONS	This method returns the HTTP methods that the server supports for the specified URI.
CONNECT	This method is used for establishing a connection to the target server over HTTP.
PATCH	This method is used for applying partial modifications to a resource identified by the URI.

We may use some of these HTTP methods, such as GET, POST, PUT, and DELETE, while building RESTful web services in the later chapters.

Continuing our discussion on HTTP, the next section discusses the HTTP header parameter, which identifies the content type for the message body.

Representing content types using HTTP header fields

When we discussed the HTTP request-response model in the *Understanding the HTTP request-response model* section, we talked about the HTTP header parameters (the name-value pairs) that define the operating parameters of an HTTP transaction. In this section, we will cover the header parameter used for describing the content types present in the request and the response message body.

The Content-Type header in an HTTP request or response describes the content type for the message body. The Accept header in the request tells the server the content types that the client is expecting in the response body. The content types are represented using the internet media type. The internet media type (also known as the MIME type) indicates the type of data that a file contains. Here is an example:

```
Content-Type: text/html
```

This header indicates that the body content is presented in the html format. The format of the content type values is a primary type/subtype followed by optional semicolon-delimited attribute-value pairs (known as parameters).

The internet media types are broadly classified into the following categories on the basis of the primary (or initial) Content-Type header:

- text: This type indicates that the content is a plain text and no special software is required to read the contents. The subtype represents more specific details about the content, which can be used by the client for special processing, if any. For instance, Content-Type: text/html indicates that the body content is html, and the client can use this hint to kick off an appropriate rendering engine while displaying the response.

- multipart: As the name indicates, this type consists of multiple parts of independent data types. For instance, Content-Type: multipart/form-data is used for submitting forms that contain the files, non-ASCII data, and binary data.

- message: This type encapsulates more messages. It allows messages to contain other messages or pointers to other messages. For instance, the Content-Type: message/partial content type allows for large messages to be broken up into smaller messages. The full message can then be read by the client (user agent) by putting all the broken messages together.

- image: This type represents the image data. For instance, Content-Type: image/png indicates that the body content is a .png image.

- audio: This type indicates the audio data. For instance, Content-Type: audio/mpeg indicates that the body content is MP3 or other MPEG audio.

- video: This type indicates the video data. For instance, Content-Type: video/mp4 indicates that the body content is an MP4 video.

- application: This type represents the application data or binary data. For instance, Content-Type: application/json; charset=utf-8 designates the content to be in the **JavaScript Object Notation (JSON)** format, encoded with UTF-8 character encoding.

JSON is a lightweight data-interchange format. If you are not familiar with the JSON format, not to worry now; we will cover this topic in Chapter 2, *Java APIs for JSON Processing.*

We may need to use some of these content types in the next chapters while developing the RESTful web services. This hint will be used by the client to correctly process the response body.

 We are not covering all possible subtypes for each category of media types here. To refer to the complete list, visit the website of the **Internet Assigned Numbers Authority (IANA)** at
`http://www.iana.org/assignments/media-types/media-types.xhtml`.

The next topic, a simple but important one, is on HTTP status codes.

HTTP status codes

For every HTTP request, the server returns a status code indicating the processing status of the request. In this section, we will see some of the frequently used HTTP status codes. A basic understanding of status codes will definitely help us later while designing RESTful web services:

- `1xx Informational`: This series of status codes indicates informational content. This means that the request is received and processing is going on. Here are the frequently used informational status codes:
    - `100 Continue`: This code indicates that the server has received the request header and the client can now send the body content. In this case, the client first makes a request (with the `Expect: 100-continue` header) to check whether it can start with a partial request. The server can then respond either with `100 Continue` (OK) or `417 Expectation Failed` (No) along with an appropriate reason.
    - `101 Switching Protocols`: This code indicates that the server is OK for a protocol switch request from the client.
    - `102 Processing`: This code is an informational status code used for long running processing to prevent the client from timing out. This tells the client to wait for the future response, which will have the actual response body.

- `2xx Success`: This series of status codes indicates the successful processing of requests. Some of the frequently used status codes in this class are as follows:
    - `200 OK`: This code indicates that the request is successful and the response content is returned to the client as appropriate.
    - `201 Created`: This code indicates that the request is successful and a new resource is created.
    - `204 No Content`: This code indicates that the request is processed successfully, but there's no return value for this request. For instance, you may find such status codes in response to the deletion of a resource.
- `3xx Redirection`: This series of status codes indicates that the client needs to perform further actions to logically end the request. A frequently used status code in this class is as follows:
    - `304 Not Modified`: This status indicates that the resource has not been modified since it was last accessed. This code is returned only when allowed by the client via setting the request headers as `If-Modified-Since` or `If-None-Match`. The client can take appropriate action on the basis of this status code.
- `4xx Client Error`: This series of status codes indicates an error in processing the request. Some of the frequently used status codes in this class are as follows:
    - `400 Bad Request`: This code indicates that the server failed to process the request because of malformed syntax in the request. The client can try again after correcting the request.
    - `401 Unauthorized`: This code indicates that authentication is required for the resource. The client can try again with appropriate authentication.
    - `403 Forbidden`: This code indicates that the server is refusing to respond to the request even if the request is valid. The reason will be listed in the body content if the request is not a `HEAD` method.
    - `404 Not Found`: This code indicates that the requested resource is not found at the location specified in the request.
    - `405 Method Not Allowed`: This code indicates that the HTTP method specified in the request is not allowed on the resource identified by the URI.

- 408 Request Timeout: This code indicates that the client failed to respond within the time window set on the server.
- 409 Conflict: This code indicates that the request cannot be completed because it conflicts with some rules established on resources, such as validation failure.

- 5xx Server Error: This series of status codes indicates server failures while processing a valid request. Here is one of the frequently used status codes in this class:
  - 500 Internal Server Error: This code indicates a generic error message, and it tells that an unexpected error occurred on the server and that the request cannot be fulfilled.

 To refer to the complete list of HTTP status codes maintained by IANA, visit http://www.iana.org/assignments/http-status-codes/http-status-codes.xhtml.

With this topic, we have finished the crash course on HTTP basics. We will be resuming our discussion on RESTful web services in the next section. Take a deep breath and be ready for an exciting journey.

The evolution of RESTful web services

Before getting into the details of REST-enabled web services, let's take a step back and define what a web service is. Then, we will see what makes a web service RESTful.

A web service is one of the most popular methods of communication between the client and server applications over the internet. In simple words, web services are web application components that can be published, found, and used over the web. Typically, a web service has an interface describing the web service APIs, which is known as **Web Services Description Language (WSDL)**. A WSDL file can be easily processed by machines, which blows out the integration complexities that you may see with large systems. Other systems interact with the web service by using **Simple Object Access Protocol (SOAP)** messages. The contract for communication is driven by the WSDL exposed by the web service. Typically, communication happens over HTTP with XML in conjunction with other web-related standards.

What kind of problems do the web services solve? There are two main areas where web services are used:

- Many of the companies specializing in internet-related services and products have opened their doors to developers using publicly available APIs. For instance, companies such as Google, Yahoo, Amazon, and Facebook are using web services to offer new products that rely on their massive hardware infrastructures. Google and Yahoo offer their search services, Amazon offers its on-demand hosting storage infrastructure, and Facebook offers its platform for targeted marketing and advertising campaigns. With the help of web services, these companies have opened the door to the creation of products that did not exist some years ago.

- Web services are being used within enterprises to connect previously disjointed departments such as marketing and manufacturing. Each department or **Line Of Business (LOB)** can expose its business processes as a web service, which can be consumed by the other departments.

- By connecting more than one department to share information by using web services, we begin to enter the territory of **Service-Oriented Architecture (SOA)**. SOA is essentially a collection of services, each talking to one another in a well-defined manner, in order to complete relatively large and logically complete business processes.

All these points lead to the fact that web services have evolved as a powerful and effective channel of communication between client and server over a period of time. The good news is that we can integrate RESTful systems into a web service-oriented computing environment without much effort. Although you may have a fair idea of RESTful web services by now, let's see the formal definition before proceeding further.

What is a RESTful web service?

Web services that adhere to the REST architectural constraints are characterized as RESTful web services. Refer to the section, *The REST architectural style*, at the beginning of this chapter if you need a quick brush up of the architectural constraints for a RESTful system.

Remember that REST is not the system's architecture in itself, but it is a set of constraints that when applied to the system's design leads to a RESTful architecture. As our definition of a web service does not dictate the implementation details of a computing unit, we can easily incorporate RESTful web services to solve large-scale problems. We can even fully use RESTful web services in the larger umbrella of the SOA, given that it inherently meets the basic values of SOA, as depicted in the following image:

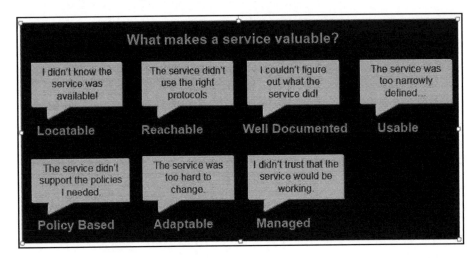

With this larger view of SOA, we begin to see how REST has the potential to impact the new computing models being developed.

 The RESTful web API or REST API is an API implemented using HTTP and the REST architectural constraints. Technically speaking, this is just another term for a RESTful web service. In this book, we will use these terms interchangeably.

The core architectural elements of a RESTful system

Having learned the basics of a RESTful system, you are now ready to meet more exciting concepts around REST. In this section, you will learn the core architectural elements that make a system RESTful.

Analogous to any software architecture, the REST architecture is also defined by a configuration of key architectural elements (components, connectors, and data) with a set of constraints, as shown in the following diagram:

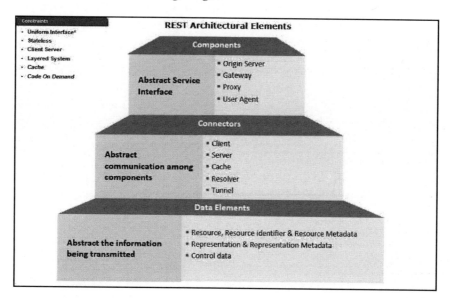

Data elements

The central feature that distinguishes the REST architectural style from other network-based styles is its emphasis on a uniform interface between components, which abstracts the information being transmitted. A uniform interface is fundamental to the architecture of any RESTful system. In plain words, this term refers to a generic interface to manage all interactions between a client and server in a unified way. All resources (or business data) involved in the client-server interactions are dealt with a fixed set of operations. The following are the core elements that form a uniform interface for a RESTful system:

- Resources and their identifiers
- The representation of resources
- Generic interaction semantics for the REST resources
- Self-descriptive messages
- Hypermedia as the engine of an application state

Let's look at these items in detail in the following section.

Resources

A RESTful resource is anything that is addressable over the web. By addressable, we mean resources that can be accessed and transferred between clients and servers. Subsequently, a resource is a logical, temporal mapping to a concept in the problem domain for which we are implementing a solution.

Here are some examples of REST resources:

- A news story
- The temperature in NY at 4:00 p.m. EST
- A tax return stored in the IRS database
- A list of code revision history in a repository such as SVN or CVS
- A student in a classroom in a school
- A search result for a particular item in a web index, such as Google

Even though a resource's mapping is unique, different requests for a resource can return the same underlying binary representation stored in the server. For example, let's say we have a resource within the context of a publishing system. Then, a request for the latest revision published and the request for revision number 12 will at some point in time return the same representation of the resource. In this example, the last revision is version 12. However, when the latest revision published is increased to version 13, a request to the latest revision will return version 13, and a request for the revision of version 12 will continue returning version 12. This implies that in a RESTful architecture, each resource can be accessed directly and independently, and sometimes, different requests may point to the same resource.

As we are using HTTP to communicate, we can transfer a variety of data types between clients and servers, as long as the data type used is supported by HTTP. For example, if we request a text file from CNN, our browser receives a text file. If we request a Flash movie from YouTube, our browser receives a Flash movie. The data is streamed in both cases over TCP/IP and the browser knows how to interpret the binary streams because of the `Content-Type` header present in the HTTP response header. Following this principle, in a RESTful system, the representation of a resource in the response body depends on the desired internet media type, which is specified within the request header sent by the client.

URI

A URI is a string of characters used to identify a resource over the web. In simple words, the URI in a RESTful web service is a hyperlink to a resource, and it is the only means for clients and servers to exchange representations.

The client uses a URI to locate the resources over web, sends a request to the server, and reads the response. In a RESTful system, the URI is not meant to change over time as it may break the contract between the client and server. More importantly, even if the underlying infrastructure or hardware changes (for example, swapping the database servers) for a server hosting the REST APIs, the URIs for the resources are expected to remain the same as long as the web service is up and running.

The representation of resources

The representation of resources is what is sent back and forth between clients and servers in a RESTful system. A representation is a temporal state of the actual data located in a storage device at the time of request. In general terms, it is a binary stream, together with its metadata, which describes how the stream is to be consumed by the client. The metadata can also contain extra information about the resource, for example, validation, encryption information, or extra code to be executed at runtime.

Throughout the life of a web service, there may be a variety of clients requesting resources. Different clients can consume different representations of the same resource. Therefore, a representation can take various forms, such as an image, a text file, an XML, or a JSON format. However, all clients will use the same URI with appropriate `Accept` header values for accessing the same resource in different representations.

For the human-generated requests through a web browser, a representation is typically in the form of an HTML page. For automated requests from other web services, readability is not as important, and a more efficient representation, such as JSON or XML, can be used.

Generic interaction semantics for REST resources

In the previous sections, we introduced the concepts of resources and representations. We learned that resources are mappings of the actual entity states that are exchanged between clients and servers. Further, we discussed that representations are negotiated between clients and servers through the communication protocol (HTTP) at runtime. In this section, you will learn about the generics of interaction semantics and self-descriptive messages followed for the client-server communication in a RESTful system.

Developing RESTful web services is similar to what we have been doing up to this point with our web applications. In a RESTful web service, resources are exchanged between the client and the server, which represent the business entities or data. HTTP specifies methods or actions for the resources. The most commonly used HTTP methods or actions are POST, GET, PUT, and DELETE. This clearly simplifies the REST API design and makes it more readable. On the other hand, in traditional application development, we can have countless actions with no naming or implementation standards. This may call for more development effort for both the client and the server and make the APIs less readable.

In a RESTful system, we can easily map our **CRUD** actions on the resources to the appropriate HTTP methods such as POST, GET, PUT, and DELETE. This is shown in the following table:

Data action	HTTP equivalent
CREATE	POST or PUT
READ	GET
UPDATE	PUT or PATCH
DELETE	DELETE

POST is also used to send an Action (Controller), (see p16? in this Restful guidelines book)

In fact, the preceding list of HTTP methods is incomplete. There are some more HTTP methods available, but they are less frequently used in the context of RESTful implementations. Of these less frequent methods, OPTIONS and HEAD are used more often than others. So, let's glance at these two method types:

- OPTIONS: This method is used by the client to determine the options or actions associated with the target resource, without causing any action on the resource or retrieval of the resource

- HEAD: This method can be used for retrieving information about the entity without having the entity itself in the response

In their simplest form, RESTful web services are networked applications that manipulate the state of resources. In this context, resource manipulation means resource creation, retrieval, updation, and deletion. However, RESTful web services are not limited to just these four basic data manipulation concepts. They can even be used for executing business logic on the server but remembering that every result must be a resource representation of the domain at hand.

A uniform interface brings all the aforementioned abstractions into focus. Consequently, putting together all these concepts, we can describe RESTful development with one short sentence--we use URIs to connect clients and servers in order to exchange resources in the form of representations.

Let's now look at the four HTTP request types in detail and see how each of them is used to exchange representations to modify the state of resources.

The HTTP GET method

The GET method is used to retrieve resources. Before digging into the actual mechanics of the HTTP GET request, we first need to determine what a resource is in the context of our web service and what type of representation we are exchanging.

For the rest of this section, we will use the example of a RESTful web service handling the department details for an organization. For this service, the JSON representation of a department looks as follows:

```
{"departmentId":10,"departmentName":"IT","manager":"John Chen"}
```

The JSON representation of the list of departments looks as follows:

```
[{"departmentId":10,"departmentName":"IT","manager":"John Chen"},
{"departmentId":20,"departmentName":"Marketing","manager":"Ameya
    J"},
{"departmentId":30,"departmentName":"HR","manager":"Pat Fay"}]
```

With our representations defined, we can now assume URIs of the form http://www.packtpub.com/resources/departments to access a list of departments, and http://www.packtpub.com/resources/departments/{name} to access a specific department with a name (unique identifier).

To keep this example simple and easy to follow, we treat the department name as a unique identifier here. Note that in real life, you can use a server-generated identifier value, which does not repeat across entities, to uniquely identify a resource instance.

We can now begin making requests to our web service. For instance, if we wanted a record for the IT department, we make a request to the following URI:

```
http://www.packtpub.com/resources/departments/IT.
```

A representation of the IT department at the time of the request may look like the following code snippet:

```
{"departmentId":10,"departmentName":"IT","manager":"John Chen"}
```

Let's have a look at the request details. A request to retrieve the details of the IT department uses the GET method with the following URI:

```
http://www.packtpub.com/resources/departments/IT
```

Let's see what happens when a client requests for the IT department with the aforementioned URI. Here is the sequence diagram for the GET request:

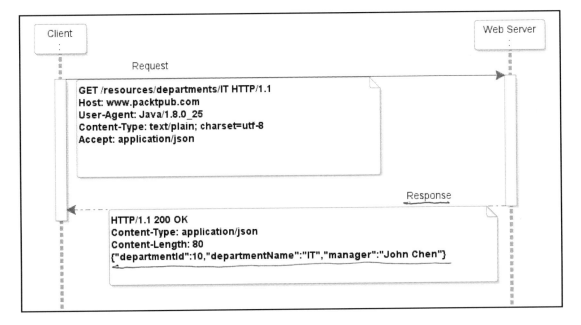

What is happening here?

1. A Java client makes an HTTP request with the GET method type and IT as the identifier for the department.
2. The client sets the representation type that it can handle through the Accept request header field. This request message is self-descriptive:

    - It uses a standard method (the GET method in this example) with known semantics for retrieving the content
    - The content type is a set to a well-known media type (text/plain)
    - This request also declares the acceptable response format

3. The web server receives and interprets the GET request to be a retrieve action. At this point, the web server passes control to the underlying RESTful framework to handle the request. Note that RESTful frameworks do not automatically retrieve resources, as that is not their job. The job of a framework is to ease the implementation of the REST constraints. Business logic and storage implementation is the role of the domain-specific Java code.
4. The server-side program looks for the IT resource. Finding the resource could mean looking for it in some data store such as a database, a filesystem, or even a call to a different web service.
5. Once the program finds the IT department details, it converts the binary data of the resource to the client's requested representation. In this example, we use the JSON representation for the resource.
6. With the representation converted to JSON, the server sends back an HTTP response with a numeric code of 200 together with the JSON representation as the payload. Note that if there are any errors, the HTTP server reports back the proper numeric code, but it is up to the client to correctly deal with the failure. Similar to the request message, the response is also self-descriptive.

All the messages between a client and server are standard HTTP calls. For every retrieve action, we send a GET request, and we get an HTTP response back, with the payload of the response being the representation of the resource or, if there is a failure, a corresponding HTTP error code (for example, 404 if a resource is not found or 500 if there is a problem with the Java code in the form of an exception).

Getting a representation for all the departments works in the same way as getting the representation for a single department, although we now use the URI as `http://www.packtpub.com/resources/departments` and the result is the JSON representation, which looks as follows:

```
[{"departmentId":10,"departmentName":"IT","manager":"John Chen"},
{"departmentId":20,"departmentName":"Marketing","manager":"Ameya
    J"},
{"departmentId":30,"departmentName":"HR","manager":"Pat Fay"}]
```

The HTTP GET method should only be used to retrieve representations, not for performing any update on the resource. A GET request must be safe and idempotent. For more information, refer to `http://www.w3.org/DesignIssues/Axioms`.

For a request to be safe, it means that multiple requests to the same resource do not change the state of the data in the server. Assume that we have a representation, R, and requests happen at time t. Then, a request at time t1 for the resource R returns R1; subsequently, a request at time t2 for the resource R returns R2, provided that no further update actions have been taken between t1 and t2. Then, R1 = R2 = R.

For a request to be idempotent, multiple calls to the same action should not change the state of the resource. For example, multiple calls to create the resource R at times t1, t2, and t3 means that R will exist only as R and the calls at times t2 and t3 are ignored.

The HTTP POST method

The POST method is used to create resources. As we are creating a department, we use the HTTP POST method. Again, the URI to create a new department in our example is `http://www.packtpub.com/resources/departments`. The method type for the request is set by the client.

Assume that the Sales department does not exist in our list, and we want to add it to the list. The Sales data representation looks like the following:

```
{"departmentName":"Sales","manager":"Tony Greig"}
```

Now, the sequence diagram of our POST request looks like the following:

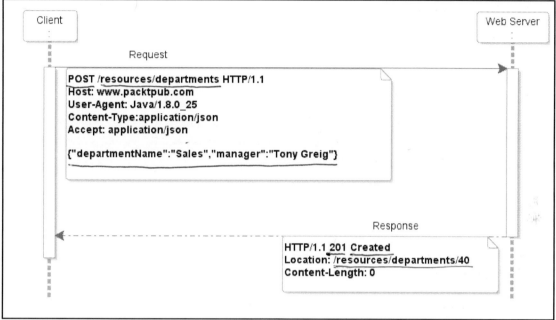

The series of steps for the POST request is as follows:

1. A Java client makes a request to the
   `http://www.packtpub.com/resources/departments` URI with the HTTP
   method set to POST.

2. The POST request carries the payload along with it in the form of a JSON
   representation of the `Sales` department.

3. The server receives the request and lets the REST framework handle it; our code
   within the framework executes the proper commands to store the representation,
   irrespective of which data persistence mechanism is used.

4. Once the new resource is stored, a response code, 2xx (representing successful
   operation), is sent back. In this example, the server sends `201 Created`, which
   implies that the server has fulfilled the request by creating a new resource. The
   newly created resource is accessible by traversing the URI given by a `Location`
   header field. If it fails, then the server sends the appropriate error code.

The HTTP PUT method

The PUT method is used to update resources. To update a resource, we first need its representation in the client. Then, at the client level, we update the resource with the new value(s) that we want. Finally, we update the resource by using a PUT request together with the representation as its payload.

In this example, let's add a manager to the Sales department, which we created in the previous example.

Our original representation of the Sales department is as follows:

```
{"departmentId":40,"departmentName":"Sales","manager":"Tony
    Greig" }
```

Let's update the manager for the Sales department; our representation is as follows:

```
{"departmentId":40,"departmentName":"Sales","manager":"Ki Gee"}
```

We are now ready to connect to our web service to update the Sales department by sending the PUT request to http://www.packtpub.com/resources/departments/Sales. The sequence diagram of our PUT request is as follows:

— how does the client know to use the word Sales?

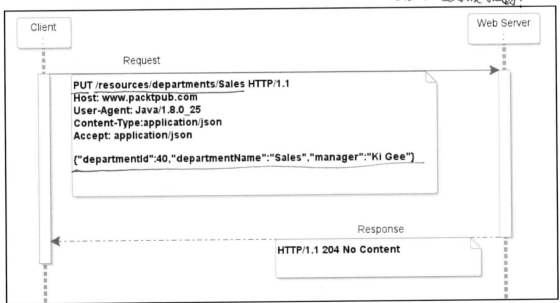

I presume there's no @PATH for Sales at the server side so it must be a Param. This means we can only have 1 level of param ie @PATH/@PARAM not @PATH/@PARAM/@PATH.

The series of steps for the PUT request is as follows:

1. A Java client makes a PUT request to `http://www.packtpub.com/resources/departments/Sales` with the JSON payload representing the modified department details.
2. The server receives the request and lets the REST framework handle it. At this point, we let our code execute the proper commands to update the representation of the Sales department. Once completed, a response is sent back. The `204 No Content` response code indicates that the server has fulfilled the request but does not return the entity body.

The HTTP DELETE method

The DELETE method is used to delete the resource. In this example, we will delete a resource by making use of the same URI that we used in the other three cases.

Assume that we want to delete the Sales department from the data storage. We send a DELETE request to our service with the following URI:
`http://www.packtpub.com/resources/departments/Sales`

The sequence diagram for our DELETE request is shown in the following diagram:

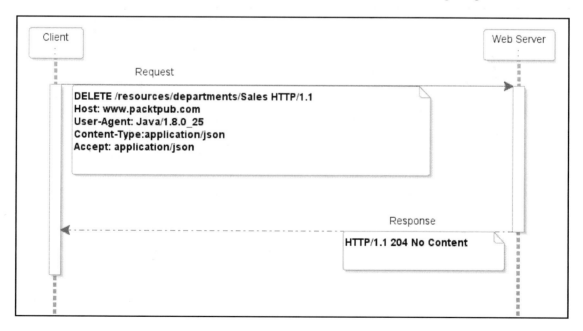

The series of steps for the `DELETE` request is as follows:

1. A Java client makes a `DELETE` request to
   `http://www.packtpub.com/resources/departments/Sales`.
2. The server receives the request and lets the REST framework handle it. At this point, the server code executes the proper commands to delete the representation of the `Sales` department.
3. Once completed, a response is sent back.

With this, we have covered all the major actions that can be carried out on resources in a RESTful web service. To keep things simple during our discussion, we did not talk about the actual implementation of the `CREATE`, `READ`, `UPDATE`, and `DELETE` operations on the resource. In all three examples, we presumed that we have a well-behaved web service that adheres to the RESTful guidelines, and the client and server communicate over HTTP. We use the communication protocol to send action requests, and our resource representations are sent back and forth through unchanging URIs. We will cover more detailed end-to-end examples later in this book.

 A point to note about our sequence diagrams is that we are assuming that all the underlying technologies are Java technologies (servers and clients). However, these are just components in the whole architecture and the explanations apply to any technology stack.

Hypermedia as the Engine of Application State

Hypermedia as the Engine of Application State (HATEOAS) is an important principle of the REST application architecture. The principle is that the model of application changes from one state to another by traversing the hyperlinks present in the current set of resource representations (model). Let's learn this principle in detail.

In a RESTful system, there is no fixed interface between the client and the server, as you may see in a conventional client-server communication model such as **Common Object Request Broker Architecture (CORBA)** and **Java Remote Method Invocation (Java RMI)**. With REST, the client just needs to know how to deal with the hypermedia links present in the response body; next, the call to retrieve the appropriate resource representation is made by using these dynamic media links. This concept makes the client-server interaction very dynamic and keeps it different from the other network application architectures.

Here is an example illustrating the HATEOAS principle. In this example, the
`http://www.packtpub.com/resources/departments/IT` URI returns the following
response to the client:

```
{"departmentId":10,
"departmentName":"IT",
"manager":"John Chen,
"links": [ {
        "rel": "employees",
        "href": "http://packtpub.com/resources/departments/IT/employees"
    } ]"}
```

This is the current state of the system. Now, to get the employees belonging to the
department, the client traverses the hyperlink present in the response body, namely
`http://www.packtpub.com/resources/departments/IT/employees`. This URI
returns the following employee list. The application state now changes into the following
form (as represented by the response content):

```
[{"employeeId":100,
 "firstName":"Steven",
 "lastName":"King",
 "links": [ {
        "rel": "self",
        "href": "http://www.packtpub.com/resources/employees/100"
    }]
 },
{"employeeId":101,
"firstName":"Neena",
"lastName":"Kochhar",
"links": [ {
        "rel": "self",
        "href": "http://www.packtpub.com/resources/employees/101"
    }]
 }]
```

In this example, the application state changes from one state to another when the client
traverses the hypermedia link. Hence, we refer to this implementation principle as
HATEOAS.

Connectors

Connectors provide decoupling between components by encapsulating the underlying implementation of resources and communication mechanisms using various connector types, as described in the following table:

Connector type	Function	Examples
Client	Initiates the request and accepts the response	Client-side web APIs (`libwww`, `libwww-perl`)
Server	Listens for connections and responds to requests	Web server APIs (Apache API, NSAPI)
Cache	Used for storing cacheable responses both at the client and server side to optimize interaction latency	Web caching solutions (Akamai, Cloudflare, Microsoft Azure CDN)
Resolver	Resolves web address to the corresponding network address	BIND, Microsoft DNS, AnswerX
Tunnel	Relays communication across a connection boundary such as firewall, gateways, or proxies.	SOCKS, HTTP Tunnel

Components

Software components required for REST are categorized by their roles as follows:

Component role	Function	Examples
Origin server	It acts as the container or definitive source for the representation of resources being requested; it must be the ultimate recipient of any requests. It uses a server connector to receive and respond to requests.	Web servers (Apache Tomcat, Microsoft IIS)
User agent	This is the user interface for the end user. It uses the client connector to initiate the request and get the response.	Web browsers (Internet Explorer, Chrome, Lynx)

| Proxy | This acts as an intermediary for requests from clients seeking resources. | CGI Proxy, CERN Proxy |
| Gateway | This involves reverse proxies providing encapsulation of services such as security (encryption), performance enhancement (load balancing), or data translation (compression). | Squid, NGINX |

The description and discovery of RESTful web services

As you may know, WSDL is used for describing the functionality offered by a SOAP web service. For a SOAP web service, this is a widely accepted standard and is supported by many enterprises today. In contrast, there is no such standard for RESTful web services, and you may find different metadata formats used by various enterprises.

However, in general, you may see the following goals in common among all these metadata formats for RESTful APIs, although they differ in their syntax and semantics:

- Entry points for the service
- Resource paths for accessing each resource
- Allowed HTTP methods to access these resources, such as GET, POST, PUT, and DELETE
- Additional parameters that need to be supplied with these methods, such as pagination parameters, while reading large collections
- Format types used for representing the request and response body contents such as JSON, XML, and TEXT
- Status codes and error messages returned by the APIs
- Human readable documentation for REST APIs, which includes documentation of the request methods, input and output parameters, response codes (success or error), API security, and business logic

Some of the popular metadata formats used for describing REST APIs are **Web Application Description Language (WADL)**, **Swagger**, **RESTful API Modeling Language (RAML)**, **API Blueprint**, and **WSDL 2.0**.

We will have a more detailed discussion on each of these items in `Chapter` `7`, *Description and Discovery of the RESTful Web Services*.

Java tools and frameworks for building RESTful web services

Over the last few years, the REST architectural style has become very popular in the industry and many enterprises have accepted it as the existent standard for building public web APIs, particularly when scalability and simplicity are major concerns for them. Today, one may see many tools and frameworks available in the market for building RESTful web services. In this section, we will briefly discuss some popular Java-based frameworks and tools for building RESTful systems.

The **Java API for RESTful Web Services (JAX-RS)** is the Java API for creating RESTful web services following the REST architectural pattern discussed in this chapter. JAX-RS is a part of the **Java Platform Enterprise Edition (Java EE)** platform and is designed to be a standard and portable solution. There are many reference implementations available for JAX-RS today. Some of the popular implementations are Jersey, Apache CXF, RESTEasy, and Restlet. At this juncture, it is worth mentioning that most of the frameworks in the preceding list, such as Jersey and Apache CXF, are not just limited to reference implementations of the JAX-RS specifications but they also offer many additional features on top of the specifications.

Apart from the JAX-RS-based frameworks (or extensions built on top of JAX-RS), you may also find some promising nonstandard (not based on JAX-RS) Java REST frameworks in the market. Some such frameworks are as follows:

- One such framework is RESTX, which is an open source Java REST framework and is primarily focused on the server-side REST API development. This is relatively new in the market and simplifies the REST API development.
- Spark is another framework that falls in this category. It is a Java web framework with support for building REST APIs. Spark 2.0 is built using Java 8, leveraging all the latest improvements of the Java language.
- Play is another framework worth mentioning in this category. It is a Java (and Scala)-based web application framework with inherent support for building RESTful web services.

Discussing all these frameworks does not come under the scope of this book. We will focus on some of the popular frameworks with many real-life use cases in mind. In the coming chapters, you will learn JAX-RS as well as the additional features available with the Jersey framework for building scalable and maintainable RESTful web services.

Summary

This chapter is intended to give an overview of RESTful web services. This is essential for an easy understanding of what you will learn in the rest of the book. As we have just started our topic, we have not covered any code samples in this chapter to keep it simple. In the following chapters, we will examine popular Java tools and frameworks available for building a RESTful web service along with many real-life examples and code samples.

In the next chapter, we will discuss the JSON representation of the REST resources and the Java APIs for JSON processing.

Java APIs for JSON Processing

2

In the previous chapter, you were introduced to the REST architectural style. Remember that REST does not prescribe any specific message format for client-server communication. One can use an appropriate format for representing messages as long as the chosen format is supported by HTTP. XML and JSON are the two popular formats used by RESTful web services today. Within these two formats, JSON is widely adopted by many vendors because of its simplicity and light weight. In this chapter, you will learn more about the JSON message format, how to represent real-life business data in the JSON format, and various processing tools and frameworks related to JSON.

The following topics are covered in this chapter:

- A brief overview of JSON
- Using the JSR 353 – Java API for processing JSON
- Using the Jackson API for processing JSON
- Using the Gson API for processing JSON
- Java EE 8 Enhancements for processing JSON

A brief overview of JSON

JSON is a lightweight, text-based, platform-neutral data interchange format in which objects are represented in the attribute-value pair format. Historically, JSON originated from JavaScript. However, nowadays, it is considered to be a language-independent format because of its wide adoption by all modern programming languages. In this section, you will learn the basics of the JSON format.

Understanding the JSON data syntax

The JSON format is very simple by design. It is represented by the following two data structures:

- An unordered collection of the name-value pairs (representing an object):
  - Attributes of an object and their values are represented in the name-value pair format; the name and the value in a pair are separated by a colon (`:`). Names in an object are strings, and values may be of any of the valid JSON data types such as number, string, Boolean, array, object, or null. Each `name:value` pair in a JSON object is separated by a comma (`,`). The entire object is enclosed in curly braces (`{}`).
  - For instance, the JSON representation of a department object is as follows:

    ```
    {"departmentId":10, "departmentName":"IT",
     "manager":"John Chen"}
    ```

  - This example shows how you can represent the various attributes of a department, such as `departmentId`, `departmentName`, and `manager` in the JSON format.

- An ordered collection of values (representing an array):
  - Arrays are enclosed in square brackets (`[]`), and their values are separated by a comma (`,`). Each value in an array may be of a different type, including another array or an object.
  - The following example illustrates the use of array notation to represent the employees working in a department. You can also see an array of locations in this example:

    ```
    {"departmentName":"IT",
      "employees":[
        {"firstName":"John", "lastName":"Chen"},
        {"firstName":"Ameya", "lastName":"Job"},
        {"firstName":"Pat", "lastName":"Fay"}
      ],
      "location":["New York", "New Delhi"]
    }
    ```

Basic data types available with JSON

While discussing the JSON syntax in the previous section, we glanced at some of the basic data types used in JSON. Let's take a detailed look at each item.

Here is the list of the basic data types available with JSON:

- **Number**: This type is used for storing a signed decimal number that may optionally contain a fractional part. Both integer and floating point numbers are represented by using this data type. The following example uses the decimal data type for storing `totalWeight`:

  ```
  {"totalWeight": 123.456}
  ```

- **String**: This type represents a sequence of zero or more characters. Strings are surrounded with double quotation marks and support a backslash escaping syntax. Here is an example for the string data type:

  ```
  {"firstName": "Jobinesh"}
  ```

- **Boolean**: This type represents either a `true` or a `false` value. The Boolean type is used for representing whether a condition is `true` or `false`, or to represent two states of a variable (`true` or `false`) in the code. Here is an example representing a Boolean value:

  ```
  {"isValidEntry": true}
  ```

- **Array**: This type represents an ordered list of zero or more values, each of which can be of any type. In this representation, comma-separated values are enclosed in square brackets. The following example represents an array of `fruits`:

  ```
  {"fruits": ["apple", "banana", "orange"]}
  ```

- **Object**: This type is an unordered collection of comma-separated attribute-value pairs enclosed in curly braces. All attributes must be strings and should be distinct from each other within that object. The following example illustrates an object representation in JSON:

  ```
  {"departmentId":10,
    "departmentName":"IT",
  "manager":"John Chen"}
  ```

- **null**: This type indicates an empty value, represented by using the word null. The following example uses null as the value for the error attribute of an object:

```
{"error":null}
```

The example in the next section illustrates how you can use the JSON data types that we discussed in this section to represent the details of employees.

Sample JSON file representing employee objects

Here is a sample JSON document file called emp-array.json, which contains the JSON array of the employee objects. The content of the file is as follows:

```
[ {"employeeId":100,"firstName":"John","lastName":"Chen",
  "email":"john.chen@xxxx.com","hireDate":"2008-10-16"},
  {"employeeId":101,"firstName":"Ameya","lastName":"Job",
  "email":"ameya.job@xxx.com","hireDate":"2013-03-06"},
  {"employeeId":102,"firstName":"Pat","lastName":"Fay",
"email":"pat.fey@xxx.com","hireDate":"2001-03-06"} ]
```

javax.json.JsonValue does not have a DATE ValueType. In the previous example, hireDate will be treated as a STRING type, so handling of DATE values requires explicit parsing as per the date format.

We will use this emp-array.json file as the input source for many examples that we will discuss later in this chapter. By now, you should have a fairly good understanding of the JSON syntax. We will later learn the various techniques for processing JSON data.

Processing JSON data

If you use Java RESTful web service frameworks, such as JAX-RS, for building RESTful web APIs, the serialization and deserialization of the request and response messages will be taken care of by the framework. However, understanding the JSON structure and tools for processing JSON will definitely help you when the default offering by the framework does not meet your requirements. The following diagram illustrates the role of the JSON marshalling (converting Java object to JSON format) and unmarshalling components (converting JSON format to Java Object) in a typical Java RESTful web service implementation:

This section will teach you the various processing models for JSON data. By the term processing, we mean reading, writing, querying, and modifying JSON data. Two widely adopted programming models for processing JSON are as follows:

- **Object model**: In this model, the entire JSON data is read into memory in a tree format. This tree can be traversed, analyzed, or modified with appropriate APIs. As this approach loads the entire content in the memory first and then starts parsing, it ends up consuming more memory and CPU cycles. However, this model gives more flexibility while manipulating the content.

- **Streaming model**: The term streaming is very generic in meaning and can be used in many aspects. In our discussion, this term means that the data can be read or written in blocks. This model does not read the entire JSON content into the memory to get started with parsing; rather, it reads one element at a time. For each token read, the parser generates appropriate events indicating the type of token, such as the start or end of an array, or the start or end of the object and attribute values. A client can process the contents by listening for appropriate events. The most important point is that instead of letting the parser push the content to the client (push parser), the client can pull the information from the parser, as it needs (pull parser). In this model, the client is allowed to skip or stop reading contents in the middle of the process if it has finished reading the desired elements. This model is also useful when you write the content to an output source in blocks.

You may want to consider using streaming APIs in the following situations:

- When the data is huge in size, and it is not feasible to load the entire content into the memory for processing the content
- When partial processing is needed and the data model is not fully available yet

We will revisit these two parsing models while discussing tools for processing JSON later in this chapter.

Using JSR 353 – Java API for processing JSON

There are many Java-based frameworks available today for processing JSON. In this section, we will learn the APIs available in the Java EE platform for processing JSON. Java EE 7 has standardized the JSON processing APIs with **Java Specification Request (JSR)**, that is, **JSR 353 – Java API for JSON Processing**. This JSR offers portable APIs to parse, generate, transform, and query the JSON data. The JSR 353 APIs can be classified into two categories on the basis of the processing model followed by the APIs:

- Object model API
- Streaming model API

We had a generic discussion on these two processing models in the previous section, *Processing JSON data*. In this section, we will see how these processing models are implemented in JSR 353.

Processing JSON with JSR 353 object model APIs

This category of APIs generates an in-memory tree model for JSON data and then starts processing it as instructed by the client. This is conceptually similar to the **Document Object Model (DOM)** API for XML.

Here is a list of the frequently used classes in the object model API of the JSR 353 specification:

Class or interface	Description
`javax.json.Json`	This class is the main factory class for creating JSON processing objects, such as `JsonReader` and `JsonWriter`.
`javax.json.JsonReader`	This interface reads the JSON content and generates a JSON object or array as appropriate.
`javax.json.JsonWriter`	This interface writes a JSON object or array to an output source.
`javax.json.JsonObjectBuilder`	This interface offers APIs for generating the `JsonObject` models from scratch.
`javax.json.JsonArrayBuilder`	This interface offers APIs for generating `JsonArray` models from scratch.
`javax.json.JsonValue`	This interface is the superinterface representing an immutable JSON value. The JSON value takes one of the following forms: • `javax.json.JsonObject` • `javax.json.JsonArray` • `javax.json.JsonNumber` • `javax.json.JsonString` • `javax.json.JsonValue.TRUE` • `javax.json.JsonValue.FALSE` • `javax.json.JsonValue.NULL`

The JSR 353 object model APIs are easy to use and rich in offerings.

Refer to the complete list of the object model APIs available in JSR 353 at `http://docs.oracle.com/javaee/7/api/javax/json/package-summary.html`.

Generating the object model from the JSON representation

The example in this section illustrates the usage of the JSR 353 object model APIs for building an object representation of the JSON data.

Downloading the example code

All the code examples that you see in this chapter are downloadable from the Packt website link mentioned at the beginning of this book, in the *Preface* section. In the downloaded source, open the rest-chapter2-jsonp folder to access all the examples discussed in this chapter.

This example uses the JSON array of the employee objects stored in the emp-array.json file as an input source. The contents of this file are listed under the *Sample JSON file representing employee objects* section. Let's see how we can convert the JSON content present in the file into a Java object model by using the JSR 353 object model API.

As you may have guessed, the first step is to read the JSON content from the emp-array.json file and store it in an appropriate data structure. The following code snippet illustrates the APIs for reading the JSON content from the file to javax.json.JsonArray:

```
//Import statements for the core classes
import java.io.InputStream;
import javax.json.JsonArray;
import javax.json.JsonReader;

//Get input stream for reading the specified resource.
InputStream inputStream =
    getClass().getResourceAsStream("/emp-array.json");
// Create JsonReader to read JSON data from a stream
Reader reader = new InputStreamReader(inputStream, "UTF-8");
JsonReader jsonReader = Json.createReader(reader);
// Creates an object model in memory.
JsonArray employeeArray = jsonReader.readArray();
```

Here is a brief description of the preceding code snippet. `javax.json.Json` is the factory class that we use for creating JSON processing objects. We will use this `Json` class to create the `javax.json.JsonReader` instance. The next step is to read the JSON content into an appropriate object model. As the JSON data that we use in this example holds an array of `employee` objects, we call `readArray()` on the `JsonReader` instance to retrieve `javax.json.JsonArray`. The `JsonArray` instance contains an ordered sequence of zero or more objects read from the input source.

> If the input is a JSON object, you can call `readObject()` on `JsonReader` to retrieve the JSON object that is presented in the input source.

Now, let's see how to convert the `JsonArray` elements into specific object types. In this example, we will convert each `JsonObject` object present in `employeeArray` into the `Employee` object. The `Employee` class used in this example is shown here for your reference:

```
//All import statements are removed for brevity
public class Employee {
    private String firstName;
    private String lastName;
    private String email;
    private Integer employeeId;
    private java.util.Date hireDate;
    //Getters and Setter for the above properties are not
    //shown in this code snippet to save space
}
```

> The Java EE 7 platform lacks a binding feature, which does the automatic conversion of the JSON content into Java classes. There is a proposal, *JSR 367: Java™ API for JSON Binding (JSON-B)* as part of Java EE 8, to provide a standard binding layer for converting Java objects into/from JSON messages, which will be discussed in the later sections.

In this example, we create the `Employee` instance for each `JsonObject` object present in `employeeArray`.

The following code snippet is a continuation of the previous example. This example converts the employeeArray array that we retrieved from the JSON input file into a list of Employee objects:

```
//import statements for the core APIs used in
//the following code snippet
import javax.json.JsonObject;
import javax.json.JsonValue;
import java.text.SimpleDateFormat;
import java.util.Date;

//Iterate over employeeArray(JsonArray)
//and process each JsonObject
List<Employee> employeeList = new ArrayList<Employee>();
for(JsonValue jsonValue : employeeArray) {
  //Get JsonObject and read desired attributes
  //and copy them to Employee object
  if(JsonValue.ValueType.OBJECT == jsonValue.getValueType()){
      JsonObject jsonObject = (JsonObject) jsonValue;
      Employee employee = new Employee();
      employee.setFirstName(jsonObject.getString("firstName"));
      employee.setLastName(jsonObject.getString("lastName"));
      employee.setEmployeeId(jsonObject.getInt("employeeId"));
      //Converts date string (from JSON) to java.util.Date object
      SimpleDateFormat dateFormat =
        new SimpleDateFormat("yyyy-MM-dd");
      Date hireDate=
        dateFormat.parse(jsonObject.getString("hireDate"))
      employee.setHireDate(hireDate);
      employeeList.add(employee);
  }
}
```

The preceding code iterates over the JsonArray instance and builds the Employee instances. Let's take a closer look at the JsonArray object to understand how it stores JSON data.

A JsonArray instance contains one or more javax.json.JsonValue elements, each representing an item present in the input source. Let's take a closer look at the representation of different value types in JSON.

JSON value types

`javax.json.JsonValue` is a top-level interface used to represent the node value types of JSON data, as shown ahead:

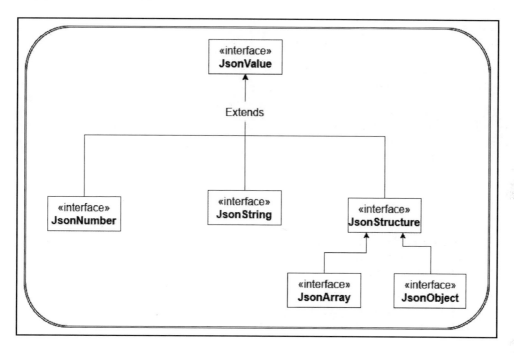

At runtime, it takes one of the following forms on the basis of the content type:

- `javax.json.JsonObject`: This form is an immutable JSON object value
- `javax.json.JsonArray`: This form is an immutable array representing an ordered sequence of zero or more JSON values
- `javax.json.JsonNumber`: This form is an immutable JSON numerical value
- `javax.json.JsonString`: This form is an immutable JSON string value
- `javax.json.JsonValue.TRUE`: This form represents the JSON TRUE value
- `javax.json.JsonValue.FALSE`: This form represents the JSON FALSE value
- `javax.json.JsonValue.NULL`: This form represents the JSON NULL value

By now, we have read the entire JSON content from the input file into the Employee objects. It is now time for some cleanup activities. The following code closes the inputStream and jsonReader objects after use. This lets the runtime release the system resources associated with the stream:

```
try(InputStream inputStream = getClass().getResourceAsStream(jsonFileName);
         Reader reader = new InputStreamReader(inputStream, "UTF-8");
         JsonReader jsonReader = Json.createReader(reader))
```

Once you have finished using the inputStream, outputStream, JsonReader, or JSonWriter objects, make sure that you close them to release the associated resources.

The try-with-resources available from Java 1.7 is used to release resources automatically once the application stops. This is applicable only when the resource implements the java.lang.AutoCloseable interface.

Generating the JSON representation from the object model

In the previous section, we discussed the APIs provided by JSR 353 to convert the JSON data into the Java object model. In this section, you will learn how to convert a Java object model into the JSON format, which is the opposite of the operation discussed in the previous section.

The very first step is to build an object model. You can use either of the following classes to generate the object model. The choice of the builder class depends on whether you want to generate a JSON object or a JSON array:

- javax.json.JsonObjectBuilder: This builder class is used for generating the JSON object model from scratch. This class provides methods to add the name-value pairs to the object model and to return the final object.
- javax.json.JsonArrayBuilder: This builder class is used for generating an array of JSON objects from scratch. This class provides methods to add objects or values to the array model and to return the final array.

The builder classes can be created either from the javax.json.Json factory class or from the javax.json.JsonBuilderFactory class. You may go for JsonBuilderFactory if you want to override the default configurations for the generated objects (configurations are specific to vendors) or if you need to create multiple instances of the builder classes.

The following code snippet illustrates the use of the `JsonArrayBuilder` APIs for converting an array of the `employee` objects into the JSON array. The client builds the JSON objects by using `JsonObjectBuilder` and adds them to `JsonArrayBuilder`. Finally, when the client calls the `build()` method, `JsonArrayBuilder` returns the associated JSON array:

```java
//import statements for the core classes used this example
//Other imports are removed for brevity
import javax.json.Json;
import javax.json.JsonArray;
import javax.json.JsonArrayBuilder;
import javax.json.JsonObject;
import javax.json.JsonObjectBuilder;
import javax.json.JsonWriter;
import java.io.FileOutputStream;
import java.io.OutputStream;


// Creates a JsonArrayBuilder instance that is
// used to build JsonArray
JsonArrayBuilder jsonArrayBuilder = Json.createArrayBuilder();

//Get a list of Employee instances.
// We are not interested in the implementation details of the
// getEmployeeList() method used in this example.
List<Employee> employees = getEmployeeList();

//Iterate over the employee list and create JsonObject for each item
for (Employee employee : employees) {

//Add desired name-value pairs to the JSON object and push
// each object in to the array.
  jsonArrayBuilder.add(
    Json.createObjectBuilder()
    .add("employeeId", employee.getEmployeeId())
    .add("firstName", employee.getFirstName())
    .add("lastName", employee.getLastName())
    .add("email", employee.getEmail())
    .add("hireDate", employee.getHireDate())
  );

}
//Return the json array holding employee details
JsonArray employeesArray = jsonArrayBuilder.build();

//write the array to file
OutputStream outputStream = new FileOutputStream
```

```
    ("emp-array.json");
JsonWriter jsonWriter = Json.createWriter(outputStream);
jsonWriter.writeArray(employeesArray);

//Close the stream to clean up the associated resources
outputStream.close();
jsonWriter.close();
```

The resulting file output content may look like the following:

```
[ {"employeeId":100,"firstName":"John","lastName":"Chen",
   "email":"john.chen@xxxx.com","hireDate":"2008-10-16"},
   {"employeeId":101,"firstName":"Ameya","lastName":"Job",
"email":"ameya.job@xxx.com","hireDate":"2013-03-06"}]
```

Processing JSON with JSR 353 streaming APIs

This category of APIs supports the streaming model for both reading and writing the JSON content. This model is designed to process a large amount of data in a more efficient way. Conceptually, this model is similar to the **Streaming API for XML (StAX)** parser that you might have used while dealing with the XML data.

Streaming APIs are grouped in the `javax.json.stream` package in the JSR specification. In this section, we will see how we can use the streaming APIs to efficiently process JSON data.

Here is a list of the frequently used classes in the streaming API provided by the JSR 353 specification:

Class	Description
`javax.json.stream.JsonParser`	This class provides forward read-only access to JSON data by using the pull parsing programming model.
`javax.json.stream.JsonGenerator`	This class writes JSON to an output source as specified by the client application. It generates the name-value pairs for the JSON objects and values for the JSON arrays.

Streaming APIs read and write the content serially at runtime in accordance with client calls, which makes them suitable for handling a large amount of data.

To refer to the complete list of the streaming APIs provided by JSR 353, visit
`http://docs.oracle.com/javaee/7/api/javax/json/stream/package-su`
`mmary.html`.

Using streaming APIs to parse JSON data

In this section, you will learn the use of streaming APIs for converting JSON data into appropriate Java classes.

This example illustrates the use of streaming APIs for converting a JSON array of the `employee` objects present in the `emp-array.json` file into an appropriate Java class representation.

The following code snippet illustrates how you can use `javax.json.stream.JsonParser`, which follows the streaming parsing model, to read the content from the `emp-array.json` file:

1. The first step is to get the input stream for reading the `emp-array.json` file. Then, you can create a `JsonParser` instance with the input stream, as follows:

```
//Other imports are removed for brevity
import javax.json.stream.JsonParser;

//Read emp-array.json file that contains JSON array of
//employees
//This file is listed under the section:
//"A sample JSON file representing employee objects"
InputStream inputStream =
  getClass().getResourceAsStream("/emp-array.json");
JsonParser jsonParser = Json.createParser(inputStream);
```

2. Start parsing the content now. The following code snippet illustrates the API use for parsing the content with the pull parsing model:

```
// Returns true if there are more parsing states
while (jsonParser.hasNext()) {
//Returns the event for the next parsing state
  Event event = jsonParser.next();
//Start of a JSON object,
//position of the parser is after'{'
  if (event.equals(JsonParser.Event.START_OBJECT)) {
    employee = new Employee();
    employeeList.add(employee);
```

```
    } else if (event.equals(JsonParser.Event.KEY_NAME)) {
      String keyName = jsonParser.getString();
      switch (keyName) {
        case "firstName":
        jsonParser.next();
        employee.setFirstName(
        jsonParser.getString());
        break;
        case "lastName":
        jsonParser.next();
        employee.setLastName(
        jsonParser.getString());
        break;
        case "email":
        jsonParser.next();
        employee.setEmail(jsonParser.getString());
        break;
        case "employeeId":
        jsonParser.next();
        employee.setEmployeeId(jsonParser.getInt());
        break;
        case "hireDate":
        jsonParser.next();
        //Converts date string (from JSON) into
        //java.util.Date object
        SimpleDateFormat dateFormat =
          new SimpleDateFormat("yyyy-MM-dd");
        Date hireDate=
          dateFormat.Parse
            (jsonObject.getString("hireDate"));
        employee.setHireDate(hireDate);
        break;
        default:
      }
    }

  }
```

Remember that `JsonParser` parses JSON by using the pull parsing programming model. In this case, the client application code controls the progress of parsing. The client calls `next()` on `JsonParser` to advance the parser to the next state after processing each element. In response to the `next()` call from the client, the parser generates the following events on the basis of the type of the next token encountered: START_OBJECT, END_OBJECT, START_ARRAY, END_ARRAY, KEY_NAME, VALUE_STRING, VALUE_NUMBER, VALUE_TRUE, VALUE_FALSE, and VALUE_NULL.

To better understand this, consider the following JSON array as the input to the parser:

```
[{"country": "IN"}]
```

The parser generates the START_ARRAY event for the first call to the next() method and the START_OBJECT event with the second call to the next() method, and so on. The following diagram illustrates the events generated while parsing each token present in the JSON representation:

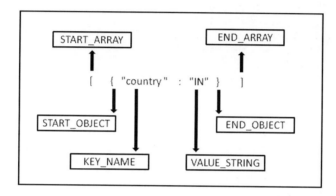

Using streaming APIs to generate JSON

You can use javax.json.stream.JsonGenerator to write JSON data to an output source as a stream of tokens. This approach does not keep the content in memory throughout the process. Once a name-value pair is written to the stream, the content used for wiring the name-value pair will be discarded from the memory.

JsonGenerator has support for writing both the JSON object and the JSON array. You can use the writeStartObject() method to generate the JSON object and then add the name-value pairs with the write() method. To finish the object representation, call writeEnd().

To generate the JSON arrays, call the writeStartArray() method and then, add values with the write() method. To finish the array representation, call writeEnd(), which writes the end of the current context.

The following example illustrates the use of streaming APIs for converting an array of employee objects into a JSON string:

```
//Other imports are removed for brevity
import javax.json.stream.JsonGenerator;
import com.packtpub.rest.ch2.model.DateUtil;
```

```
//Get the employee list that needs to be converted to JSON
List<Employee> employees = getEmployeeList();
//Create file output stream for writing data to a File
OutputStream outputStream = new FileOutputStream(
  "emp-array.json");
//Generates JsonGenerator which converts data to JSON
JsonGenerator jsonGenerator = Json.createGenerator(outputStream);
// Writes the JSON 'start array' character : [
jsonGenerator.writeStartArray();
for(Employee employee : employees) {
  // Writes the JSON object for each Employee object
  jsonGenerator.writeStartObject()
  .write("employeeId", employee.getEmployeeId())
  .write("firstName", employee.getFirstName())
  .write("lastName", employee.getLastName())
  .write("email", employee.getEmail())
  .write("hireDate",DateUtil.getDate(employee.getHireDate()))
  .writeEnd();

}
// Writes the end of the current context(array).
jsonGenerator.writeEnd();
```

The use of the `JsonGenerator` class is very straightforward. Therefore, we are not going to discuss the methods in detail here.

With this, we are ending our discussion on JSR 353 – Java API for JSON processing. In the next section, we will discuss Jackson, which is another popular framework available in the industry for processing JSON.

Using the Jackson API for processing JSON

Jackson is a multipurpose data processing Java library. The primary capability of this tool is the support for processing JSON. It also has additional modules for processing the data encoded in other popular formats, such as Apache Avro (a data serialization system), **Concise Binary Object Representation** (CBOR), a binary JSON format, Smile (a binary JSON format), XML, **comma-separated values** (CSV), and YAML. In this section, you will learn how to use Jackson APIs to process JSON.

Jackson provides the following three methods for processing JSON:

- **Tree model APIs**: This method provides APIs for building a tree representation of a JSON document
- **Data binding API**: This method provides APIs for converting a JSON document into and from Java objects
- **Streaming API**: This method provides streaming APIs for reading and writing a JSON document

We will discuss the preceding three methods in detail in this section.

To learn the dependencies of Jackson2 APIs, visit
`https://github.com/FasterXML/jackson-docs/wiki/Using-Jackson2-wi`
`th-Maven`.

Processing JSON with Jackson tree model APIs

The Jackson tree model API provides an in-memory representation of the JSON data. A client can optionally modify the object model representation. Here is a list of the core classes that you may need to know while dealing with tree model APIs in Jackson:

Class	Description
`com.fasterxml.jackson.databind.ObjectMapper`	This mapper class provides the functionality for converting between Java objects and matching JSON representations.
`com.fasterxml.jackson.databind.JsonNode`	This class is the base class for all JSON nodes, which form the basis of the JSON tree model in Jackson.

Using Jackson tree model APIs to query and update data

You will use the `com.fasterxml.jackson.databind.ObjectMapper` class to convert the JSON data into a tree representation. This class has a variety of APIs to build a tree from the JSON data. The tree representation built from JSON is made up of `com.fasterxml.jackson.databind.JsonNode` instances. This is similar to the DOM nodes in an XML DOM tree. You can also navigate through `JsonNode` to identify specific elements present in the tree hierarchy. The following example illustrates the use of Jackson tree model APIs.

This example generates a tree hierarchy for the JSON array of `employee` objects and then queries the generated tree for the `employee` nodes with the null `email` value. This example updates all the null `email` values with the system-generated email addresses for later processing.

The `readTree(InputStream in)` instance defined on the `com.fasterxml.jackson.databind.ObjectMapper` class helps you to deserialize the JSON content as a tree (expressed using a set of `JsonNode` instances). To query `JsonNode` for a specific field name, you can call `path(String fieldName)` on the underlying `JsonNode` instance. The following code snippet will help you understand the use of these APIs:

```
//Other imports are removed for brevity
import com.fasterxml.jackson.databind.JsonNode;
import com.fasterxml.jackson.databind.ObjectMapper;
import com.fasterxml.jackson.databind.node.ObjectNode;

// Read in the JSON employee array form emp-array.json file
InputStream inputStream =
  getClass().getResourceAsStream("/emp-array.json");
//Create ObjectMapper instance
//ObjectMapper provides functionality for creating tree
//structure for JSON content
ObjectMapper objectMapper = new ObjectMapper();

//Read JSON content in to tree
JsonNode rootNode = objectMapper.readTree(inputStream);

//Check if the json content is in array form
if (rootNode.isArray()) {
//Iterate over each element in the array
  for (JsonNode objNode : rootNode) {
    //Find out the email node by traversing tree
```

```
      JsonNode emailNode = objNode.path("email");
      //if email is null, then update with
      //a system generated email
      if(emailNode.textValue() == null ){
        String generatedEmail=getSystemGeneratedEmail();
        ((ObjectNode)objNode).put("email", generatedEmail );
      }
    }
  }
//Write the modified tree to a json file
objectMapper.writeValue(new File("emp-modified-array.json"),
  rootNode);
if(inputStream != null)
  inputStream.close();
```

The tree model API discussed in this section produces a generalized tree representation for the JSON content. To learn how to generate a more specific object representation for JSON, refer to the next section.

Processing JSON with Jackson data binding APIs

Jackson data binding is used to convert the JSON representation into and from **Plain Old Java Object (POJO)** by using property accessors or annotations. With this API, you can either generate generic collection classes or more specific Java objects, such as the Employee object, for representing JSON data. Let's take a quick look at these two variants available for representing the JSON data.

Simple Jackson data binding with generalized objects

Sometimes, you may need to deal with highly dynamic JSON content where you may not be able to map data to a specific Java object, as the structure of the data changes dynamically. In such a scenario, you can use the simple binding APIs offered by the Jackson framework. You will use the Java maps, lists, strings, numbers, Booleans, and nulls for representing dynamic JSON data.

The following code snippet converts a JSON string into a map object. The `com.fasterxml.jackson.core.type.TypeReference` class is used for passing a generic type definition, which defines a type to bind to, as follows:

```
String jsonString =
  "{\" firstName\":\"John\",\"lastName\":\"Chen\"}";
ObjectMapper objectMapper = new ObjectMapper();
//properties will store name and value pairs read from jsonString
Map<String, String> properties = objectMapper.readValue(
  jsonString, new TypeReference<Map<String, String>>() { });
```

Full Jackson data binding with specialized objects

If the JSON data format, which a client receives, is well-structured, you can directly map the content to a concrete Java class. A full data binding solution fits well in such a scenario. For instance, you can create an `Employee` class for representing the `employee` data presented in the JSON format as long as the JSON content structure does not change. The following example uses the data binding offering from Jackson to convert the JSON content from the `emp.json` file into an `Employee` object. This example calls `readValue(InputStream src, Class<T> valueType)` on `ObjectMapper` to get the Java representation for the JSON content:

```
// emp.json file has following contents:
//{"employeeId":100,"firstName":"John","lastName":"Chen"}
ObjectMapper objectMapper = new ObjectMapper();
Employee employee = objectMapper.readValue(new File("emp.json"),
  Employee.class);
```

The next example demonstrates how you can create a Java collection containing the `Employee` objects from a JSON array of employees. Here, we need to construct a Java collection type, indicating the type of elements in the collection. To create a collection type, you can call the `constructCollectionType()` method on the `com.fasterxml.jackson.databind.type.TypeFactory` instance returned by `ObjectMapper`:

```
ObjectMapper objectMapper = new ObjectMapper();
CollectionType collectionType =
  objectMapper.getTypeFactory().constructCollectionType
  (List.class, Employee.class);
//"emp-array.json" file contains JSON array of employee data
List<Employee> emp = objectMapper.readValue(new File
  ("emp-array.json"), collectionType);
```

To convert a Java object into the JSON representation, you can call the `writeValue(OutputStream out, Object value)` method on `ObjectMapper`. The `writeValue()` method serializes any Java value to JSON and writes it to the output stream present in the method call. The following code snippet converts the `employee` object into the JSON structure and writes the content to the `emp.json` file:

```
//Get the employee object
Employee employee = getEmployeeEntity();
//Convert the object in to JSON and write to a file
objectMapper.writeValue(new File("emp.json"), employee);
```

How does Jackson map JSON object values to a Java class?

The default mapping mechanism used by Jackson is based on the bean naming properties. The binding layer copies the matching properties from the source to the destination. This implies that all the names present in a JSON object need to match the Java class properties for the default mapping mechanism to work. However, you can override the default mapping behavior by annotating a desired field (or by the `getter` and `setter` methods) with `@JsonProperty`. This annotation is used to override the default property name that is used during the serialization and deserialization process. To learn more, visit `http://wiki.fasterxml.com/JacksonAnnotations`.

Processing JSON with Jackson streaming APIs

The Jackson framework supports the streaming API for reading and writing JSON contents. You will use `org.codehaus.jackson.JsonParser` to read the JSON data and `org.codehaus.jackson.JsonGenerator` to write the data. The following table lists the important classes in the streaming model API:

Class	Description
`com.fasterxml.jackson.core.JsonParser`	This class is used for reading the JSON content.
`com.fasterxml.jackson.core.JsonGenerator`	This class is used for writing the JSON content.

com.fasterxml.jackson.core.JsonFactory	This is the main factory class of the Jackson package. It is used to generate JsonParser and JsonWriter.

Using Jackson streaming APIs to parse JSON data

The following example illustrates Jackson streaming APIs for reading JSON data. This example uses streaming APIs to generate a Java model for the JSON array of employee objects. As in the earlier examples, the emp-array.json file is used as the input source. The steps are as follows:

1. Create the com.fasterxml.jackson.core.JsonParser instance by using com.fasterxml.jackson.core.JsonFactory. The JsonParser class reads the JSON content from the file input stream.

2. The next step is to start parsing the JSON content read from the input source. The client may call the nextToken() method to forward the stream enough to determine the type of the next token. Based on the token type, the client can take an appropriate action. In the following sample code, the client checks for the start of an object (JsonToken.START_OBJECT) in order to copy the current JSON object to a new Employee instance. We use ObjectMapper to copy the content of the current JSON object to the Employee class:

```
//Step 1: Finds a resource with a given name.
InputStream inputStream = getClass().getResourceAsStream(
  "/emp-array.json");
//Creates Streaming parser
JsonParser jsonParser = new
   JsonFactory().createParser(inputStream);

//Step 2: Start parsing the contents
//We will use data binding feature from ObjectMapper
//for populating employee object
ObjectMapper objectMapper = new ObjectMapper();
//Continue the parsing till stream is opened or
//no more token is available
while (!jsonParser.isClosed()) {
  JsonToken jsonToken = jsonParser.nextToken();
  // if it is the last token then break the loop
  if (jsonToken == null) {
    break;
  }
  //If this is start of the object, then create
```

```
  //Employee instance and add it to the result list
  if (jsonToken.equals(JsonToken.START_OBJECT)) {
    //Use the objectMapper to copy the current
    // JSON object to Employee object
    employee = objectMapper.readValue(jsonParser,
      Employee.class);
    //Add the newly copied instance to the list
    employeeList.add(employee);

  }


}
//Close the stream after the use to release the resources
if (inputStream != null) {
  inputStream.close();
}
if (jsonParser != null) {
  jsonParser.close();
}
```

 To learn all the possible token types returned by `JsonParser` in the Jackson framework, refer to
http://fasterxml.github.io/jackson-core/javadoc/2.5/com/fasterxml/jackson/core/JsonToken.html.

Using Jackson streaming APIs to generate JSON

The following example illustrates Jackson streaming APIs for writing JSON data. This example reads a list of `Employee` objects, converts them into JSON representations, and then writes to the `OutputStream` object. The steps are as follows:

1. The following code snippet generates
   `com.fasterxml.jackson.core.JsonGenerator` by using
   `com.fasterxml.jackson.core.JsonFactory`:

   ```
   OutputStream outputStream = new
       FileOutputStream("emp-array.json");JsonGenerator jsonGenerator =
   new
       JsonFactory().createGenerator(outputStream,
         JsonEncoding.UTF8);
   ```

2. The next step is to build the JSON representation for the list of employees. The `writeStartArray()` method writes the starting marker for the JSON array ([). Now, write the marker for the object ({) by calling `writeStartObject()`. This is followed by the name-value pairs for the object by calling an appropriate write method. To write the end marker for the object (}), call `writeEndObject()`. Finally, to finish writing an array, call `writeEndArray()`:

```
jsonGenerator.writeStartArray();
List<Employee> employees = getEmployeesList();
for (Employee employee : employees) {
  jsonGenerator.writeStartObject();
  jsonGenerator.writeNumberField("employeeId",
    employee.getEmployeeId());
jsonGenerator.writeStringField("firstName",
    employee.getFirstName());  jsonGenerator.writeStringField("lastName",
    employee.getLastName());
  jsonGenerator.writeEndObject();

}
//JsonGenerator class writes the JSON content to the
//specified OutputStream.

jsonGenerator.writeEndArray();
```

3. Close the stream object after use:

```
//Close the streams to release associated resources
jsonGenerator.close();
outputStream.close();
```

With this topic, we are ending our discussion on Jackson. In this section, we discussed the various categories of APIs for processing JSON. An in-depth coverage of the Jackson API is beyond the scope of this book. More details on Jackson are available at `https://github.com/FasterXML/Jackson`.

The link that answers some of the generic queries that you may have around Jackson is `https://github.com/FasterXML/jackson/wiki/FAQ`.

In the next section, we will discuss Gson, yet another framework for processing JSON.

Using the Gson API for processing JSON

Gson is an open source Java library that can be used for converting Java objects into JSON representations and vice versa. The Gson library was originally developed by Google for its internal use and later open sourced under the terms of Apache License 2.0.

To learn the dependencies of Gson APIs, refer to `https://github.com/google/gson/blob/master/UserGuide.md#TOC-Gson-With-Maven`.

Processing JSON with object model APIs in Gson

The main class in the Gson library that you will use for building an object model from the JSON data is the `com.google.gson.Gson` class. Here is a list of the core Gson classes from the object model API category:

Class	Description
`com.google.gson.GsonBuilder`	This class is useful when you need to construct a Gson instance, overriding the default configurations such as custom date format, pretty printing, and custom serialization.
`com.google.gson.Gson`	This class is the main class for using Gson. This class does conversions from JSON to Java objects and the other way round.
`com.google.gson.reflect.TypeToken<T>`	This class is used for getting a generic type for a class. The resulting type can be used for serializing and deserializing JSON data.

Generating the object model from the JSON representation

Gson offers simpler APIs to convert the JSON representation into Java objects. To do this, you can call the `fromJson(Reader json, Class<T> classOfT)` method on the `com.google.gson.Gson` object. The following example will help you understand the end-to-end use of Gson APIs for deserializing the JSON content to Java objects:

1. The first step is to create a `Gson` instance. The `Gson` class offers all the necessary methods for serializing and deserializing JSON data. You can simply create an instance by calling `new Gson()`. However, in this example, we use `com.google.gson.GsonBuilder` to create a `Gson` instance. This is because `GsonBuilder` lets you override the default configuration for a `Gson` instance. We use this feature to override the default date format used for serializing and deserializing the date fields present in the JSON content. The following code snippet creates a `Gson` instance:

    ```
    //Other imports are removed for brevity
    import com.google.gson.Gson;
    import com.google.gson.GsonBuilder;

    // Get GsonBuilder object
    GsonBuilder gsonBuilder = new GsonBuilder();
    //Set date format for converting date presented in
    //form (in JSON data)  to java.util.Date
    gsonBuilder.setDateFormat("yyyy-MM-dd");
    //Get gson object
    Gson gson = gsonBuilder.create();
    ```

2. The next step is to convert the JSON content into an appropriate Java class. You can do this by invoking `fromJson(Reader json, Class<T> classOfT)` on the `Gson` instance. The following sample code converts the JSON representation of the `employee` object into the `employee` Java object:

    ```
    //Read the json input file with current class's class
    //loader
    // emp.json contains JSON employee objectInputStream inputStream =
      getClass().getResourceAsStream("/emp.json");
    BufferedReader reader = new BufferedReader(
      new InputStreamReader(inputStream));
    //Converts JSON string to Employee object
    Employee employee = gson.fromJson(reader, Employee.class);
    ```

Generating the parameterized Java collection from the JSON representation

The previous example demonstrated the Gson APIs for converting a JSON representation of a single `employee` object into a Java object. This section discusses how to convert a JSON object array into a Java collection. You can do this by calling the `fromJson(JsonReader reader, Type typeOfT)` method on the `Gson` instance. Let's take an example to better understand this API. The steps are as follows:

1. The `emp-array.json` file used in this example contains a JSON array of the `employee` objects.

2. This example converts the JSON array read from the input file into the `List<Employee>` collection object, which is a parameterized collection type (generic type). We use `com.google.gson.reflect.TypeToken<T>` to define the collection type that holds the `Employee` objects.

3. To deserialize the JSON data read from the file into the `List<Employee>` object, call `fromJson(Reader json, Type typeOfT)` on the `Gson` object with the file input stream reader and the desired `TypeToken` object as the parameter.

The following code snippet illustrates these steps:

```
//Step 1: Read emp-array.json
InputStream inputStream =
getClass().getResourceAsStream(("/emp-array.json");
BufferedReader reader = new BufferedReader(new
  InputStreamReader(inputStream));
// Step 2: Define TypeToken
// Define a  parameterized collection type to hold the List
// of Employees returned by Gson::fromJSon method call.
Type listType = new TypeToken<ArrayList<Employee>>(){}
  .getType();
//Step 3: Convert JSON array to List<Employee>
//Generates list of employees by calling Gson::fromJson()
Gson gson = new Gson();
List<Employee> employees = gson.fromJson(reader, listType);
```

How does Gson map a JSON object to a Java class?

The default mapping mechanism used by Gson is based on bean properties. The binding layer copies the matching properties from the source to the destination. This implies that all the names present in a JSON object need to match the Java class properties for the default mapping mechanism to work. However, you can override the default mapping behavior by annotating the desired attribute with `@SerializedName`. This annotation indicates that the annotated member should be serialized to JSON with the provided name value as its field name.

Generating the JSON representation from the object model

Gson has simplified APIs to convert the object model into the JSON content. Depending upon the type of the object model, you can use either of the following APIs to get the JSON representation:

- To convert a Java object into JSON, you can call the `toJson(Object src)` method. Here is an example:

```
// Get Employee object that needs
//to be converted into JSON
Employee emp=getEmployee();
Gson gson = new Gson();
// create JSON String from Object
String jsonEmp = gson.toJson(emp);
```

- To convert a parameterized collection into a JSON string, you can use `toJson(Object src, Type typeOfSrc)`. Here is an example:

```
//Get Employee list that needs to be converted into JSON
List<Employee>  employees= getEmployeeList();
Gson gson = new Gson();
//Specify collection type that you want
//to convert into JSON
Type typeOfSource = new
  TypeToken<List<Employee>>(){}.getType();
// create JSON String from Object
String jsonEmps = gson.toJson(employees, typeOfSource);
```

Processing JSON with Gson streaming APIs

In addition to the object model APIs, the Gson library supports the streaming APIs for reading and writing the JSON representations. The streaming APIs in Gson follow the pull parser model. Here is a list of the important streaming API classes in Gson:

Class	Description
`com.google.gson.stream.JsonReader`	This class reads the JSON-encoded value as a stream of tokens. Tokens are read in the same order as they appear in the JSON document.
`com.google.gson.stream.JsonWriter`	This class writes a JSON-encoded value to the stream, one token at a time.

Reading JSON data with Gson streaming APIs

The following example demonstrates the use of the Gson streaming APIs for reading JSON data.

This example converts the JSON array of `employee` objects present in the `emp-array.json` file into a list of `Employee` objects. The steps are as follows:

1. Gson provides `com.google.gson.stream.JsonReader` to read the JSON encoded value as a stream of tokens. You can create a `JsonReader` instance by supplying the `InputStreamReader` instance as input.

2. As the next step, start parsing the contents. The tokens returned by `JsonReader` are traversed in the same order as they appear in the JSON document. As this example uses an array of JSON objects as input, the parser starts off by calling `beginArray()`. This call consumes the array's opening bracket. The client then calls `beginObject()` to consume the object's opening brace. This call is followed by a series of `nextName()` and `next<DataType>`, such as `nextString()`, to read the name value representing the object. After reading the entire object, the client calls `endObject()` to consume the next token from the JSON stream and asserts that it is the end of the current object. Once all the objects are read, the client invokes `endArray()` to consume the next token from the JSON stream and asserts that it is the end of the current array.

The following code snippet implements the two preceding steps:

```
//Step 1: Read emp-array.json file containing JSON
// array of employees
InputStream inputStream =
  getClass().getResourceAsStream("/emp-array.json");
InputStreamReader inputStreamReader = new
  InputStreamReader(inputStream);

//Step 2: Start parsing the contents
List<Employee> employeeList = new ArrayList<Employee>();
JsonReader reader = new JsonReader(inputStreamReader);
reader.beginArray();
while (reader.hasNext()) {
  // The method readEmployee(...) is listed below
  Employee employee = readEmployee(reader);
  employeeList.add(employee);
}
reader.endArray();
reader.close();
```

Here is the definition of the `readEmployee(JsonReader reader)` method used in the preceding code snippet:

```
// This method is referred in the above code snippet to create
// Employee object
private Employee readEmployee(JsonReader reader) throws
    IOException {
  Employee employee = new Employee();

  reader.beginObject();
  while (reader.hasNext()) {
    String keyName = reader.nextName();
    switch (keyName) {
      case "firstName":
        employee.setFirstName(reader.nextString());
      break;
      case "lastName":
        employee.setLastName(reader.nextString());
      break;
      case "email":
        employee.setEmail(reader.nextString());
      break;
      case "employeeId":
        employee.setEmployeeId(reader.nextInt());
      break;
      default:
    }
```

```
    }
    reader.endObject();
    return employee;
}
```

Writing JSON data with Gson streaming APIs

You can use `com.google.gson.stream.JsonWriter` to write the JSON-encoded value to the stream. The following example demonstrates the use of Gson streaming APIs for writing JSON data. This example writes the JSON array representation of `employee` objects to the `emp-array.json` file. The steps are as follows:

1. To write the JSON content, build the `JsonWriter` object, which takes the implementation of `java.io.Writer` as the input.

2. Once the `JsonWriter` instance is created, start writing the JSON content. As this example writes an array of the `employee` objects, we start by invoking the `beginArray()` method. This call begins encoding a new array. Then, call `beginObject()` to start encoding a new object. This is followed by the encoding of the name and the value. To finish the encoding of the current object, call `endObject()`, and to finish the encoding of the current array, call `endArray()`:

```java
//Step 1: Build JsonWriter to read the JSON contents
OutputStream outputStream = new FileOutputStream(
    "emp-array.json");
BufferedWriter bufferedWriter= new BufferedWriter(
new OutputStreamWriter(outputStream));
//Creates JsonWriter object
JsonWriter writer = new JsonWriter(bufferedWriter);

//Step 2: Start writing JSON contents

//Starts with writing array
writer.beginArray();
List<Employee> employees = getEmployeesList();
for (Employee employee : employees) {
  //start encoding the object
  writer.beginObject();
  //Write name:value pair to the object
  writer.name("employeeId").value
      (employee.getEmployeeId());
  writer.name("firstName").value(employee.getFirstName());
  writer.name("lastName").value(employee.getLastName());
  writer.name("email").value(employee.getEmail());
  //Finish encoding of the object
```

```
        writer.endObject();
    }
    //Finish encoding of the array
    writer.endArray();
    writer.flush();
    //close writer
    writer.close();
```

An in-depth coverage of the Gson API is beyond the scope of this book. To learn more about Gson, visit https://code.google.com/p/google-gson/. The Gson API documentation is available at https://www.javadoc.io/doc/com.google.code.gson/gson/2.3.1.

With this, we have finished our discussion on the three popular JSON processing frameworks that you may find today. We may revisit some of these tools and frameworks with more complex use cases later in the book. In the following section, let's explore the proposed enhancements in Java EE8 for processing JSON.

Java EE 8 enhancements for processing JSON

While Java EE8 is on its way and expected by the end of 2017, one of the most-awaited enhancement in Java EE 8 is related to JSON processing, covered by *JSR 374 – Java API for JSON Processing 1.1*.

With JSON becoming widely used in service-oriented patterns (such as reusable contract and lightweight endpoint), another key feature planned in Java EE8 is the JSR 367 Java API for **JSON Binding (JSON-B)**. Similar to GSON, JSR 367 brings in the capability of marshalling/unmarshalling Java objects to JSON representation. JSON-B will be the standard binding layer for converting Java objects to/from JSON messages, similar to JAXB for XML binding.

Service-oriented patterns cover a variety of design patterns used to address the pain points that inhibit adopting Service-oriented principles. For example, reusable contract pattern avoids tight coupling by having a generic interface. Similarly lightweight endpoint can be applied to expose specific capabilities of an entity consumer in interest, with well-suited patterns for building fine-grained services.

Using the JSR 374 – Java API for JSON Processing 1.1

JSR 374: Java API for JSON Processing 1.1 supercedes JSR 353: Java API for JSON Processing, to accomplish the following key objectives:

- Support for JSON Pointer and JSON Patch
- Add editing/transformation operations to the JSON object model
- Update the API to work with Java SE 8

These goals are met with the help of the following key APIs mentioned in the JSR:

Interface	Description
`javax.json.JsonPointer`	This interface represents an immutable implementation of a JSON Pointer, as defined by RFC 6901 (`https://tools.ietf.org/html/rfc6901`). JSON Pointer can be used to perform the following functions: • Add `JsonValue` at the referenced location in the specified target • Replace `JsonValue` at the referenced location in the specified target with the supplied value • Check for the presence of the value in the specified target • Fetch `JsonValue` at the referenced location in the specified target • Remove `JsonValue` at the referenced location in the specified target
`javax.json.JsonPatch`	This interface represents an immutable implementation of a JSON Patch as defined by RFC 6902 (`https://tools.ietf.org/html/rfc6902`). JSON Patch operates on the target JSON document by applying the `add`, `copy`, `move`, `replace`, `remove`, and `test` functions.

Refer to the complete list of the object model APIs available in JSR 374 at `https://jcp.org/aboutJava/communityprocess/final/jsr374/index.html`.

Understanding the JSON Pointer

Similar to XPATH for XML processing, JSON Pointer is used to reference a specific value within a JSON document. JSON Pointer is intended to be easily expressed in JSON string values as well as URI RFC3986 fragment identifiers:

Syntax type	Syntax
String	Unicode string containing a sequence of zero or more reference tokens, each prefixed by a '/' (%x2F) character. Because the characters, '~' (%x7E) and '/' (%x2F), have special meanings in JSON Pointer, '~' needs to be encoded as '~0' and '/' needs to be encoded as '~1' when these characters appear in a reference token.
URI	A JSON Pointer can be represented in a URI fragment identifier by encoding it into octets using UTF-8 RFC3629, while percent-encoding the characters not allowed by the fragment rule in RFC3986.

For example, let's consider the following JSON document:

```
{
"departmentId":10,
"departmentName":"IT",
"country":"US",
"manager":{"firstName":"John","lastName":"Chen","email":"john.chen@xxx.com"
,"doj":"2012-04-23T18:25:43.511Z"},
"directReportIds":["12345","67890"]
}
```

Let's examine how the values in the preceding JSON document can be referenced using JSON Pointer:

JSON pointer (string syntax)	JSON pointer (URI syntax)	Referenced value
""	#	The whole document
"/departmentId"	#/departmentId	10
"/manager"	#/manager	{firstName:John,lastName:Chen, email:john.chen@xxx.com,doj:2012-04-23T18:25:43.511Z}
"/manager/firstName"	#/manager/firstName	John
"/directReportIds/0"	#/directReportIds/0	12345

Processing JSON using JSON Pointer

The following example reads the JSON representation of the employee object from the
emp.json file and uses the javax.json.JsonPointer API to reference
the firstName value inside the JSON document and modify its contents.

First, create an instance of JsonObject using JsonReader. Then, define the JsonPointer
for the firstName reference. Using JsonPointer, access or modify the value defined
against firstName:

```java
public class JSR374JsonPointerExample {

  private static final Logger logger =
Logger.getLogger(JSR374JsonPointerExample.class.getName());

  public static void main(String[] args) throws IOException {
  logger.setLevel(Level.INFO);

  //Step-1 Read the Target JSON Document using JSR 353 API as mentioned in
the previous sections
  String jsonFileName = "/emp.json";
  InputStream inputStream =
JSR374JsonPointerExample.class.getResourceAsStream(jsonFileName);
  Reader reader = new InputStreamReader(inputStream, "UTF-8");

  JsonReader jsonReader = Json.createReader(reader);
  JsonObject jsonObject = (JsonObject) jsonReader.read();

  //Step-2: Create the JSON Pointer passing the reference location
  JsonPointer pointer = Json.createPointer("/firstName");

  //Step-3: Fetch the firstName from target object using the pointer
  JsonValue value = pointer.getValue(jsonObject);

  logger.log(Level.INFO, "Fetched First Name:{0}", value.toString());

  //Step-4: Alter the first name to different value
  JsonValue replaceFirstName = Json.createValue("Mike");
  jsonObject = pointer.add(jsonObject, replaceFirstName);

  //Step-5: Fetch the modified firstName from target object using the
pointer
  value = pointer.getValue(jsonObject);

  logger.log(Level.INFO, "Modified First Name:{0}", value.toString());
  }
}
```

The preceding program reads the `emp.json` file and prints the input and modified employee first name, as shown ahead:

```
Output of the Program:
Fetched First Name:"John"
Modified First Name:"Mike"
```

Understanding the JSON Patch

JSON Patch is a format (identified by the media type, `application/ json-patch+json`) for expressing changes to a target JSON document intended for use with the HTTP PATCH method to apply partial modification of the target resource. JSON Patch operations are expressed in the JSON document, as follows:

Operation	JSON Patch document
`Add`: Used to add the `<value>` to the specified `<location>`.	`{ op: add, path: <location>, value: <value> }`
`Remove`: Used to remove the value at the specified `<location>`.	`{ op: remove, path: <location>}`
`Replace`: Used to update the given `<value>` at the specified `<location>`.	`{ op: replace, path: <location>, value: <value> }`
`Copy`: Used to copy a value from the `<from-location>` to the `<destination-location>`.	`{ op: copy, from: <from-location>, path: <destination-location> }`
`Move`: Used to move a value from the `<from-location>` to the `<destination-location>`.	`{ op: move, from: <from-location>, path: <destination-location> }`
`Test`: Used to test the presence of a given `value` at the specified `location`. The Result of the test operation can be used to decide before performing other patch operations.	`{ op: test, path: <location>, value: <value> }` `]`

Processing JSON using JSON Patch

The following example reads the JSON representation of the employee object from the emp.json file and uses the javax.json.JsonPatch API to add the gender value and remove hiredate inside the JSON document:

1. Read the target JSON document using JsonReader
2. Instantiate PatchBuilder
3. Use PatchBuilder to add gender data
4. Use PatchBuilder to remove hiredate
5. Construct and apply patch operations on the target JSON document

The implementation of the previous steps is demonstrated in the following program:

```
public class JSR374JsonPatchExample {

 private static final Logger logger =
Logger.getLogger(JSR374JsonPointerExample.class.getName());

 public static void main(String[] args) throws IOException {
 logger.setLevel(Level.INFO);

 //Step-1 Read the Target JSON Document using JSR 353 API as mentioned in
 the //previous sections
 String jsonFileName = "/emp.json";
 InputStream inputStream =
JSR374JsonPointerExample.class.getResourceAsStream(jsonFileName);
 Reader reader = new InputStreamReader(inputStream, "UTF-8");

 JsonReader jsonReader = Json.createReader(reader);
 JsonObject jsonObject = (JsonObject) jsonReader.read();

 logger.log(Level.INFO, "Input Employee:{0}", jsonObject.toString());

 //Step-2: Instantiate the Patch Builder to include patch operations
 JsonPatchBuilder patchBuilder = Json.createPatchBuilder();

 //Step-3: Add gender data to Employee data
 patchBuilder.add("/gender", "Male");
 //Step-4:Remove the hireDate from Employee data
 patchBuilder.remove("/hireDate");

 //Step-5: Construct and apply the patch operations on the
 //target object
 JsonPatch patch = patchBuilder.build();
 jsonObject = patch.apply(jsonObject);
```

```
logger.log(Level.INFO, "Output Employee:{0}", jsonObject.toString());
}
```

The preceding program reads the `emp.json` file and prints the input and patched `JsonObject`, as shown ahead:

Output of the Program:
```
Input
Employee:{"employeeId":100,"firstName":"John","lastName":"Chen","email":"jo
hn.chen@xxxx.com","hireDate":"2008-10-16"}
Output
Employee:{"employeeId":100,"firstName":"John","lastName":"Chen","email":"jo
hn.chen@xxxx.com","gender":"Male"}
```

Using the JSR 367 – Java API for JSON Binding

Similar to JAXB for XML processing, the JSR 367: Java API for **JSON Binding (JSON-B)** defines the binding layer for transforming Java objects to JSON messages and vice-versa, as depicted ahead:

Now let's look at the key components of JSON-B:

Class or Interface	Description
`javax.json.bind.Jsonb`	This is the core API that provides the functions to serialize a Java object to JSON and deserialize to Java object from a JSON input.
`javax.json.bind.JsonbConfig`	This class provides functions for formatting and encoding to create customized JSON data.
`javax.json.bind.JsonbBuilder`	As the name suggests, this API abstracts the creation of JSON-B instances for the specified configuration or provider.

`javax.json.bind.adapter.JsonbAdapter`	JSON-B supports mapping for a majority of Java data types to JSON. There may be instances when some of the custom Java types may not map to JSON (for example, by default, JSON-B uses ISO date formats required to handle custom date formats. Also, in cases where a client is querying for employee details, we need to respond back with a part of the employee details masking personal details). To handle these situations `JsonbAdapter` provides the abstraction to implement custom mapping of Java type to JSON and vice-versa.

Processing JSON using JSON-B

The following example reads the JSON representation of the Employee object from the emp.json file and uses the javax.json.bind.JsonBuilder to create an instance of javax.json.bind.Jsonb to map the Employee object to JSON representation and vice-versa:

1. Read the target JSON document using JsonReader
2. Create an instance of JSON-B using JsonbBuilder
3. Unmarshal the JSON object to the Employee Java object
4. Create a Jsonb instance with formatting enabled
5. Marshal the Employee Java object to JSON

The implementation of the preceding steps is demonstrated in the following program:

```
public class JSR367JsonbDefaultBindingExample {

 private static final Logger logger =
Logger.getLogger(JSR367JsonbDefaultBindingExample.class.getName());

 public static void main(String[] args) throws IOException {
 logger.setLevel(Level.INFO);

 //Step-1:Read the Target JSON Document
 String jsonFileName = "/emp.json";
 InputStream inputStream =
JSR374JsonPointerExample.class.getResourceAsStream(jsonFileName);
 Reader reader = new InputStreamReader(inputStream, "UTF-8");
```

```
JsonReader jsonReader = Json.createReader(reader);
JsonObject jsonObject = (JsonObject) jsonReader.read();

//Step-2: Create instance of Jsonb using JsonbBuilder
Jsonb jsonb = JsonbBuilder.create();

//Step-3:Map JSON to Employee Object
Employee employee = jsonb.fromJson(jsonObject.toString(), Employee.class);

logger.log(Level.INFO, "Employee Object constructed from JSON:{0}",
employee);

//Step-4:Create Jsonb instance with formatting enabled
JsonbConfig config = new JsonbConfig().withFormatting(Boolean.TRUE);
jsonb = JsonbBuilder.create(config);

//Step-5:Map Employee Object to JSON
String employeeJson = jsonb.toJson(employee);
logger.log(Level.INFO, "JSON constructed from Employee object:{0}",
employeeJson);
    }
```

The preceding program reads the emp.json file and prints the Employee object and JSON, as shown ahead:

```
Output of the Program:
Employee Object constructed from JSON:Employee{employeeId=100,
firstName=John, lastName=Chen, email=john.chen@xxxx.com,
hireDate=2008-10-16}
JSON constructed from Employee object:
{
  "email": "john.chen@xxxx.com",
  "employeeId": "100",
  "firstName": "John",
  "hireDate": "2008-10-16",
  "lastName": "Chen"
}
```

Summary

In this chapter, you were introduced to the various processing models for the JSON content and some of the popular Java-based JSON processing frameworks available today. We also explored the upcoming enhancements for processing JSON in Java EE8. This chapter is essential for understanding how the JSON-based request and response messages are bound to the Java model while building REST APIs later in the book.

This chapter is not meant to recommend any specific JSON framework for your application but to help you understand the popular frameworks available today for processing JSON, and their offerings in general.

In the next chapter, we will build our first REST service by using JAX-RS APIs.

3
Introducing the JAX-RS API

In the previous chapters, we covered the basics of RESTful web services and looked at Java APIs for JSON processing. By now, you have a good understanding of the RESTful architectural style and the main components, such as resources, URI, and so on, that form a REST API. It is time for us to put all this knowledge into practice. In this chapter, we will build simple RESTful web services using the JAX-RS APIs. This chapter covers the following topics:

- An overview of the JAX-RS annotations
- Understanding data binding in JAX-RS
- Building your first RESTful web service with JAX-RS
- Client APIs for accessing RESTful web services

An overview of JAX-RS

There are many tools and frameworks available in the market today for building RESTful web services. You can use tools of your choice as long as the REST implementation meets the RESTful architectural constraints discussed in the first chapter. There are some recent developments with respect to the standardization of various framework APIs by providing unified interfaces for a variety of implementations. Let's take a quick look at this effort.

As you may know, Java EE is the industry standard for developing portable, robust, scalable, and secure server-side Java applications. The Java EE 6 release took the first step towards standardizing RESTful web service APIs by introducing a Java API for RESTful web services (JAX-RS). JAX-RS is an integral part of the Java EE platform, which ensures portability of your REST API code across all Java EE-compliant application servers. The first release of JAX-RS was based on JSR 311. The next version, JAX-RS 2 (based on JSR 339), was released as part of the Java EE 7 platform. The latest version, JAX-RS 2.1 (based on JSR 370), is part of the Java EE8 platform. There are multiple JAX-RS implementations available today by various vendors. Some of the popular JAX-RS implementations are as follows:

- **Jersey RESTful web service framework**: This framework is an open source framework for developing RESTful web services in Java. It serves as a JAX-RS reference implementation. You can learn more about this project at `https://jersey.github.io/`.
- **Apache CXF**: This framework is an open source web services framework. CXF supports both JAX-WS and JAX-RS web services. To learn more about CXF, refer to `http://cxf.apache.org`.
- **RESTEasy**: This framework is an open source project from JBoss, which provides various modules to help you build a RESTful web service. To learn more about RESTEasy, refer to `http://resteasy.jboss.org`.
- **Restlet**: This framework is a lightweight open source RESTful web service framework. It has good support for building both scalable RESTful web service APIs and lightweight REST clients (which suits mobile platforms well). You can learn more about Restlet at `http://restlet.com`.

We will be using the Jersey implementation of JAX-RS for running the examples discussed in this book (unless otherwise specified). Remember that you are not locked down to any specific vendor here; the RESTful web service APIs that you build using JAX-RS will run on any JAX-RS implementation as long as you do not use any vendor-specific APIs in the code.

JAX-RS annotations

The main goal of the JAX-RS specification is to make the RESTful web service development easier than it has been in the past. As JAX-RS is a part of the Java EE platform, your code becomes portable across all Java EE-compliant servers. In this section, we will familiarize ourselves with some JAX-RS annotations for building RESTful web services based on their usage context:

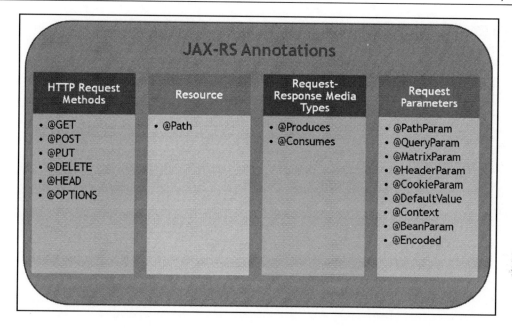

Specifying the dependency of the JAX-RS API

To use JAX-RS APIs in your project, you need to add the `javax.ws.rs-api` JAR file to the class path. If the consuming project uses Maven for building the source, the dependency entry for the `javax.ws.rs-api` JAR file in the **Project Object Model** (POM) file may look like the following:

```
<dependency>
    <groupId>javax.ws.rs</groupId>
    <artifactId>javax.ws.rs-api</artifactId>
    <version>2.0.1</version><!-- set the right version -->
    <scope>provided</scope><!-- compile time dependency -->
</dependency>
```

Refer to https://mvnrepository.com/artifact/javax.ws.rs/javax.ws.rs-api for the latest versions of JAX-RS API.

Using JAX-RS annotations to build RESTful web services

Java annotations provide the metadata for your Java class, which can be used during compilation, deployment, or at runtime in order to perform designated tasks. The use of annotations allows us to create RESTful web services as easily as we develop a POJO class. Here, we leave the interception of the HTTP requests and representation negotiations to the framework and concentrate on the business rules necessary to solve the problem at hand.

> If you are not familiar with Java annotations, go through the tutorial available
> at: http://docs.oracle.com/javase/tutorial/java/annotations/.

We will take a quick look at some of the very frequently used JAX-RS annotations in this section. Note that the next section does not provide a comprehensive list of all the JAX-RS annotations; we will see more annotations as we proceed further in this chapter.

Annotations for defining a RESTful resource

REST resources are the fundamental elements of any RESTful web service. A REST resource can be defined as an object that is of a specific type with the associated data and is optionally associated with other resources. It also exposes a set of standard operations corresponding to the HTTP method types, such as the HEAD, GET, POST, PUT, and DELETE methods, using the @HttpMethod annotation.

> Resource classes are Java POJO classes, which use JAX-RS annotations to implement a web service. Each resource class must have at least one method annotated with @Path or a request method designator (@HttpMethod). Only public methods of a resource class can be exposed as resource methods.

@Path

The @javax.ws.rs.Path annotation indicates the URI path to which a resource class or a class method must respond. The value that you specify for the @Path annotation is relative to the URI of the server where the REST resource is hosted. This annotation can be applied at both the class and method levels.

TIP

A @Path annotation value is not required to have leading or trailing slashes (/), as you may see in some examples. The JAX-RS runtime will parse the URI path templates in the same way even if they have leading or trailing slashes.

Specifying the @Path annotation on a resource class

The following code snippet illustrates how you can make a POJO class respond to a URI path template containing the /departments path fragment:

```
import javax.ws.rs.Path;

@Path("departments")
public class DepartmentService {
  //Rest of the code goes here
}
```

The /department path fragment that you see in this example is relative to the base path in the URI. The base path typically takes the http://host:port/<context-root>/<application-path> URI pattern. You will learn how to set an application path for a JAX-RS application in the *Specifying application path* section, which comes later in this chapter.

Specifying the @Path annotation on a resource class method

The following code snippet shows how you can specify @Path on a method in a REST resource class. Note that for an annotated method, the base URI is the effective URI of the containing class. For instance, you will use the URI of the /departments/count form to invoke the getTotalDepartments() method defined in the DepartmentService class, where departments is the @Path annotation set on the class:

```
import javax.ws.rs.GET;
import javax.ws.rs.Path;
import javax.ws.rs.Produces;
@Path("departments")
public class DepartmentService {
    @GET
    @Path("count")
    @Produces("text/plain")
    public Integer getTotalDepartments() {
        return findTotalRecordCount();
    }
  //Rest of the code goes here
}
```

no parameter in this case, as no variable in path.

Specifying variables in the URI path template

Very often, a client will want to retrieve the data for a specific object by passing the desired parameter to the server. JAX-RS allows you to do this via the URI path variables, as discussed here.

The URI path template allows you to define the variables that appear as placeholders in the URI. These variables will be replaced at runtime with the values set by the client.

The following example illustrates the use of the path variable to request for a specific department resource. The URI path template looks like this: `/departments/{id}`. At runtime, the client can pass an appropriate value for the `id` parameter to get the desired resource from the server. For instance, the URI path of the `/departments/10` format returns the IT department details to the caller.

The following code snippet illustrates how you can pass the department ID as a path variable for deleting a specific department record. The path URI looks like `/departments/10`:

```
import javax.ws.rs.Path;
import javax.ws.rs.DELETE;

@Path("departments")
public class DepartmentService {

    @DELETE
    @Path("{id}")
    public void removeDepartment(@PathParam("id")
    short id) {
        removeDepartmentEntity(id);
    }
    //Other methods removed for brevity
}
```

 The annotation value is automatically encoded. For example, `@Path ("department list/{id}")` is the same as `@Path ("department%20list/{id}")`.

In the preceding code snippet, the `@PathParam` annotation is used for copying the value of the path variable to the method parameter. We will discuss this in detail in the *Annotations for accessing request parameters* section.

Restricting values for path variables with regular expressions

JAX-RS lets you use regular expressions in the URI path template for restricting the values set for the path variables at runtime by the client. By default, the JAX-RS runtime ensures that all the URI variables match the following regular expression: [^/]+?. The default regular expression allows the path variable to take any character except the forward slash (/). What if you want to override this default regular expression imposed on the path variable values? Good news is that JAX-RS lets you specify your own regular expression for the path variables. For example, you can set the regular expression as given in the following code snippet in order to ensure that the department name variable present in the URI path consists only of lowercase and uppercase alphanumeric characters:

```
@DELETE
@Path("{name: [a-zA-Z][a-zA-Z_0-9]}")
public void removeDepartmentByName(@PathParam("name")
   String deptName) {
     //Method implementation goes here
}
```

If the path variable does not match the regular expression set of the resource class or method, the system reports the status back to the caller with an appropriate HTTP status code, such as 404 Not Found, which tells the caller that the requested resource could not be found at the moment.

Annotations for specifying request-response media types

The Content-Type header field in HTTP describes the body's content type present in the request and response messages. The content types are represented using standard internet media types. A RESTful web service makes use of this header field to indicate the type of content in the request or response message body. We discussed the Content-Type header fields in the *Representing content types using HTTP header fields* section in Chapter 1, *Introducing the REST Architectural Style*.

JAX-RS allows you to specify which internet media types of representation a resource can produce or consume by using the @javax.ws.rs.Produces and @javax.ws.rs.Consumes annotations, respectively. You will learn these two annotations with examples in this section.

@Produces

The @javax.ws.rs.Produces annotation is used for defining the internet media type(s) that a REST resource class method can return to the client. You can define this either at the class level (which will get defaulted for all methods) or at the method level. The method-level annotations override the class-level annotations. The possible internet media types that a REST API can produce are as follows:

- application/atom+xml
- application/json
- application/octet-stream
- application/svg+xml
- application/xhtml+xml
- application/xml
- text/html
- text/plain
- text/xml

The following example uses the @Produces annotation at the class level in order to set the default response media type as JSON for all the resource methods in this class. At runtime, the binding provider will convert the Java representation of the return value to the JSON format. This is discussed in the *Understanding the data binding rules in JAX-RS* section, which comes later in this chapter:

```
import javax.ws.rs.Path;
import javax.ws.rs.Produces;
import javax.ws.rs.core.MediaType;

@Path("departments")
@Produces(MediaType.APPLICATION_JSON)
public class DepartmentService{
   //Class implementation goes here...
}
```

@Consumes

The @javax.ws.rs.Consumes annotation defines the internet media type(s) that the resource class methods can accept. You can define the @Consumes annotation either at the class level (which will get defaulted for all methods) or at the method level. The method-level annotations override the class-level annotations. The possible internet media types that a REST API can consume are as follows:

- application/atom+xml
- application/json
- application/octet-stream
- application/svg+xml
- application/xhtml+xml
- application/xml
- text/html
- text/plain
- text/xml
- multipart/form-data
- application/x-www-form-urlencoded

The following example illustrates how you can use the @Consumes attribute to designate a method in a class to consume a payload presented in the JSON media type. The binding provider will copy the JSON representation of an input message to the Department parameter of the createDepartment() method:

```
import javax.ws.rs.Consumes;
import javax.ws.rs.core.MediaType;
import javax.ws.rs.POST;

@POST
@Consumes(MediaType.APPLICATION_JSON)
public void createDepartment(Department entity) {
  //Method implementation goes here...
}
```

 The javax.ws.rs.core.MediaType class defines constants for all the media types supported in JAX-RS. To learn more about the MediaType class, visit the API documentation available at http://docs.oracle.com/javaee/7/api/javax/ws/rs/core/MediaType.html.

Annotations for processing HTTP request methods

In general, RESTful web services communicate over HTTP with the standard HTTP verbs (also known as method types) such as GET, PUT, POST, DELETE, HEAD, and OPTIONS. In this section, we will see annotations provided by JAX-RS for enabling a POJO class to process the standard HTTP method types. If you need a quick brush-up of the HTTP method types used by a RESTful system, refer to the *Understating HTTP request methods* section in Chapter 1, *Introducing the REST Architectural Style*.

@GET

A RESTful system uses the HTTP GET method type for retrieving the resources referenced in the URI path. The @javax.ws.rs.GET annotation designates the method of a resource class to respond to the HTTP GET requests.

The following code snippet illustrates the use of the @GET annotation to make a method respond to the HTTP GET request type. In this example, the REST URI for accessing the findAllDepartments() method may look like /departments. The complete URI path may take the http://host:port/<context-root>/<application-path>/departments URI pattern:

```
//imports removed for brevity
@Path("departments")
public class DepartmentService {
  @GET
  @Produces(MediaType.APPLICATION_JSON)
  public List<Department> findAllDepartments() {
    //Find all departments from the data store
    List<Department> departments = findAllDepartmentsFromDB();
    return departments;
  }
  //Other methods removed for brevity
}
```

@PUT

The HTTP `PUT` method is used for updating or creating the resource pointed by the URI. The `@javax.ws.rs.PUT` annotation designates the method of a resource class to respond to the HTTP `PUT` requests. The `PUT` request generally has a message body carrying the payload. The value of the payload could be any valid internet media type, such as the JSON object, XML structure, plain text, HTML content, or binary stream. When a request reaches a server, the framework intercepts the request and directs it to the appropriate method that matches the URI path and the HTTP method type. The request payload will be mapped to the method parameter as appropriate by the framework.

The following code snippet shows how you can use the `@PUT` annotation to designate the `editDepartment()` method to respond to the HTTP `PUT` request. The payload present in the message body will be converted and copied to the `department` parameter by the framework:

```
@PUT
@Path("{id}")
@Consumes(MediaType.APPLICATION_JSON)
public void editDepartment(@PathParam("id") Short id,
    Department department) {
  //Updates department entity to data store
  updateDepartmentEntity(id, department);
}
```

in path *in payload ie. body*

@POST

The HTTP `POST` method posts data to the server. Typically, this method type is used for creating a resource. The `@javax.ws.rs.POST` annotation designates the method of a resource class to respond to the HTTP `POST` requests.

The following code snippet shows how you can use the `@POST` annotation to designate the `createDepartment()` method to respond to the HTTP `POST` request. The payload present in the message body will be converted and copied to the `department` parameter by the framework:

in payload

```
@POST
public void createDepartment(Department department) {
  //Create department entity in data store
  createDepartmentEntity(department);
}
```

LETE

The HTTP DELETE method deletes the resource pointed by the URI. The @javax.ws.rs.DELETE annotation designates the method of a resource class to respond to the HTTP DELETE requests.

The following code snippet shows how you can use the @DELETE annotation to designate the removeDepartment() method to respond to the HTTP DELETE request. The department ID is passed as the path variable in this example:

```
@DELETE
@Path("{id}")
public void removeDepartment(@PathParam("id") Short id) {
    //remove department entity from data store
    removeDepartmentEntity(id);
}
```

@HEAD

The @javax.ws.rs.HEAD annotation designates a method to respond to the HTTP HEAD requests. The HEAD method is the same as the GET request, but it only transfers the status line along with the header section (without the response body) to the client. This method is useful for retrieving the metadata present in the response headers, without having to retrieve the message body from the server. You can use this method to check whether a URI pointing to a resource is active or to check the content size by using the Content-Length response header field.

The JAX-RS runtime will offer the default implementations for the HEAD method type if the REST resource is missing explicit implementation. The default implementation provided by the runtime for the HEAD method will call the method designated for the GET request type, ignoring the response entity returned by the method.

@OPTIONS

The @javax.ws.rs.OPTIONS annotation designates a method to respond to the HTTP OPTIONS requests. This method is useful for obtaining a list of HTTP methods allowed for a resource.

The JAX-RS runtime will offer a default implementation for the OPTIONS method type if the REST resource is missing an explicit implementation. The default implementation offered by the runtime sets the Allow response header to all the HTTP method types supported by the resource.

The JAX-RS annotations that we discussed in this section are the commonly used APIs for building a typical RESTful web service application. If you want to try out a simple JAX-RS application at this moment, you can jump to the *Building your first RESTful web service with JAX-RS* section. Later, you can come back and finish reading the rest of the topics discussed in this chapter.

Annotations for accessing request parameters

In addition to the parameters mentioned in the previous section, JAX-RS offers annotations to pull some information out of a request. You can use this offering to extract the following parameters from a request: a query, URI path, form, cookie, header, and matrix. Mostly, these parameters are used in conjunction with the GET, POST, PUT, and DELETE methods.

@PathParam

A URI path template, in general, has a URI part pointing to the resource. It can also take the path variables embedded in the syntax; this facility is used by the clients to pass parameters to the REST APIs, as appropriate. The @javax.ws.rs.PathParam annotation injects (or binds) the value of the matching path parameter present in the URI path template into a class field, a resource class bean property (the getter method for accessing the attribute), or a method parameter. Typically, this annotation is used in conjunction with the HTTP method type annotations, such as @GET, @POST, @PUT, and @DELETE.

The following example illustrates the use of the @PathParam annotation to read the value of the path parameter, id, into the deptId method parameter. The URI path template for this example looks like /departments/{id}:

```
//Other imports removed for brevity
javax.ws.rs.PathParam

@Path("departments")
public class DepartmentService {
    @DELETE
    @Path("{id}")
    public void removeDepartment(@PathParam("id") Short deptId) {
        removeDepartmentEntity(deptId);
    }
    //Other methods removed for brevity
}
```

The REST API call to remove the department resource identified by id=10 looks like
DELETE /departments/10 HTTP/1.1.

We can also use multiple variables in a URI path template. For example, we can have the URI path template embedding the path variables to query a list of departments from a specific city and country, which may look like /departments/{country}/{city}. The following code snippet illustrates the use of @PathParam to extract variable values from the preceding URI path template:

```
@Produces(MediaType.APPLICATION_JSON)
@Path("{country}/{city} ")
public List<Department> findAllDepartments(
  @PathParam("country")
String countyCode,    @PathParam("city") String cityCode) {
  //Find all departments from the data store for a country
  //and city
  List<Department> departments =
    findAllMatchingDepartmentEntities(countyCode,
      cityCode );
   return departments;
}
```

@QueryParam

The @javax.ws.rs.QueryParam annotation injects the value(s) of a HTTP query parameter into a class field, a resource class bean property (the getter method for accessing the attribute), or a method parameter.

The following example illustrates the use of @QueryParam to extract the value of the desired query parameter present in the URI. This example extracts the value of the query parameter, name, from the request URI and copies the value into the deptName method parameter. The URI that accesses the IT department resource looks like /departments?name=IT:

```
@GET
@Produces(MediaType.APPLICATION_JSON)
public List<Department>
  findAllDepartmentsByName(@QueryParam("name") String deptName) {
    List<Department> depts= findAllMatchingDepartmentEntities
      (deptName);
  return depts;
}
```

The following example illustrates the use of @QueryParam to extract the value of the query parameter, locationId, from the request URI and copies the value into the deptLocationId class field. The URI that accesses the IT department resource looks like /departments/queryByLocation?locationId=1700:

```
//Usage of QueryParam for injecting class field
 @QueryParam("locationId")
 Short deptLocationId;

/**
 * Returns list of departments by location
 *
 * @param locationId
 * @return
 */
@GET
@Produces(MediaType.APPLICATION_JSON)
@Path("queryByLocation")
public List<Departments> findAllDepartmentsByLocation() {
//Find all departments from the data store
    Query queryDepartmentsByLocation =
           entityManager.createNamedQuery("Departments.findByLocationId");
    queryDepartmentsByLocation.setParameter("locationId", deptLocationId);
    List<Departments> departments =
queryDepartmentsByLocation.getResultList();
    logger.log(Level.INFO, departments.toString());
    return departments;
}
```

@MatrixParam

Matrix parameters are another way of defining parameters in the URI path template. The matrix parameters take the form of name-value pairs in the URI path, where each pair is preceded by a semicolon (;). For instance, the URI path that uses a matrix parameter to list all departments in Bangalore city looks like /departments;city=Bangalore.

The @javax.ws.rs.MatrixParam annotation injects the matrix parameter value into a class field, a resource class bean property (the getter method for accessing the attribute), or a method parameter.

The following code snippet demonstrates the use of the `@MatrixParam` annotation to extract the matrix parameters present in the request. The URI path used in this example looks like `/departments/matrix;name=IT;city=Bangalore`:

```
@GET @Produces(MediaType.APPLICATION_JSON) @Path("matrix")
public List<Department> findAllDepartmentsByNameWithMatrix(
                               @MatrixParam("name") String deptName,
                               @MatrixParam("city") String locationCode) {
    List<Department> depts=findAllDepartmentsFromDB(deptName, city);
    return depts;
}
```

You can use `PathParam`, `QueryParam`, and `MatrixParam` to pass the desired search parameters to the REST APIs. Now, you may ask, "When to use what?"
Although there are no strict rules here, a very common practice followed by many is to use `PathParam` to drill down to the entity class hierarchy and locate the specific resource. For example, you may use the URI of the following form to identify an employee working in a specific department: `/departments/{dept}/employees/{id}`.
`QueryParam` can be used for specifying attributes to locate the resources. For example, you may use URI with `QueryParam` to identify employees who joined on January 1, 2015, which may look like `/employees?doj=2015-01-01`.

The `MatrixParam` annotation is not used frequently. This is useful when you need to make a complex REST style query to multiple levels of resources and subresources. `MatrixParam` is applicable to a particular path element, while the query parameter is applicable to the entire request.

@HeaderParam

The HTTP header fields provide the necessary information about the request and response contents in HTTP. For example, the header field, `Content-Length: 348`, for an HTTP request says that the size of the request body content is 348 octets (8-bit bytes). The `@javax.ws.rs.HeaderParam` annotation injects the header values present in the request into a class field, a resource class bean property (the getter method for accessing the attribute), or a method parameter.

The following example extracts the `referrer` header parameter and logs it for audit purposes. The `referrer` header field in HTTP contains the address of the previous web page from which a request to the currently processed page originated:

```
@POST
public void createDepartment(@HeaderParam("Referer")
String referer,  Department entity) {
  logSource(referer);
  createDepartmentInDB(department);
}
```

Remember that HTTP provides a very wide selection of headers that cover most of the header parameters that you are looking for. Although you can use custom HTTP headers to pass some application-specific data to the server, try using standard headers whenever possible. Furthermore, avoid using a custom header for holding properties specific to a resource, the state of the resource, or parameters directly affecting the resource. For such scenarios, you can consider the other approaches discussed in this section, namely `PathParam`, `QueryParam`, or `MatrixParam`.

@CookieParam

The `@javax.ws.rs.CookieParam` annotation injects the matching cookie parameters present in the HTTP headers into a class field, a resource class bean property (the getter method for accessing the attribute), or a method parameter.

The following code snippet uses the `Default-Dept` cookie parameter present in the request to return the default department details:

```
@GET
@Path("cook")
@Produces(MediaType.APPLICATION_JSON)
public Department getDefaultDepartment(@CookieParam("Default-Dept")
  short departmentId) {
 Department dept=findDepartmentById(departmentId);
 return dept;
}
```

@FormParam

The @javax.ws.rs.FormParam annotation injects the matching HTML form parameters present in the request body into a class field, a resource class bean property (the getter method for accessing the attribute), or a method parameter. The request body carrying the form elements must have the content type specified as application/x-www-form-urlencoded.

Consider the following HTML form that contains the data capture form for a department entity. This form allows the user to enter the department entity details:

```
<!DOCTYPE html>
<html>
  <head>
  <title>Create Department</title>
  </head>
  <body>
    <form method="POST" action="/resources/departments">
    Department Id:
    <input type="text" name="departmentId">
    <br>
    Department Name:
      <input type="text" name="departmentName">
      <br>
      <input type="submit" value="Add Department" />
    </form>
  </body>
</html>
```

Upon clicking on the **submit** button on the HTML form, the department details that you entered will be posted to the REST URI, /resources/departments. The following code snippet shows the use of the @FormParam annotation for extracting the HTML form fields and copying them to the resource class method parameter:

```
@Path("departments")
public class DepartmentService {

  @POST
  //Specifies content type as
  //"application/x-www-form-urlencoded"
  @Consumes(MediaType.APPLICATION_FORM_URLENCODED)
  public void createDepartment(@FormParam("departmentId") short
    departmentId,
      @FormParam("departmentName") String departmentName) {
      createDepartmentEntity(departmentId, departmentName);
  }
}
```

@DefaultValue

The @javax.ws.rs.DefaultValue annotation specifies a default value for the request parameters accessed using one of the following annotations: PathParam, QueryParam, MatrixParam, CookieParam, FormParam, or HeaderParam. The default value is used if no matching parameter value is found for the variables annotated using one of the preceding annotations.

The following REST resource method will make use of the default value set for the from and to method parameters if the corresponding query parameters are found missing in the URI path:

```
@GET
@Produces(MediaType.APPLICATION_JSON)
public List<Department> findAllDepartmentsInRange
  (@DefaultValue("0")  @QueryParam("from") Integer from,
    @DefaultValue("100")  @QueryParam("to") Integer to) {
    findAllDepartmentEntitiesInRange(from, to);
}
```

@Context

The JAX-RS runtime offers different context objects, which can be used for accessing information associated with the resource class, operating environment, and so on. You may find various context objects that hold information associated with the URI path, request, HTTP header, security, and so on. Some of these context objects also provide the utility methods for dealing with the request and response content. JAX-RS allows you to reference the desired context objects in the code via dependency injection. JAX-RS provides the @javax.ws.rs.Context annotation, which injects the matching context object into the target field. You can specify the @Context annotation on a class field, a resource class bean property (the getter method for accessing the attribute), or a method parameter.

The following example illustrates the use of the @Context annotation to inject the javax.ws.rs.core.UriInfo context object into a method variable. The UriInfo instance provides access to the application and request URI information. This example uses UriInfo to read the query parameter present in the requested URI path template, /departments/IT:

```
@GET
@Produces(MediaType.APPLICATION_JSON)
public List<Department> findAllDepartmentsByName(
  @Context UriInfo  uriInfo){
  String deptName =
    uriInfo.getPathParameters().getFirst("name");
```

```
    List<Department> depts= findAllMatchingDepartmentEntities
        (deptName);
    return depts;
}
```

Here is a list of the commonly used classes and interfaces, which can be injected using the
@Context annotation:

- `javax.ws.rs.core.Application`: This class defines the components of a JAX-RS application and supplies additional metadata
- `javax.ws.rs.core.UriInfo`: This interface provides access to the application and request URI information
- `javax.ws.rs.core.Request`: This interface provides a method for request processing, such as reading the method type and precondition evaluation
- `javax.ws.rs.core.HttpHeaders`: This interface provides access to the HTTP header information
- `javax.ws.rs.core.SecurityContext`: This interface provides access to security-related information
- `javax.ws.rs.ext.Providers`: This interface offers the runtime lookup of a provider instance, such as `MessageBodyReader`, `MessageBodyWriter`, `ExceptionMapper`, and `ContextResolver`
- `javax.ws.rs.ext.ContextResolver<T>`: This interface supplies the requested context to the resource classes and other providers
- `javax.servlet.http.HttpServletRequest`: This interface provides the client request information for a servlet
- `javax.servlet.http.HttpServletResponse`: This interface is used to send a response to a client
- `javax.servlet.ServletContext`: This interface provides methods for a servlet to communicate with its servlet container
- `javax.servlet.ServletConfig`: This interface carries the servlet configuration parameters

@BeanParam

The `@javax.ws.rs.BeanParam` annotation allows you to inject all the matching request parameters into a single bean object. The `@BeanParam` annotation can be set on a class field, a resource class bean property (the getter method for accessing the attribute), or a method parameter. The bean class can have fields or properties annotated with one of the request parameter annotations, namely `@PathParam`, `@QueryParam`, `@MatrixParam`, `@HeaderParam`, `@CookieParam`, or `@FormParam`. Apart from the request parameter annotations, the bean can have the `@Context` annotation if there is a need.

Consider the example that we discussed for `@FormParam`. The `createDepartment()` method that we used in that example has two parameters annotated with `@FormParam`:

```
public void createDepartment(
  @FormParam("departmentId") short departmentId,
   @FormParam("departmentName") String departmentName)
```

Let's see how we can use `@BeanParam` for the preceding method to give a more logical and meaningful signature by grouping all the related fields into an aggregator class, thereby avoiding too many parameters in the method signature.

The `DepartmentBean` class that we use for this example is as follows:

```
public class DepartmentBean {

  @FormParam("departmentId")
    private short departmentId;

  @FormParam("departmentName")
    private String departmentName;

  //getter and setter for the above fields
  //are not shown here to save space
}
```

The following code snippet demonstrates the use of the `@BeanParam` annotation to inject the `DepartmentBean` instance that contains all the `FormParam` values extracted from the request message body:

```
@POST
public void createDepartment(@BeanParam DepartmentBean deptBean)
{
  createDepartmentEntity(deptBean.getDepartmentId(),
    deptBean.getDepartmentName());
}
```

@Encoded

By default, the JAX-RS runtime decodes all the request parameters before injecting the extracted values into the target variables annotated with one of the following annotations: `@FormParam`, `@PathParam`, `@MatrixParam`, or `@QueryParam`. You can use `@javax.ws.rs.Encoded` to disable the automatic decoding of the parameter values. With the `@Encoded` annotation, the value of parameters will be provided in the encoded form itself. This annotation can be used on a class, method, or parameters. If you set this annotation on a method, it will disable decoding for all the parameters defined for this method. You can use this annotation on a class to disable decoding for all the parameters of all the methods. In the following example, the value of the `name` path parameter is injected into the method parameter in the URL encoded form (without decoding). The method implementation should take care of the decoding of the values in such cases:

```
@GET
@Produces(MediaType.APPLICATION_JSON)
public List<Department>
   findAllDepartmentsByName(@QueryParam("name") String deptName) {
  //Method body is removed for brevity
}
```

 URL encoding converts a string into a valid URL format, which may contain alphabetic characters, numerals, and some special characters supported in the URL string. To learn more about the URL specification, visit http://www.w3.org/Addressing/URL/url-spec.html.

Annotation inheritance

JAX-RS annotations defined in a class or interface method are inherited by the corresponding subclass or implementation class method, provided that the method and its parameters do not define their own annotations. Let's familiarize ourselves with this with a simple example; the `IEmployeeService` interface defines REST API functions with the annotations required for `EmployeeService` to implement:

```
public interface IEmployeeService {

  @GET
  @Path("{id}")
  @Produces(MediaType.APPLICATION_JSON)
  public Employee findEmployee(@PathParam("id") Short id);

  @GET
  @Path("{age}")
  @Produces(MediaType.APPLICATION_JSON)
```

```
    public List<Employee> findEmployeesByAge(@PathParam("age") Short age);
    }

public class EmployeeService implements IEmployeeService{
    public Employee findEmployee(Short id) {
        //....
    }

    @Produces(MediaType.TEXT_XML)
    public List<Employee> findEmployeesByAge(Short age) {
        //....
    }
}
```

The `EmployeeService findEmployee` method inherits the annotations from the `IEmployeeService` interface. Conversely, the `findEmployeesByAge` method does not inherit the annotations from the `IEmployeeService` interface, as it has overridden its own annotation.

 Class or interface annotations inheritance are not supported; only annotations used on the method and method parameters can be inherited.

Returning additional metadata with responses

We discussed a few examples in the previous section for retrieving resources via the HTTP `GET` request. The resource class implementations that we used in these examples were simply returning plain Java constructs in response to the method call. What if you want to return extra metadata, such as the `Cache-Control` header or the status code, along with the result (resource representation)?

JAX-RS allows you to return additional metadata via the `javax.ws.rs.core.Response` class, which wraps the entity and any additional metadata, such as the HTTP headers, HTTP cookie, and status code. You can create a `Response` instance by using `javax.ws.rs.core.Response.ResponseBuilder` as a factory. The following example demonstrates the use of the `Response` class to return the response content along with the additional HTTP header fields:

```
//Other imports removed for brevity
import javax.ws.rs.core.CacheControl;
```

```
import javax.ws.rs.core.Response;
import javax.ws.rs.core.Response.ResponseBuilder;

@GET
@Produces(MediaType.APPLICATION_JSON)
public Response findAllDepartmentsByName(@QueryParam("name")
   String deptName) {
  List<Department> depts= findAllMatchingDepartmentEntities
    (deptName);
  //Sets cache control directive to the response
  CacheControl cacheControl = new CacheControl();
  //Cache the result for a day
  cacheControl.setMaxAge(86400);
  return Response.ok().
    cacheControl(cacheControl).entity(depts).build();
}
```

Understanding data binding rules in JAX-RS

While injecting variable values from the URI path and query parameter into the resource class or while mapping the request-response entity body with Java types, the JAX-RS runtime follows certain rules for the Java types present in the resource class. We will discuss this topic in this section.

Mapping the path variable with Java types

At runtime, the framework automatically detects and copies the parameter values present in the inbound request into the appropriate Java types based on the request parameter type. In general, the mapping is performed on the basis of the following rules for each of the request parameter annotation types, except for the @Context annotation:

- All primitive types, such as short, int, float, double, and Boolean, except char.
- All the wrapper classes of primitive types, such as short, integer, BigDecimal, and Boolean, except char.
- All classes with a constructor that accept a single string type argument. In this case, you can define your own class with a single string type constructor and use it as a method parameter or member variable with an appropriate annotation for reading the parameter value.

- Any class with the static method named `valueOf(String)` that accepts a single string argument.
- Have a registered implementation of `ParamConverterProvider` JAX-RS extension SPI that returns a `ParamConverter` instance, capable of a *from string* conversion for the type.
- If the parameters contain more than one value for the same name, you can have `java.util.List<T>`, `java.util.Set<T>`, or `java.util.SortedSet<T>` as the Java variable type at the receiving end, where `T` represents the types that satisfy the first two criteria that we defined.

It would be interesting to see how the framework initializes the Java class types when there are no matching request parameters found. The following outcomes will occur if there is no matching value found in the request URI for a Java variable type and if `@DefaultValue` is not defined:

- All the primitive Java types follow the default value rules set for the primitive types in Java, which are listed at
  `http://docs.oracle.com/javase/tutorial/java/nutsandbolts/datatypes.htm l`
- All Java objects will be set to null
- `List`, `set`, or `SortedSet` will have a corresponding empty collection instance

Now, let's see how the mapping is done between the request-response body content and Java types.

Mapping the request and response entity body with Java types

JAX-RS uses `javax.ws.rs.ext.MessageBodyReader` for mapping the HTTP request entity body to an appropriate Java type. On the other hand, `javax.ws.rs.ext.MessageBodyWriter` is used for mapping the Java type returned by a resource class method to the appropriate HTTP response entity body representation, such as JSON, XML, and text. The `MessageBodyReader` and `MessageBodyWriter` implementations will raise `javax.ws.rs.WebApplicationException` if they do not know how to convert the input data.

JAX-RS offers the default content handlers (entity providers) for all common data types. Here is a list of the Java types supported by JAX-RS by default:

- JAX-RS supports mapping between the following Java data types and request-response entity bodies for all media forms: `byte[]`, `java.lang.String`, `java.io.InputStream`, `java.io.Reader`, `java.io.File`, `javax.activation.DataSource`, and `javax.xml.transform.Source`

- JAX-RS supports the `javax.ws.rs.core.MultivaluedMap<K,V>` type for reading or writing the form content, whose media type is `application/x-www-form-urlencoded`

- JAX-RS supports the `javax.xml.bind.JAXBElement` type for reading or writing content represented using the XML media types (`text/xml`, `application/xml`, and `application/*+xml`)

- JAX-RS supports the `java.lang.Boolean`, `java.lang.Character`, and `java.lang.Number` types for reading and writing the Boolean strings (`true` or `false`), characters, and numerical content presented in the `text/plain` media type

Using JAXB to manage the mapping of the request and response entity body to Java objects

If you want more control over the marshalling and unmarshalling of objects, such as skipping some fields or renaming field names, you can use the **Java Architecture for XML Binding (JAXB)** annotations to indicate this to the runtime. Let's take a quick look at this feature.

JAXB allows Java developers to access and process the XML data without worrying about the XML structure of the content. JAXB offers annotations that map XML to the Java class and vice versa, letting you work on the Java objects. JAX-RS can automatically read and write both XML and JSON by using JAXB. Our discussions in this section are focused on using the JAXB annotation for managing the serialization of Java objects.

Here is a brief description of the commonly used JAXB annotations to control the serialization of Java objects:

- `@javax.xml.bind.annotation.XmlRootElement`: When a top-level class is annotated with the `@XmlRootElement` annotation, the JAX-RS runtime takes care of the serialization of all its instances at runtime.

- @javax.xml.bind.annotation.XmlAccessorType: This annotation controls whether the fields or JavaBean properties are serialized by default. It takes the following values:
    - XmlAccessType.FIELD: Every non-static, non-transient field will be copied in an XML or JSON representation
    - XmlAccessType.NONE: No fields are copied
    - XmlAccessType.PROPERTY: Every getter/setter pair will be copied in an XML or JSON representation
    - XmlAccessType.PUBLIC_MEMBER: Every public field and public getter/setter pair will be copied in an XML or JSON representation

- @javax.xml.bind.XmlElement: This value maps a JavaBean property to an XML or JSON element derived from the property name
- @javax.xml.bind.XmlTransient: This value prevents the mapping of a JavaBean property/type to JSON

Consider the following Department object with the JAXB annotation to manage the serialization of contents:

```
//Other imports removed for brevity
import javax.xml.bind.annotation.XmlAccessType;
import javax.xml.bind.annotation.XmlAccessorType;
import javax.xml.bind.annotation.XmlElement;
import javax.xml.bind.annotation.XmlRootElement;
import javax.xml.bind.annotation.XmlTransient;

@XmlRootElement(name="department")
@XmlAccessorType(XmlAccessType.FIELD)
public class Department implements Serializable {
  @XmlElement(name="departmentId")
  private Short id;
  private String departmentName;
  @XmlTransient
  public List<Employee> employees;
  //Rest of the code removed for brevity
}
```

Let's see how the JAX-RS runtime makes use of the JAXB annotations while serializing results returned by a resource method into the JSON representation:

1. The following resource class method returns the `Department` object in response to a GET request, for example, `GET /departments/10 HTTP/1/1`:

```
@GET
@Path("{id}")
@Produces(MediaType.APPLICATION_JSON)
public Department find(@PathParam("id") Short id) {
  return findDepartmentEntity(id);
}
```

2. The JAX-RS runtime deploys entity providers that implement `javax.ws.rs.ext.MessageBodyWriter` to serialize Java objects into an appropriate output stream representation, such as JSON or XML. The `MessageBodyWriter` implementation scans through the JAXB annotations defined on the `Department` class and converts values to the JSON data, as appropriate.

The sample JSON output produced by the preceding resource class method will look like the following code:

```
{"departmentId":30,
  "departmentName":"HR"}
```

Note that the `List<Employee> employees` field that you see in the `Department` class is not present in the JSON output data because this field is marked as `@XmlTransient` in the class definition. Furthermore, `@XmlElement(name="departmentId")` for the `id` field causes the provider to rename `id` to `departmentId` in the JSON representation.

You now have enough information on all the commonly used JAX-RS annotations that you will need for a RESTful web service. Let's move on and build a simple RESTful web service by using JAX-RS to get a real feel of the topics that we have discussed so far in this chapter.

EclipseLink MOXy is the default entity provider used by the Jersey framework for converting the message body content to and from Java types. The JAX-RS framework allows you to override the default entity provider with the implementation of your choice. The provider that you choose should implement the `javax.ws.rs.ext.MessageBodyReader` interface for converting a stream into a Java type and the `javax.ws.rs.ext.MessageBodyWriter` interface for converting the Java types into a stream. For example, the Jackson framework, discussed in Chapter 2, *Java APIs for JSON Processing*, implements all the necessary contracts set by JAX-RS for binding Java types with the message body content. Your JAX-RS application can automatically discover and register the Jackson entity provider if it is found in the class path.

Building your first RESTful web service with JAX-RS

In the earlier sections, we discussed the commonly used annotations and APIs in JAX-RS that you may need to be aware of while building REST APIs with JAX-RS. It is now time for us to put all these theories into practice. In this section, we will build a simple yet complete end-to-end RESTful web service by using JAX-RS.

Setting up the environment

This example uses the following software and tools:

- Java SE Development Kit 8 or newer
- NetBeans IDE 8.2 (with Java EE bundle) or newer
- Glassfish Server 4.1 or newer
- Maven 3.2.3 or newer
- Oracle Database Express Edition 11g Release 2 or newer with HR sample database schema
- Oracle Database JDBC Driver (`ojdbc7.jar` or newer)

Detailed instructions for procuring and setting up all the required tools for running the examples used in this book are discussed in the appendix.

Make sure that your machine has all the tools ready before starting with the tutorial. In this tutorial, we will build a RESTful web service by using the JAX-RS APIs. We will use Maven as a build tool for our sample application, as it does a great job in the dependency management department for the application and provides a standard structure for the source code. NetBeans has great support for building Maven-based applications, and this is one of the reasons we chose NetBeans as the IDE for this exercise.

Once the development environment is set up, you are ready to launch the NetBeans IDE for application development.

Building a simple RESTful web service application using the NetBeans IDE

To create a JAX-RS application, perform the following steps:

1. Launch the NetBeans IDE.
2. In the main toolbar, navigate to **File** | **New Project**.
3. On the **New Project** dialog screen, navigate to **Maven** | **Web Application** for building the RESTful web service. Proceed to the next screen by clicking on the **Next** button.
4. In the **Name and Location** screen, enter **Project Name**, **Project Location** (for storing the source), **Group Id**, **Version** (for the Maven project), and **Package** (for the Java source files), as follows:
   - **Project Name**: `rest-chapter3-service`
   - **Group Id**: `com.packtpub`
   - **Package**: `com.packtpub.rest.ch3.service`

Refer to the following screenshot for the values used for this example:

If you are not familiar with Maven, enter the same values as you see in the preceding screenshot to save time and to stay focused. Otherwise, there is nothing preventing you from having your own values for any of the fields that you see in the wizard. After setting all the values, click on **Next** to continue to the **Settings** screen in the wizard.

5. On the **Settings** screen, select **GlassFish Server**, which you installed along with the NetBeans IDE as **Server** for running your JAX-RS application. Then, click on **Java EE 7 Web** as the Java EE version for the application that you'll build.

6. The server list on this screen may appear empty if you have not configured any server for the IDE yet. To add a new server reference, perform the following steps:

    1. Click on the **Add** button. In the **Add Server Instance** wizard, choose **GlassFish** as the server and click on **Next** to continue the wizard.

    2. Set **Server Location** to the folder where you installed **GlassFish**. Select **Local Domain** and click on **Next** to continue the wizard.

    3. On the **Domain Name** screen, enter `domain1` in the **Domain** field (which is the default one) and `localhost` in the **Host** field. Click on **Finish** to complete the server creation.

7. Now, the IDE will take you back to the **Settings** screen once again where you can choose **GlassFish** (that you added in the previous step) as the server and Java EE 7 Web as the Java EE version.

8. You can now click on the **Finish** button to finish the project configuration wizard. NetBeans will now set up a Maven-based web project for you, as shown in the following screenshot:

9. The next step is to build a simple RESTful web service implementation by using a POJO class to get a feel of the JAX-RS APIs.

10. To build a POJO class, you can right-click on the project and navigate to **New | Java Class** in the menu. In the **New Java Class** editor, enter `DepartmentService` in the **Class Name** field and enter `com.packtpub.rest.ch3.service` in the **Package** field. This class will contain the service implementation for this example. We will add `@Path("departments")` to this class so that `DepartmentService` becomes a REST resource class and responds to the REST API calls with the URI path fragment, `\departments`. Let's add a simple `helloWorld()` method to this class and add `@Path("hello")` to this method. Add the `@GET` annotation to designate this method to respond to the HTTP GET methods. The `DepartmentService` class now looks like the following:

```
package com.packtpub.rest.ch3.service;
import javax.ws.rs.GET;
import javax.ws.rs.Path;
import javax.ws.rs.Produces;
import javax.ws.rs.core.MediaType;

@Path("departments")
```

```
public class DepartmentService{
  @GET
  @Path("hello")
  @Produces(MediaType.APPLICATION_JSON)
  public String helloWorld(){
    return "Hello world";
  }
}
```

11. To configure resources, add a REST configurations class, which extends
    `javax.ws.rs.core.Application`. This class defines the components of a JAX-
    RS application and supplies additional metadata if any. The configuration class
    looks like the following:

```
package com.packtpub.rest.ch3.jaxrs.service;

import java.util.Set;
import javax.ws.rs.core.Application;

@javax.ws.rs.ApplicationPath("webresources")
public class RestAppConfig extends Application {
// Get a set of root resource and provider classes.
  @Override
  public Set<Class<?>> getClasses() {
    Set<Class<?>> resources =
      new java.util.HashSet<>();
    resources.add(com.packtpub.rest.ch3.service.
      DepartmentService.class);
    return resources;
  }
}
```

Specifying the application path

The `@javax.ws.rs.ApplicationPath` annotation that you see in the
preceding code snippet identifies the application path that serves as the
base URI for all the resources defined in this application.

Alternatively, you can define the application path in `web.xml`, as shown in the
following code. However, to keep things simple, we will not use `web.xml` for
configuring resources in this example:

```
<servlet>
  <servlet-name>javax.ws.rs.core.Application
  </servlet-name>
  <load-on-startup>1</load-on-startup>
```

```
</servlet>
<servlet-mapping>
  <servlet-name>javax.ws.rs.core.Application
  </servlet-name>
  <url-pattern>/webresources/*</url-pattern>
</servlet-mapping>
```

12. With this step, we have finished building a very simple JAX-RS RESTful web service. To deploy and run the RESTful web service application, you can right-click on the `rest-chapter3-service` project and click on **Run**. This will build and deploy the application to the **GlassFish** server integrated with the NetBeans IDE.

13. To test the desired REST API, right-click on the appropriate HTTP methods, as shown in the following screenshot, and select **Test Resource Uri**. This action will open up the default browser with the response content returned by the REST call. The URI for accessing the `helloWorld` RESTful web API will look like `http://localhost:8080/rest-chapter3-service/webresources/dep artments/hello`:

Adding CRUD operations on the REST resource class

In the previous section, we built a very basic RESTful web API by using JAX-RS. In this section, we will enhance this example by introducing more realistic real-life use cases. We will add a department model class to the application and then introduce the REST APIs to perform the CRUD operations on the `department` object.

We will use the `DEPARTMENT` table from the HR database schema as the data source for this example. This example uses the **Java Persistence API (JPA)** for mapping the database table with the Java objects. JPA is a specification for the persistence of Java objects to any relational data store. If you are not familiar with JPA, read the official documentation available at `https://docs.oracle.com/javaee/7/tutorial/persistence-intro.htm`.

 The Oracle Database XE database comes with a sample database schema user named `HR`. We will use this schema for building most of the examples in this book. To learn more about the HR sample schema in Oracle XE, visit

`https://docs.oracle.com/cd/E17781_01/admin.112/e18585/toc.htm`.

Here are the detailed steps for building a model for the project:

1. Open the `rest-chapter3-service` project that we built in the previous section in the NetBeans IDE (if it is not opened).

2. Add a `department` JPA entity class to the project. To do this, right-click on the `rest-chapter3-service` project opened in the **Projects** pane and then navigate to **New | Entity Classes from Database** from the menu.

3. On the **Database Table** screen, you can choose a data source to which your application wants to connect. We will use the HR schema for this example. If you have not yet created the data source for connecting to the HR database schema, perform the following steps:

   1. To connect to the HR database schema, click on the **Data Source** drop-down list and select the **New Data Source** option.

   2. In the **Create Data Source** dialog, enter the **JNDI** field (for example, `HRDS`) and then select **New Database Connection** from the **Database Connection** drop-down list. You will see a **New Connection** wizard window now. In the **Locate Driver** screen, click on the **Oracle Thin** driver, and add the path to the folder where you have downloaded `ojdbc7.jar`. Click on **Next** to continue with the wizard.

3. On the **Customize Connection** screen, enter the connection details to connect to your local Oracle XE instance (or any Oracle database, which has the HR schema). This is shown in the following screenshot. The parameter that you enter on this screen depends on your Oracle database settings. Click on the **Finish** button to create the connection. Once the connection is created, the wizard will take you back to the **Database Tables** screen:

4. On the **Database Tables** screen, choose the data source that you have created for connecting to the HR database schema (for example, HRDS). Uncheck the **Include Related Tables** checkbox as we want to generate the model only for the DEPARTMENTS table for this project. Select the DEPARTMENTS table and shuttle it to the right. Click on **Next** to generate the entity class for the selected table.
5. On the **Entity Classes** creation screen, change the package to com.packtpub.rest.ch3.model and leave all other default values as is; then click on **Next** to continue.

6. On the **Mapping Options** screen, check **Generate Fields for Unresolved Relationships** and click on **Finish** to generate the entity class and standard JPA configuration files such as the `persistence.xml` file. The IDE now has `Departments.java` and `persistence.xml`:

   - `Departments.java`: This file is a JPA entity class mapped to the DEPARTMENTS table.
   - `persistence.xml`: This file is a standard configuration file in JPA. It is located in the META-INF folder of the project source.

In this part of the tutorial, we will convert the `DepartmentService` POJO class that we created in the first part to a stateless session bean by annotating it with the `@javax.ejb.Stateless` annotation. A stateless session bean (being an Enterprise JavaBean) offers declarative security, container-managed transactions, and instance-pooling capabilities. Next, add a method that returns a list of departments queried from the DEPARTMENTS table by using the JPA.

With the introduction of the JPA entity into the `DepartmentService` class, we will need the `javax.persistence.EntityManager` instance to manage the entities. You can use the `@PersistenceContext` annotation to inject the `EntityManager` instance into the stateless session bean. As the last step in this exercise, you should define methods that use the standard JPA APIs to perform the CRUD operations on the `Departments` entity and expose them as REST APIs. The implementation of `DepartmentService` now looks like the following:

```
package com.packtpub.rest.ch3.service;

import com.packtpub.rest.ch3.model.Departments;
import java.util.List;
import javax.ejb.Stateless;
import javax.persistence.EntityManager;
import javax.persistence.PersistenceContext;
import javax.ws.rs.GET;
import javax.ws.rs.Path;
import javax.ws.rs.Produces;
import javax.ws.rs.core.MediaType;

@Path("departments")
@Stateless
public class DepartmentService {
//Inject EntityManager instance
  @PersistenceContext(unitName =
    "com.packtpub_rest-chapter3-service_war_1.0-
       SNAPSHOTPU")
  private EntityManager entityManager;
```

```
//Method that responds to HTTP GET request
//Returns list of departments
@GET
@Produces(MediaType.APPLICATION_JSON)
public List<Departments> findAllDepartments() {
  //Find all departments from the data store
  javax.persistence.criteria.CriteriaQuery cq =
    entityManager.getCriteriaBuilder()
      .createQuery();
  cq.select(cq.from(Departments.class));
  List<Departments> departments =
    entityManager.createQuery(cq).getResultList();
  return departments;
}

//Method that responds to HTTP POST request
//Creates a new department object
@POST
@Consumes(MediaType.APPLICATION_JSON)
public void createDepartment(Departments entity) {
  entityManager.persist(entity);
}

//Method that responds to HTTP PUT request
//Modifies the department identified by 'id' path param
@PUT
  @Path("{id}")
@Consumes(MediaType.APPLICATION_JSON)
public void editDepartment(@PathParam("id") Short id,
  Departments entity) {
  entityManager.merge(entity);
}

//Method that responds to HTTP DELETE request
//Removes the department identified by 'id' path param
@DELETE
@Path("{id}")
public void removeDepartment(@PathParam("id") Short id)
{

  Departments entity =
    entityManager.find(Departments.class,
      id);
  entityManager.remove(entityManager.merge(entity));

}

}
```

Wow... congratulations! You are done with the implementation.

To deploy and run the web application, you can right-click on the `rest-chapter3-service` project and click on **Run**. This will build and deploy the application to the integrated **GlassFish** server.

> The source code for the preceding example is available on the Packt website. You can download the example from the Packt website link mentioned at the beginning of this book, in the *Preface* section.

To test the REST API, you can either build a Java client or use one of the many ready-made REST client testing tools available in the industry today. **Postman**, a REST client, is a popular API testing tool, which comes as a Google Chrome extension. You can learn more about this tool at `https://www.getpostman.com/`.

The following screenshot demonstrates how you can use the Postman REST client for testing the `GET` operation on the `/departments` resource. Similarly, you can use Postman to test the other HTTP methods, such as `PUT`, `DELETE`, and `POST`, on the `/departments` resource:

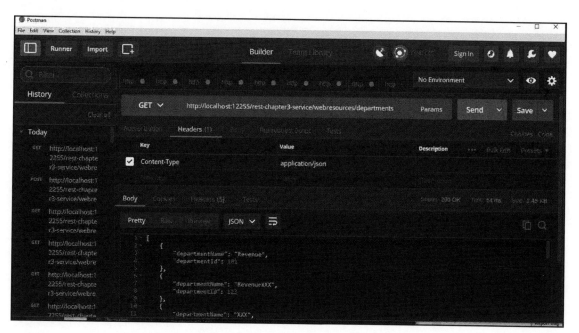

The following table will help you to quickly identify the REST URI path for accessing each REST API used in this example. The REST URI paths shown in this table are subject to change on the basis of the actual server name and port used:

HTTP method	Sample URI	REST resource
GET	`http://localhost:8080/rest-chapter3-service/webresources/departments`	`DepartmentService::` `findAllDepartments()`
POST	`http://localhost:8080/rest-chapter3-service/webresources/departments`	`DepartmentService` `::createDepartment(Departments)`
PUT	`http://localhost:8080/rest-chapter3-service/webresources/departments/300`	`DepartmentService ::` `editDepartment (Departments)`
DELETE	`http://localhost:8080/rest-chapter3-service/webresources/departments/30`	`DepartmentService ::` `removeDepartment(Short)`

We will look at the JAX-RS client APIs for building the REST API client in the next section.

Client APIs for accessing RESTful web services

There are many frameworks available for building a Java client for accessing REST. The JAX-RS specification standardizes the client APIs and provides fluent APIs for interaction with the RESTful web service.

Fluent APIs allow you to chain method calls to perform the desired operation, which improves the readability of the code. The return value of the called method gives a context for the next call and is terminated through the return of a void context. You can learn more about the fluent APIs at `https://en.wikipedia.org/wiki/Fluent_interface`.

Specifying a dependency of the JAX-RS client API

To use the client part of the JAX-RS specification, the client application needs to depend only on the client part of the JAX-RS libraries. If you use the Jersey implementation, the dependency entry in `pom.xml` will look like the following:

```
<dependency>
    <groupId>org.glassfish.jersey.core</groupId>
    <artifactId>jersey-client</artifactId>
    <version>2.19</version><!-sets the correct version -->
</dependency>
```

This is the minimum dependency that the application needs to have for using the Jersey implementation of the JAX-RS client APIs. You need to add additional modules for availing specific runtime features. For instance, to enable the automatic conversion of the response content type (for example, JSON) to a desired Java class at runtime, you need to add a dependency to the `jersey-media-moxy` JAR file, as shown here:

```
<dependency>
   <groupId>org.glassfish.jersey.media</groupId>
   <artifactId>jersey-media-moxy</artifactId>
   <version>2.5.1</version>
</dependency>
```

Calling REST APIs using the JAX-RS client

The JAX-RS client API encapsulates the uniform interface constraint, which is a key constraint of the REST architectural style, and offers many convenient APIs for accessing the web resources. We will start by looking at the JAX-RS client API for reading a simple RESTful web service.

You will use the `javax.ws.rs.client.ClientBuilder` factory class as the entry point to the client API. The `javax.ws.rs.client.Client` instance returned by `ClientBuilder` exposes a set of high-level APIs for accessing the web resources.

Let's now apply what we've learned and see how we can access the REST resource identified by the following URI:
`http://localhost:8080/rest-chapter3-service/webresources/departments`.

The preceding URI has the following two parts:

- Base URI:
  `http://localhost:8080/rest-chapter3-service/webresources`
- URI path fragments that identify the REST resource: `/departments`

We will build `WebTarget` pointing to the base URI as follows:

```
import javax.ws.rs.client.Client;
import javax.ws.rs.client.ClientBuilder;
import javax.ws.rs.client.WebTarget;

Client client = javax.ws.rs.client.ClientBuilder.newClient();
String BASE_URI =
  "http://localhost:8080/rest-chapter3-service/webresources";
//Builds a web resource target pointing to BASE_URI
WebTarget  webTarget = client.target(BASE_URI);
```

You can append `/departments` to the base web target instance in order to complete the URI for the REST API, which returns the JSON representation of the `department` objects. You can do this by calling `path(String path)` on the `WebTarget` instance as follows:

```
webTarget.path("departments");
```

This call creates a new `WebTarget` instance by appending the input path to the URI of the current target instance.

Once you have a `WebTarget` instance pointing to a valid REST resource, you can start building a request to the targeted REST API by calling the `request()` method. In the request method, you can specify the desired media types for the response, such as `text/html`, `text/plain`, `text/xml`, and `application/json`:

A resource class method implementation can return resources in different representations, such as JSON, XML, and plain text. The client can indicate the content types that are acceptable for response via the HTTP `Accept` request header. The process of agreeing on the content format used for sending messages between the client and server is known as **Content Negotiation**.
To learn more about the HTTP request headers, refer to
`http://www.w3.org/Protocols/rfc2616/rfc2616-sec14.html`.

The `request()` method returns the `javax.ws.rs.client.Invocation.Builder` object, which can be used for building the appropriate innovation handlers. The last step in this process is to invoke the request and get a response.

The following code snippet illustrates all the steps that we discussed till now for calling the REST APIs:

```
Client client = javax.ws.rs.client.ClientBuilder.newClient();
String BASE_URI =
   "http://localhost:8080/rest-chapter3-service/webresources";
WebTarget  webTarget = client.target(BASE_URI);
//Append departments URI path to Base URI
WebTarget resource = webTarget.path("departments");

// Build appropriate request type by specifying the content
// type for the response
Builder builder=resource.
   request(javax.ws.rs.core.MediaType.APPLICATION_JSON);
//Build a GET request invocation
Invocation invocation=builder.buildGet();
//Invoke the request and receive the response in
// specified format type.
GenericType responseType=new GenericType<List<Department>>() { };
List<Department> depts = invocation.invoke(responseType);
```

While calling the `invoke(Class<T> responseType)` method on the `Invocation` object, you can specify the desired response Java type as the input. The runtime will automatically convert the response message content into the desired Java type.

Simplified client APIs for accessing REST APIs

Apart from the preceding approach, you can use a simplified version of the client API available on the `Invocation.Builder` object, such as `head()`, `get()`, `post()`, `update()`, `put()`, or `delete()`, to invoke the appropriate REST API. The following code snippet invokes the HTTP GET method on the `department` resource API in a more simplified way:

```
// Obtain a client reference
Client client = javax.ws.rs.client.ClientBuilder.newClient();
// Bind the target to the REST service
String BASE_URI =
   "http://localhost:8080/rest-chapter3-service/webresources";
WebTarget  resource = client.target(BASE_URI).path("departments");
GenericType responseType=new GenericType<List<Department>>() { };
// Invoke GET  method on the resource
List<Department> depts =
   resource.request(javax.ws.rs.core.MediaType.APPLICATION_JSON).
     get(responseType);
```

The following code snippet illustrates how you can invoke the PUT method on a REST resource. This example updates the Department resource and posts the modified content to the RESTful web API:

```
departments/{id}. }
//Get the modified department object
Department department = getModifiedDepartment();
String id = department.getDepartmentId();
Client client = javax.ws.rs.client.ClientBuilder.newClient();
String BASE_URI =
  "http://localhost:8080/rest-chapter3-service/webresources";
WebTarget resource = client.target(BASE_URI).path("departments")
  .path(java.text.MessageFormat.format("{0}", new Object[]{id}));
Builder builder =
  resource.request(javax.ws.rs.core.MediaType.APPLICATION_JSON);
//Invoke PUT method on resource to update the contents on server
builder.put( javax.ws.rs.client.Entity.entity(department,
  javax.ws.rs.core.MediaType.APPLICATION_JSON));
```

 The NetBeans IDE has good support for building the RESTful web service client by using the JAX-RS client APIs. To avail this offering, navigate to **File | New | Web Services | RESTful Java Client** and follow the steps in the wizard.

Summary

With the use of annotations, the JAX-RS API provides a simple development model for RESTful web service programming. In this chapter, we covered the frequently used features of the JAX-RS framework and developed a non-trivial RESTful web service to get a feel of the offerings.

In the next chapter, we will discuss the advanced features of JAX-RS, such as asynchronous REST APIs, advanced topics on filters and interceptors, validations and error handling, custom message body providers, and custom media types. Take a deep breath and be prepared for a deep dive.

4
Advanced Features in the JAX-RS APIs

In the previous chapter, we introduced you to the JAX-RS APIs for building RESTful web services. We also discussed how to build interceptors and filters for a RESTful web service application and their usage in real-life use cases. This chapter is a continuation of what we discussed in the previous chapter. This chapter will take you further into the JAX-RS APIs, and some complex use cases and their solutions.

The following topics are covered in this chapter:

- Understanding subresources and subresource locators in JAX-RS
- Dynamic dispatching and request matching
- Response builder explained
- Exception handling in JAX-RS
- Introducing validations in JAX-RS applications
- Supporting custom request-response message formats
- Asynchronous RESTful web services
- Asynchronous RESTful web service client
- Server-Sent Events
- Managing the HTTP cache in a RESTful web service
- Understanding filters and interceptors in JAX-RS
- Understanding the JAX-RS resource life cycle

Discussions on the JAX-RS framework would not be complete without covering the advanced features offered by the framework for building subresources, validations, exception handling, and extensions for handling various message types. Take a deep breath and get ready for a deep dive into the JAX-RS API.

Understanding subresources and subresource locators in JAX-RS

While discussing the JAX-RS APIs in the previous chapter, we covered the resource class and the resource class methods in RESTful web APIs. If you need a quick brush-up on this topic, refer to the *Annotations for defining a RESTful resource* section in Chapter 3, *Introducing the JAX-RS API*. In this section, you will get introduced to two new concepts, namely subresources and subresource locators in REST. You will find them very useful while designing well-structured RESTful web APIs.

Subresources in JAX-RS

In the previous chapter, we discussed the @Path annotation that identifies the URI path that a resource class or class method will serve requests for. A class annotated with the @Path annotation (at the class level) is called the **root resource** class. You can also use the @Path annotation on the methods of the root resource classes. If a resource method with the @Path annotation is annotated with request method designators such as @GET, @POST, @PUT, or @DELETE, it is known as a subresource method.

The concept of subresources is to have a root resource class that resolves a generic URI path and to have the @Path annotated methods in the class to further resolve the request. This helps you to keep the REST resource class implementation more structured and readable.

Let's consider a simple example to understand this topic better. Look at the following code snippet:

```
//imports are omitted for brevity
@Path("hr")
public class HRService {

    @GET
    @Path("departments")
    @Produces(MediaType.APPLICATION_JSON)
    public List<Department> findAllDepartmnets () {
        List<Department> departments =
            findAllDepartmentEntities();
        return departments;
    }

    @GET
    @Path("departments/{id}")
    @Produces(MediaType.APPLICATION_JSON)
```

```
    public Department findDepartment(@PathParam("id") Short id) {

        Department department = findDepartmentEntity(id);
        return department;
    }
}
```

When a client calls the HTTP GET method with the URI hr/departments, the JAX-RS
runtime on the server resolves the hr portion of the URI first. In this example, the hr path
fragment resolves to the HRService class. Next, it identifies a subresource that matches the
remaining part of the URI for the given HTTP request type. This part is resolved to the
findAllDepartmnets() method. However, if the request URI is hr/departments/10,
the URI path will be resolved to the findDepartment() subresource method.

Subresource locators in JAX-RS

Having discussed subresources, we will now see a subresource locator.

It is perfectly legal to use the @Path annotations on methods in a REST resource class
without any resource method designators such as @GET, @POST, @PUT, or @DELETE. The
objects returned by these methods will be used for resolving the incoming HTTP request
further. These methods are called the subresource locators. These locators are useful when
requests need to be further resolved dynamically by other objects. This gives you more
flexibility in implementation.

In the following example, DepartmentResource is the root resource and the
findManagerForDepartment() method is a subresource locator method. The
findManagerForDepartment() method has only the @Path annotation in the code
snippet. The EmployeeResource object returned by this method further resolves the HTTP
request:

```
// Imports are omitted for brevity
@Path("departments")
public class DepartmentResource {
    //Sub-resource locator method
    @Path("{id}/manager")
    public EmployeeResource
        findManagerForDepartment(@PathParam("id")
        Short deptId) {
        //Find the department for id
        Department department = findDepartmentEntity(deptId);
        //Create the instance of Employee object
        //This instance will be used for further resolving request
```

```
            EmployeeResource employeeResource = new
                EmployeeResource(department.getManagerId());
            return employeeResource;
    }
//Other methods are omitted for brevity
}

/**
  *This class that defines the subresource used in
  *DepartmentResource
*/
//imports are omitted for brevity
public class EmployeeResource{
    Short employeeId;
    public EmployeeResource(Short employeeId){
        this.employeeId=employeeId;
    }
    //Resolves GET request to findEmployee() method
    @GET
    @Produces(MediaType.APPLICATION_JSON)
    public Employee findEmployee(){
        Employee employee = findEmployeeEntity(employeeId);
        return employee;
    }
    //Other methods are omitted for brevity
}

}
```

In this example, let's see what happens on the server when a client calls the HTTP GET method with the following URI: departments/10/manager.

The JAX-RS runtime on the server resolves the URI part of the HTTP request to the findManagerForDepartment() method defined on the DepartmentResource class. The runtime further resolves the request on the EmployeeResource object returned by the findManagerForDepartment() method and identifies the findEmployee() that matches the HTTP request type. The HTTP request will be then dispatched to the findEmployee() method defined on the EmployeeResource instance.

In the preceding example, you are managing the life cycle of the subresource by creating an instance of EmployeeResource in the code and returning it from the findManagerForDepartment() method. You can ask the JAX-RS runtime to manage the subcomponent instance by returning the class instead of an instance, as given in the following code:

```
@Path("{id}/manager")
public Class<EmployeeResource>
```

```
findManagerForDepartment(@PathParam("id") Short deptId) {
    return EmployeeResource.class;
}
```

In this case, the runtime will manage the initialization of the subresource instance (`EmployeeResource`), including all dependency injections via **Context and Dependency Injection (CDI)**, if any. If you are not familiar with CDI, go through the tutorial available at `http://docs.oracle.com/javaee/7/tutorial/partcdi.htm`.

Dynamic dispatching

In real-life scenarios, a subresource locator method can return different implementations of the subresource class on the basis of various conditions. This makes the implementation more flexible and dynamic.

Let's say we need to operate on the `DepartmentResource` or `EmployeeResource`. This can be accomplished as follows, with the `getResource` method returning the `DepartmentResource` or `EmployeeResource` class, based on the user-specified resource type. JAX-RS will introspect the returned type to dynamically dispatch the request to the target resource:

```
@Path("enterprise")
public class EnterpriseResource {

@Path("{resourcetype}")
public Class getResource(@PathParam("resourcetype") String resourceId) {
  if (resourceId.equals("department") ) {
      return DepartmentResource.class;
    } else {
      return EmployeeResource.class;
    }
  }
}
```

Request matching

JAX-RS uses the `@Path` annotation for dispatching requests to corresponding resource or sub-resource methods using the following steps:

1. Identify a set of candidate root resource classes matching the request.
2. Obtain a set of candidate resource methods for the request.

3. Identify the method that will handle the request.

4. If no matching resource method or sub-resource method can be found, then an appropriate error response is returned.

Now let us illustrate, for the following services, Service1 and Service2, how request dispatching happens when a client requests the target resources:

```java
@Path("/s1")
public class Service1 {
    /**
     * Creates a new instance of Service1
     */
    public Service1() {
    }

    @GET
    @Path("{name : .+}")
    @Produces(MediaType.APPLICATION_JSON)
    public String get1(@PathParam("name") String name) {
        System.out.println("Service1.get1 Invoked");
        return "Service1.get1."+name;
    }

    @GET
    @Path("{name : .+}/g2")
    @Produces(MediaType.APPLICATION_JSON)
    public String get2(@PathParam("name") String name) {
        System.out.println("Service1.get2 Invoked");
        return "Service1.get2."+name;
    }
}
```

Let's see how it works with Service 2 here:

```java
@Path("/{any : .*}")
public class Service2 {
    /**
     * Creates a new instance of Service2
     */
    public Service2() {
    }

    @GET
    @Produces(MediaType.APPLICATION_JSON)
    public String get1() {
        System.out.println("Service2.get1 Invoked");
        return "Service2.get1";
```

```
    }

    @PUT
    @Consumes(MediaType.APPLICATION_JSON)
    public void put1(String content) {
        System.out.println("Service2.put1 Invoked");
        System.out.println(content);
    }
}
```

Now let us look at how the different client requests get resolved to the corresponding target resource:

Client request	Request matching steps
HTTP GET request /s1/g1	• Matching root resource class is Service1 as @Path ("/s1") best matches the Service1 class. • Candidate resource methods is get1 as the @Path expression resolves to {name : .+}. The .+ is a regular expression that will match any stream of characters after /s1. • The method that will handle the request is get1 in this case.
HTTP GET request /s1/x/g2	• Matching root resource class is Service1 as @Path ("/s1") best matches the Service1 class. • Candidate resource methods is get2 as the @Path expression resolves to {name : .+}/g2. The .+ is a regular expression that will match any stream of characters after /s1 that ends with g2. • The method that will handle the request is get2 in this case.
HTTP GET request /s1/x/g1	• Matching root resource class is Service1 as @Path ("/s1") best matches the Service1 class. • Candidate resource methods is get1 as the @Path expression resolves to {name : .+}. The .+ is a regular expression that will match any stream of characters after /s1. • The method that will handle the request is get1 in this case.
HTTP GET request /s2/g1	• Matching root resource class is Service2 as @Path ("{any : .*}") best matches the Service2 class. • Candidate resource methods is get1, which is the only available GET method in this class. • The method that will handle the request is get1 in this case.

HTTP PUT request /s2/g1	• Matching root resource class is Service2 as @Path("{any : .*}") best matches the Service2 class. • Candidate resource methods is put1, as that is the only available PUT method in this class. • The method that will handle the request is put1 in this case.
HTTP PUT request /s1/g1	• Matching root resource class is Service1 as @Path("/s1") best matches the Service1 class. • Candidate resource methods is get1 as the @Path expression resolves to {name : .+}. The .+ is a regular expression that will match any stream of characters after /s1. • As get1 does not support PUT requests, the server responds saying HTTP Status 405 - Method Not Allowed.

JAX-RS response builder explained

The JAX-RS resource methods return type is generally based on the entity being operated on. For example, getDepartment returns the Department type. This return value is wrapped by JAX-RS in the default response message body and response status; additional metadata like content length, media type are added by the default JAX-RS implementation provider, which is not transparent to us. If we intend to explicitly control the response sent back to the client, the resource methods can return an instance of javax.ws.rs.core.Response. The Response class is an abstract class which contains methods required to get access to the different attributes of Response sent back to the client. Listed here are a few key methods of Response class:

Method	Purpose
getCookies	Get cookies set on the response message.
getDate	Get the response message date.
getEntity	Get the response message entity object. In case of HTTP, this will be the entity object set in the HTTP message body.
getHeaders	Get a view of the response headers and their object values.
getHeaderString	Get a message header value as a string value.
getLength	Get the content length value.
getMediaType	Get the media type of the message entity.

getStatus	Get the status code associated with the response.
getStatusInfo	Get the complete status information associated with the response.

Instances of `Response` object cannot be created directly; instead they are created from `javax.ws.rs.core.Response.ResponseBuilder` instances returned by one of the following static helper methods of the `Response` class:

Method	Purpose
ok	Create a new `ResponseBuilder` with the OK status.
status	Create a new `ResponseBuilder` with the supplied status.
serverError	Create a new `ResponseBuilder` with the server error status.
temporaryRedirect	Create a new `ResponseBuilder` for a temporary redirection to the specified URI.
noContent	Create a new `ResponseBuilder` for an empty response.
notAcceptable	Create a new `ResponseBuilder` for a not acceptable response.
notModified	Create a new `ResponseBuilder` with a not-modified status.

The `javax.ws.rs.core.Response.ResponseBuilder` class provides easy-to-use utility methods for creating the `javax.ws.rs.core.Response` instance by using a builder pattern. `ShoppingService` illustrates the usage of `javax.ws.rs.core.Response.ResponseBuilder` to construct the `javax.ws.rs.core.Response` with the `OK` status:

```
@Path("/shopping")
public class ShoppingService {
   @GET
   public Response productExists((@PathParam("productId") String productId)
{
      NewCookie cookie = new NewCookie("shopping-id", "uid");
      //Check if the specified product exists
      ResponseBuilder builder = Response.ok("Y", "text/plain");
      return builder.cookie(cookie).build();
   }
}
```

`javax.ws.rs.core.NewCookie` is used to create a new HTTP cookie to be sent as part of `javax.ws.rs.core.Response`.

Exception handling in JAX-RS

Exceptions in Java are a way to tell the client that an abnormal condition has occurred while executing specific statements in the code. In this section, you will see how a REST resource method handles exceptions.

Reporting errors using ResponseBuilder

The `Response` instance can hold metadata, such as the HTTP status code, along with the entity body. The REST resource method can return the `Response` object to report back on the status of the REST API call to the caller.

For example, the following resource method returns `HTTP 404 Not Found` (represented by the following Enum constant: `Response.Status.NOT_FOUND`) if the `department` entity object is not found in the data store:

```
@DELETE
@Path("departments/{id}")
public Response remove(@PathParam("id") Short id) {
    Department department = entityManager.find(Department.class,
        id);
    if(department == null){
        //Department to be removed is not found in data store
        return Response.status(Response.Status.NOT_FOUND).entity
            ("Entity not found for : " + id).build();
    }
    entityManager.remove(entityManager.merge(department));
    return  Response.status(Response.Status.OK).build();
}
```

Although the approach of using the `Response` object for reporting errors back to the caller works for basic use cases, it may not really scale up in real life. With this approach, every resource method in a class should have the `Response` object as the return type. Furthermore, developers may need to catch all exceptions in the resource method and convert them to the `Response` object programmatically. This may eventually result in repetitive coding, silly coding errors, and maintenance issues. JAX-RS addresses this issue by allowing you to directly throw exceptions from the REST resource methods to report errors back to the caller. This model is explained in the next two sections.

Reporting errors using WebApplicationException

The JAX-RS framework provides `javax.ws.rs.WebApplicationException` which you can throw from the JAX-RS resource methods or provider implementations to report exceptions back to the caller. Later, in the request processing cycle, the default exception mapper class deployed by the JAX-RS runtime will intercept the exception thrown by the method and will generate an appropriate HTTP response object. `WebApplicationException` can be created by wrapping the response content, error text, or HTTP status code. As `WebApplicationException` is extended from `RuntimeException`, the methods that throw this exception do not need to have the `throws` clause for `WebApplicationException` in the method signature. When a method throws `WebApplicationException`, the server stops the execution of the request and sends the response created from `WebApplicationException` back to the client. Here is an example:

```
@DELETE
@Path("departments/{id}")
public void removeDepartment(@PathParam("id") Short id) {
    //Read department from data store for id
    Department department = findDepartmentEntity(id);
    //throw exception if department to be deleted is not found
    if(department == null){
        throw new
            WebApplicationException(Response.Status.NOT_FOUND);
    }
    removeDepartmentEntity(department);
}
```

The preceding example throws `WebApplicationException` with the HTTP status `404 Not Found` if the department is not found in the data store. You can use different HTTP status codes, depending upon the use case. The `javax.ws.rs.core.Response.Status` class holds the commonly used status codes defined by HTTP. We discussed the HTTP status codes and their meaning in the *HTTP status codes* section in `Chapter 1`, *Introducing the REST Architectural Style*.

There are many exceptions available in JAX-RS, subclassed from
javax.ws.rs.WebApplicationException. You can use the most appropriate one in your
use case. Some of the exceptions extended from WebApplicationException are as
follows: BadRequestException, ForbiddenException, NotAcceptableException,
NotAllowedException, NotAuthorizedException, NotFoundException,
NotSupportedException, RedirectionException, InternalServerErrorException,
and ServiceUnavailableException.

> Refer to the API documentation to learn more about the child exceptions
> derived from WebApplicationException available at
> http://docs.oracle.com/javaee/7/api/javax/ws/rs/WebApplicationEx
> ception.html.

You can also extend WebApplicationException to hold more meaningful error messages
for your application, as shown in the following code:

```java
import javax.ws.rs.WebApplicationException;
import javax.ws.rs.core.MediaType;
import javax.ws.rs.core.Response;

public class DepartmentNotFoundWebAppException extends
    WebApplicationException {

    /**
     * Generates a HTTP 404 (Not Found) exception.
     */
    public DepartmentNotFoundWebAppException() {
        super(Response.Status.NOT_FOUND);
    }

    /**
     * Generates a HTTP 404 (Not Found) exception.
     * @param message
     */
    public DepartmentNotFoundWebAppException(String message) {
        super(Response.status(Status.NOT_FOUND).
        entity(message).type(MediaType.TEXT_PLAIN).build());
    }
}
```

WebApplicationException is subclassed from RuntimeException. This fits well for handling unexpected exceptions that may occur in the REST API implementation. However, for a typical business application, there may be many modules and certain modules may be reused in a non-REST context as well. So, you cannot live with WebApplicationException (which is automatically handled by the JAX-RS runtime) for all scenarios. The next section discusses the usage of the checked business exception in the JAX-RS application.

Reporting errors using application exceptions

It is recommended to use a checked application exception for recoverable error scenarios. In this section, we will see how a checked exception can be used in a RESTful web API implementation.

Here is a checked business exception definition for use in the JAX-RS resource method:

```
//Business exception class
public class DeprtmentNotFoundBusinessException extends Exception{

    public DeprtmentNotFoundBusinessException(String message) {
        super(message);
    }

    public DeprtmentNotFoundBusinessException(String message,
        Throwable cause) {
        super(message, cause);
    }

    //Rest of the implementation code goes here
}
```

The following code snippet uses `DeprtmentNotFoundBusinessException` for reporting the `DepartmentNotFound` error to the caller:

```
@DELETE
@Path("departments/{id}")
public void remove(@PathParam("id") Short id) throws
    DeprtmentNotFoundBusinessException {
    //Read department from data store for id
    Department department = findDepartmentEntity(id);
    // throw exception if department to be deleted is not found
    if(department == null){
        throw new DeprtmentNotFoundBusinessException
            ("Department is missing in store");

    }
    removeDepartmentEntity(department);
}
```

The preceding implementation is simple and easy to follow. However, you may want to perform an additional step to map exceptions to the HTTP response body content. Note that the JAX-RS runtime, by default, does not know how to generate the right response content for the custom application exception thrown by a method. All the unhandled exceptions are handled by the underlying servlet container, which may wrap or swallow your application exception. The solution is to use the exception mapper feature offered by JAX-RS. JAX-RS allows you to deploy a custom exception mapper implementation, which will map the business exception to the appropriate response message. The next section discusses this topic in detail.

Mapping exceptions to a response message using ExceptionMapper

You can use the `javax.ws.rs.ext.ExceptionMapper` class to map the checked or unchecked exceptions to the appropriate HTTP response content. At runtime, when an exception is thrown by a method, the JAX-RS runtime will scan through all registered exception mappers to find the best match for handling the exception. If there is no exact match found, runtime considers a mapper class that matches with the parent class of the checked exception class. After identifying the exception mapper class for handling an exception, the framework invokes the `toResponse()` method on the exception mapper instance to generate the appropriate HTTP response content for the exception.

Here is an example for the `ExceptionMapper` class, which creates the HTTP response for `DepartmentNotFoundBusinessException`:

```
import javax.ws.rs.core.Response;
import javax.ws.rs.ext.ExceptionMapper;
import javax.ws.rs.ext.Provider;

@Provider
public class DepartmentNotFoundExceptionMapper implements
    ExceptionMapper<DeprtmentNotFoundBusinessException> {

    // Map an exception to a Response
    @Override
    public Response toResponse(DeprtmentNotFoundBusinessException
        exception) {
        return Response.status(
            Response.Status.NOT_FOUND).
        entity(exception.getMessage()).build();
    }

}
```

When the runtime fails to find an exception mapper for the custom exceptions, the exception will be propagated to the underlying container, which will eventually result in `javax.servlet.ServletException`, sending the `HTTP 500` status back to the client.

Introducing validations in JAX-RS applications

Validation is the process of ensuring the completeness and sanity of business data before posting it to the underlying data source. Validating the client input is very important for any REST API that you build. In this section, we will see the offering in JAX-RS for validating client input.

The JAX-RS 2.x release allows you to validate the resource class and methods via **Java Bean Validation**. This framework is a Java specification, which lets you specify the validation rules on the objects or hierarchy of objects via the built-in annotations; it also lets you write the reusable validation rules for handling various use cases. Bean Validation is integrated into the Java EE platform, allowing developers to easily define and enforce the validation rules across various components that come as a part of Java EE. The following is a list of Java EE components that support Bean Validation: `JAX-RS`, `JAXB`, `JPA`, `EJB`, `JSF`, and `CDI`.

The latest release of Bean Validation is Version 2.0, which is based on JSR 380 and formerly JSR 349. You can learn more about JSR 380 at `http://beanvalidation.org/2.0/spec/#introduction`.

A brief introduction to Bean Validation

The Bean Validation framework allows you to specify the validation rules in the form of annotations on a field, method, or a Java class. You can either use built-in constraints offered by Bean Validation or build custom constraints by using the extension mechanisms offered by the framework. The following table summarizes the built-in constraints offered by Bean Validation that are applicable to all data types:

Validation constraints	Supported Java types	Details of the imposed constraints
`@NotNull`	Applicable to all Java types	The annotated variable must not be `null`.
`@Null`	Applicable to all Java types	The annotated variable must be `null`.

The following table summarizes the built-in constraints offered by Bean Validation that are applicable to the Boolean data types:

Validation constraints	Supported Java types	Details of the imposed constraints
`@AssertFalse`	• `java.lang.Boolean` • Boolean	The annotated variable must be `false`.
`@AssertTrue`	• `java.lang.Boolean` • Boolean	The annotated variable must be `true`.

The following table summarizes the built-in constraints offered by Bean Validation that are applicable to the number data types:

Validation constraints	Supported Java types	Details of the imposed constraints
@DecimalMax	• java.math.BigDecimal • java.math.BigInteger • java.lang.String • byte, short, int, long, and their wrapper types	The annotated variable must not exceed the maximum specified limit.
@DecimalMin	• java.math.BigDecimal • java.math.BigInteger • java.lang.String • byte, short, int, long, and their wrapper types	The annotated variable must be higher than or equal to the minimum specified value.
@Digits	• java.math.BigDecimal • java.math.BigInteger • java.lang.String • byte, short, int, long, and their wrapper types	The annotated variable must be a number within the acceptable range.
@Max	• java.math.BigDecimal • java.math.BigInteger • byte, short, int, long, and their wrapper types	The annotated variable must be a number with a value less than or equal to the specified maximum value.
@Min	• java.math.BigDecimal • java.math.BigInteger • byte, short, int, long, and their wrapper types	The annotated variable must be a number with a value larger than or equal to the specified minimum value.

The following table summarizes the built-in constraints offered by Bean Validation that are applicable to the date data types:

Validation constraints	Supported Java types	Details of the imposed constraints
@Future	• `java.util.Date` • `java.util.Calendar`	The annotated variable must be a date in the future.
@Past	• `java.util.Date` • `java.util.Calendar`	The annotated variable must be a date in the past.

The following table summarizes the built-in constraints offered by Bean Validation that are applicable to the string data types:

Validation constraints	Supported Java types	Details of the imposed constraints
@Pattern	`java.lang.String`	The annotated string must match the regular expression specified.

The following table summarizes the built-in constraints offered by Bean Validation that are applicable to the collection and string data types:

Validation constraints	Supported Java types	Details of the imposed constraints
@Size	• `java.lang.String` (string length is evaluated) • `jav.util.Collection` (collection size is evaluated) • `java.util.Map` (map size is evaluated) • * `java.lang.Array` (array length is evaluated)	The annotated string or collection size must be between the specified boundaries (included).

The following code snippet illustrates the use of built-in validation constraints provided by Bean Validation for validating an input to a JAX-RS method call. This example validates the input parameter for a positive number:

```
@GET
@Path("departments/{id}")
@Produces(MediaType.APPLICATION_JSON)
public Department findDepartment(@PalhParam("id")
    @Min(value = 0, message = "Department Id must be a
    positive value")
    Short id, @Context Request request) {

    Department department = findDepartmentEntity(id);
    return department;
}
```

Building custom validation constraints

In the previous section, we had a quick look at the built-in validation constraints offered by the Bean Validation framework. There may be cases where you may want to build your own validation constraints. The Bean Validation framework supports that as well.

The core contracts that you should implement for a custom validation constraint are as follows:

- Annotation for the custom validation constraint
- Implementation of the `javax.validation.ConstraintValidatorContext` interface. This class contains your custom validation logic
- Definition of a default error message

Let's build a custom validation constraint for checking whether a department with the same name already exists for a given location. This constraint avoids the duplicate department entities.

The first step is to build an annotation for the custom constraint that you are going to construct. The Bean Validation framework specification demands the following attribute definitions in a constraint annotation:

- `message`: This attribute returns the default key for reading the validation error messages.
- `groups`: This attribute specifies the validation groups to which this constraint belongs to. This is default to an empty array of the `Class<?>` type.
- `payload`: This attribute can be used by clients for assigning custom payload objects to a constraint. This attribute is not used here.

Let's define an annotation for the custom validation constraint, `ValidDepartmentValidator`, which we are going to build next:

```
//Other import statements are omitted for brevity
import java.lang.annotation.ElementType;
import java.lang.annotation.Retention;
import java.lang.annotation.Target;
import java.lang.annotation.RetentionPolicy;
import javax.validation.Constraint;
import javax.validation.Payload;

//@Constraint links a constraint annotation with
//its constraint validation implementations.
@Constraint(validatedBy = {ValidDepartmentValidator.class})
@Target({ElementType.FIELD, ElementType.PARAMETER})
@Retention(value = RetentionPolicy.RUNTIME)
public @interface ValidDepartment {

    //The message key for validation error message
    //fails the validation.
    String message() default
    "{com.packtpub.rest.validation.deptrule}";
    Class<?>[] groups() default {};
    Class<? extends Payload>[] payload() default {};
}
```

As the next step, we need to provide the implementation for the custom validation constraint called `ValidDepartmentValidator`. Here is the code snippet:

```
//Other import statements are omitted for brevity
import javax.validation.ConstraintValidator;
import javax.validation.ConstraintValidatorContext;

//Defines the logic to validate the constraint 'ValidDepartment'
//for the object type 'Department'
public class ValidDepartmentValidator implements
    ConstraintValidator<ValidDepartment, Department> {

    @Override
    public void initialize(ValidDepartment constraintAnnotation) {
    }

    @Override
    public boolean isValid(Department department,
        ConstraintValidatorContext context) {
        //Implementation of isDeptExistsForLoc() is not shown here
        //to save space. This method return true if the given
        // department id is found in the database
        if(isDeptExistsForLoc(department.getDepartmentId(),
            department.getDepartmentName(),
            department.getLocationId())) {
            return false;

        }

        return true;
    }
    //Rest of the code goes here

}
```

The last step is to define the error message in a resource bundle in order to localize the validation error messages. This file should be added to the root folder with the following name: `ValidationMessages.properties`. The file contents may look like the following code:

```
com.packtpub.rest.validation.deptrule= Department already exists
```

This feature lets you localize the validation error messages. For example, `ValidationMessages_fr.properties` contains messages for the French locale. The custom validation constraint for checking a duplicate department entity is ready for use now!

You can apply this constraint on the method parameters or class fields, as shown in the following code snippet:

```
@POST
@Path("departments")
@Consumes(MediaType.APPLICATION_JSON)
public void create(@ValidDepartment Department entity) {
    createDepartmentEntity(entity);
}
```

To learn more about Bean Validation, visit the following link: `http://beanvalidation.org/`. The official tutorial for Bean Validation is available at `http://docs.oracle.com/javaee/7/tutorial/partbeanvalidation.htm`.

What happens when Bean Validation fails in a JAX-RS application?

The framework throws `javax.validation.ValidationException` or its subclass exceptions, such as `javax.validation.ConstraintViolationException`, when the Bean Validation rules that you set on the model class fails at runtime. The JAX-RS runtime will report the validation error back to the client with a `500` (internal server error) HTTP status code. You can override the default validation exception handling by providing a custom `javax.ws.rs.ext.ExceptionMapper` class. We discussed `ExceptionMapper` a while ago in the *Mapping exceptions to the response message using ExceptionMapper* section.

Supporting custom request-response message formats

The JAX-RS framework uses entity provider components for the marshaling and unmarshaling of the message body content (entity) present in the response and request objects, respectively. It is the entity provider component that maps an entity with the associated Java types.

The following table lists the default entity mappings provided by the JAX-RS runtime via a set of built-in entity providers. When you use one of the internet media types present in the following table to represent the request or response entity body, the framework takes care of the conversion and reconversion of the entity body to the associated Java type:

Data types	Internet media type
`byte[]`	`*/*`
`java.lang.String`	`*/*`
`java.io.Reader`	`*/*`
`java.io.File`	`*/*`
`javax.activation.DataSource`	`*/*`
`javax.ws.rs.core.StreamingOutput`	`*/*`
All primitive types	`text/plain`
`java.lang.Boolean`	`text/plain`
`java.lang.Character`	`text/plain`
`java.lang.Number`	`text/plain`
`javax.xml.transform.Source`	`text/xml`, `application/xml`, and `application/*+xml`
`javax.xml.bind.JAXBElement`	`text/xml`, `application/xml`, and `application/*+xml`
Application supplied JAXB annotated objects (types annotated with `@XmlRootElement` or `@XmlType`)	`text/xml`, `application/xml`, and `application/*+xml`
`javax.ws.rs.core.MultivaluedMap<String, String>`	`application/x-www-form-urlencoded`

What if you want to build your own media type for representing the message content? Or what if you want to customize the marshaling and unmarshaling process for specific media types?

JAX-RS has a solution for both these use cases. The JAX-RS extension API allows you to handle the request or response message bodies via custom entity providers. You can have custom entity providers configured for an application for serializing the Java type into the appropriate media type. They can also be used for deserializing the message body content present in a request to the appropriate Java types. In this section, we will learn how to use the JAX-RS provider APIs for building custom message handlers.

The JAX-RS providers are application components that offer a way to extend and customize the runtime behavior. There are mainly three categories of providers: entity provider, context provider, and exception provider. Each JAX-RS provider class must be annotated with the `@javax.ws.rs.ext.Provider` annotation. During deployment, the server scans through the deployment units for the `@Provider` annotations and automatically registers all the identified provider components. You do not need to do any extra configurations or API calls for integrating the provider components.

The JAX-RS extension API offers the following two contracts (interfaces) for managing the marshaling and unmarshaling of the entity body present in the request and response messages:

- `javax.ws.rs.ext.MessageBodyWriter<T>`: This interface provides the contract for the conversion of a Java type to the output stream. The class that implements this interface converts the message payload represented in Java into the one on the internet media type representation format that is sent over the wire to the client.
- `javax.ws.rs.ext.MessageBodyReader<T>`: This interface provides the contract for the conversion of the input stream to a Java type. The provider class that implements this interface reads the message body representation from the input stream and converts the incoming message body into an appropriate Java type.

Building custom entity provider

Let's have some fun now! In this section, we will build a custom entity provider for handling the request and response message content represented using the application/csv media type. Note that JAX-RS, by default, does not support the CSV media type. The custom entity providers, which we will build in a short while, leverage the runtime extension mechanism offered by JAX-RS via the MessageBodyWriter and MessageBodyReader interfaces.

Marshaling Java objects to the CSV representation with MessageBodyWriter

The JAX-RS framework uses MessageBodyWriter to serialize the Java representation of resources returned by the REST web API into an appropriate format, which is sent back to the client. The JAX-RS runtime natively supports the serialization of the commonly used Java types, such as java.lang.String, java.io.InputStream, and Java custom objects annotated with JAXB binding annotations. You can provide your own implementation of MessageBodyWriter if you find that the default implementation provided by JAX-RS is not meeting your use case requirements.

A javax.ws.rs.ext.MessageBodyWriter<T> provider should implement the following methods:

- isWriteable(): This method checks whether this MessageBodyWriter implementation supports converting the Java type present in the method argument to the designated internet media type. This method is invoked when the framework tries to find a MessageBodyWriter implementation for serializing the Java objects returned by a resource method to the designated internet media type.
- getSize(): JAX-RS 2.0 deprecated this method, and the value returned by the method is ignored by the JAX-RS runtime. You can return -1 from this method.
- writeTo(): This method writes a Java type object to an HTTP message.

Keep a note of the following points when building a `MessageBodyWriter` implementation:

- A `MessageBodyWriter` provider implementation may be annotated with `@Produces` to restrict the media types for which it will be considered suitable
- A `MessageBodyWriter` provider implementation must be either programmatically registered in the JAX-RS runtime or must be annotated with `@Provider` annotation

The API documentation for `MessageBodyWriter` is available at `https://docs.oracle.com/javaee/7/api/javax/ws/rs/ext/MessageBody Writer.html`.

The following example shows how you can build a custom `MessageBodyWriter` implementation that converts a list of the `Department` Java objects into the CSV format:

```
//Other imports omitted for brevity
import javax.ws.rs.Produces;
import javax.ws.rs.WebApplicationException;
import javax.ws.rs.core.MediaType;
import javax.ws.rs.core.MultivaluedMap;
import javax.ws.rs.ext.MessageBodyWriter;
import javax.ws.rs.ext.Provider;
import org.supercsv.io.CsvBeanWriter;
import org.supercsv.io.ICsvBeanWriter;
import org.supercsv.prefs.CsvPreference;

@Provider
@Produces("application/csv")
public class CSVMessageBodyWriter implements
MessageBodyWriter<List<Department>> {

    /**
     * Ascertain if MessageBodyWriter supports
     * a particular type.
     */
    @Override
    public boolean isWriteable(Class<?> type, Type genericType,
        Annotation[] annotations, MediaType mediaType) {
        //Is this MessageBodyWriter implementation capable
        //of serializing the object type returned by
        //the current REST API call?
        return (List.class.isAssignableFrom(type));
    }

    /**
```

```
    *Deprecated by JAX-RS 2.0 and ignored by Jersey runtime
    */
@Override
public long getSize(List<Department> t, Class<?> type, Type
    genericType, Annotation[] annotations,
        MediaType mediaType) {
    return 0;
}

/**
 * Converts Java to desired media type and Writes it
 * to an HTTP response
 */
@Override
public void writeTo(List<Department> dataList, Class<?> type,
    Type genericType, Annotation[] annotations, MediaType
        mediaType, MultivaluedMap<String, Object> httpHeaders,
            OutputStream entityStream) throws IOException,
                WebApplicationException {
    // This class uses CsvBeanWriter for converting
    // Java to CSV. It is an open source framework
    // that writes a CSV file by mapping each field
    // on the bean to a column in the CSV file
    //(using the supplied name mapping).
    ICsvBeanWriter writer = new CsvBeanWriter(
        new PrintWriter(entityStream),
            CsvPreference.STANDARD_PREFERENCE);
    //No data then return
    if (dataList == null || dataList.size() == 0) {
        return;
    }
    //Columns headers in CSV
    String[] nameMapping ={"departmentId","departmentName",
    "managerId","locationId"} ;

    //CsvBeanWriter writes the header with the property names
    writer.writeHeader(nameMapping);
    for (Object p : dataList) {
        //Write each row
        writer.write(p, nameMapping);
    }
    writer.close();
}
}
```

The following RESTful web service call illustrates a sample output (in CSV format) generated by the CSVMessageBodyWriter implementation:

```
GET /api/hr/departments HTTP/1.1
Host: localhost:8080
Accept: application/csv

departmentId,departmentName,locationId,managerId
1001,"Finance",1700,101
1002,"Office Administration",1500,205
```

Marshaling CSV representation to Java objects with MessageBodyReader

In the previous section, we discussed the entity provider that supports the marshaling of the Java object to media types. In this section, we will see the entity provider that does the reverse process, unmarshaling of the input stream to the Java types.

The JAX-RS framework uses MessageBodyReader to deserialize the message body into the Java type. The JAX-RS runtimes natively supports the deserialization of input stream to the commonly used Java types. You can use the custom MessageBodyReader implementation to control the deserialization of the input stream, which is not supported by JAX-RS, by default.

A javax.ws.rs.ext.MessageBodyReader<T> provider should implement the following methods and contracts:

- isReadable(): This method checks whether the MessageBodyReader interface can produce an instance of a particular Java type. This method is invoked when the framework tries to find a matching MessageBodyReader interface for reading the input stream into a Java type parameter present in the resource method.
- readFrom(): This method reads the input stream into the designated Java type.

Keep a note of the following points when building a MessageBodyReader interface:

- A MessageBodyReader implementation may be annotated with @Consumes to restrict the media types for which it will be considered suitable
- A MessageBodyReader provider implementation must be either programmatically registered in the JAX-RS runtime or must be annotated with the @Provider annotation

The following example illustrates a custom `MessageBodyReader` implementation, which converts the CSV representation of the department items present in the input stream to list the `Department` Java objects:

```java
//Other imports are omitted for brevity
import javax.ws.rs.Consumes;
import javax.ws.rs.WebApplicationException;
import javax.ws.rs.core.MediaType;
import javax.ws.rs.core.MultivaluedMap;
import javax.ws.rs.ext.MessageBodyReader;
import javax.ws.rs.ext.Provider;

import org.supercsv.cellprocessor.ift.CellProcessor;
import org.supercsv.io.CsvBeanReader;
import org.supercsv.io.ICsvBeanReader;
import org.supercsv.prefs.CsvPreference;

@Provider
@Consumes("application/csv")
public class CSVMessageBodyReader implements
MessageBodyReader<List<Department>> {

    /**
     * Ascertain if the MessageBodyReader can produce
     * an instance of a particular type.
     */
    @Override
    public boolean isReadable(Class<?> type, Type genericType,
        Annotation[] annotations, MediaType mediaType) {
        return Collection.class.isAssignableFrom(type);
    }

    /**
     * Read a type from InputStream.
     */
    @Override
    public List readFrom(Class<List<Department>> type, Type
        genericType, Annotation[] annotations,
        MediaType mediaType,
        MultivaluedMap<String, String> httpHeaders,
        InputStream entityStream)
        throws IOException, WebApplicationException {

        ArrayList list = new ArrayList();
        //Following code uses Super CSV lib for reading CSV data
        //Define the type for each column in CSV
        final CellProcessor[] processors = new CellProcessor[]{
            new NotNull(new ParseShort()), // departmentId
```

```
                    new NotNull(), // departmentName
                    new NotNull(new ParseShort()), // locationId
                    new Optional(new ParseInt()) //managerId
            };
            //Reads CSV input stream
            ICsvBeanReader beanReader = new CsvBeanReader(new
                InputStreamReader(entityStream),
                CsvPreference.STANDARD_PREFERENCE);
            //Start building object from CVS
            String[] header = beanReader.getHeader(false);
            Object obj = null;
            while ((obj = beanReader.read(Department.class,
        header, processors)) != null) {
                list.add(obj);
                logger.log(Level.INFO, obj.toString());
            }

            return list;
        }
    }
```

The following RESTful web service call illustrates how a JAX-RS application can use `CSVMessageBodyReader` for taking input in CSV format:

```
POST /api/hr/departments HTTP/1.1
Host: localhost:8080
Content-Type: application/csv

departmentId,departmentName,locationId,managerId
1001,"Finance",1700,101
1002,"Office Administration",1500,205
```

You can download this example from the Packt website link mentioned at the beginning of this book, in the *Preface*. See the `CSVMessageBodyReader.java` and `CSVMessageBodyWriter.java` files in the `<rest-chapter4-service>` project.

Asynchronous RESTful web services

All the discussions on RESTful web services that we have had so far were based on the synchronous request and response model. When a client invokes a RESTful web API synchronously, the server keeps the request handling thread engaged till its request is processed. In this case, the entire request is processed in a single thread on the server. This model works if the request processing is finished quickly. The problem starts when a request takes more time to finish. In such a case, the thread used by the container to handle the long-running request will remain busy till the processing is over. This may adversely affect the scalability of the application when the load (concurrent requests) increases because the server will not have enough threads in the pool to handle the incoming requests. The asynchronous processing feature in JAX-RS solves this by processing the long-running requests asynchronously, as depicted in the following flow diagram. The client sends the request using AsyncInvoker to the target with a callback handler, thereby releasing the thread that is handling the current request back to the container. AsyncResponse responds later with response data once the processing is complete; this essentially increases the throughput of the server:

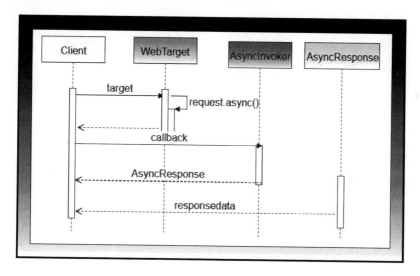

The following example demonstrates how to use the asynchronous REST API in JAX-RS. This example exposes the findAllDepartments() resource class method as an asynchronous REST API. You can do this by injecting javax.ws.rs.container.AsyncResponse as a parameter to the desired resource method, as shown in the following code snippet:

```
@GET
@Path("departments")
@Produces(MediaType.APPLICATION_JSON)
public void findAllDepartments(@Suspended AsyncResponse asyncResponse)
```

The @Suspended annotation used for injecting AsyncResponse tells the JAX-RS runtime that this method is expected to be executed in asynchronous mode and the client connection should not be automatically closed by the runtime when the method returns. The asynchronous REST resource method can use the injected AsyncResponse instance to send the response back to the client by using another thread. The AsyncResponse instance that is injected to methods is bound to the running request and can be used to asynchronously provide the request processing result. The core operations available on this instance are as follows:

- cancel(): This method cancels the request processing and passes the message to the suspended thread that was handling the current client request.
- resume(): This method resumes the request processing and passes the message to the suspended thread that was handling the current client request.
- register():This method is used for registering callbacks such as CompletionCallback, which is executed when the request finishes or fails, and ConnectionCallback, which is executed when a connection to a client is closed or lost.
- setTimeout(): This method is used for specifying the timeout value for the asynchronous process. Upon timeout, the runtime will throw javax.ws.rs.ServiceUnavailableException, which will be translated into the 503 Service Unavailable HTTP status code and sent back to the caller. You can even plug in a custom timeout handler implementation (which implements javax.ws.rs.container.TimeoutHandler) by invoking the setTimeoutHandler(TimeoutHandler) method on the AsyncResponse object.

The following code snippet illustrates a complete asynchronous method implementation for your reference. This method reads the department's records from the database in a different thread. Upon successful retrieval of records, the result is set on the `AsyncResponse` instance and resumes the suspended request processing. The resumed request is processed in a new thread as a normal request. The framework executes all configured filters, interceptors, and exception mappers before sending the response back to the client.

```
//Other imports are omitted for brevity
import javax.ws.rs.container.AsyncResponse;
import javax.ws.rs.container.Suspended;
import javax.ws.rs.container.TimeoutHandler;

@Stateless
@Path("hr/asynch")
public class HRAsynchService {
    private final ExecutorService
executorService=Executors.newCachedThreadPool();
    @GET
    @Path("departments")
    @Produces(MediaType.APPLICATION_JSON)
    public void findAllDepartments(@Suspended final AsyncResponse
asyncResponse)
    {
        //Set time out for the request
        asyncResponse.setTimeout(10, TimeUnit.SECONDS);
        Runnable longRunningDeptQuery = new Runnable(){
            EntityManagerFactory emf =
Persistence.createEntityManagerFactory("HRPersistenceUnit");
            EntityManager entityManagerLocal = emf.createEntityManager();

            public void run() {
                CriteriaQuery cq =
                    entityManagerLocal.getCriteriaBuilder().createQuery();
                cq.select(cq.from(Department.class));
                List<Department> depts =
                    entityManagerLocal.createQuery(cq).getResultList();
                GenericEntity<List<Department>> entity
                    = new GenericEntity<List<Department>>(depts) { };
                asyncResponse.resume(Response.ok().entity(entity).build());
            }
        };
        executorService.execute(longRunningDeptQuery);
    }
}
```

Asynchronous RESTful web service client

This section describes the usage of the asynchronous JAX-RS API on the client for calling the RESTful web APIs.

To invoke a REST API asynchronously on the client, you use `javax.ws.rs.client.AsyncInvoker`. The `AsyncInvoker` instance is obtained from the call of the `Invocation.Builder.async()` method, as shown in the following code:

```
//Other imports are omitted for brevity
import javax.ws.rs.client.AsyncInvoker;
import javax.ws.rs.client.Client;
import javax.ws.rs.client.WebTarget;
import javax.ws.rs.core.GenericType;
import javax.ws.rs.core.Response;

String BASE_URI =
    "http://localhost:8080/hr-services/webresources";
Client client = ClientBuilder.newClient();
WebTarget webTarget =
    client.target(BASE_URI).path("hr").path("departments");
AsyncInvoker asyncInvoker =
    webTarget.request(APPLICATION_JSON).async();
Future<Response> responseFuture = asyncInvoker.get();
Response response = responseFuture.get();
List<Department> depts = response.readEntity(new
    GenericType<List<Department>>() { });
response.close();
client.close();
```

The JAX-RS client-side API allows you to listen to events generated during the asynchronous invocation of the REST APIs by registering the callback handlers. To do this, you may need to implement `javax.ws.rs.client.InvocationCallback` and pass this instance as a parameter to the appropriate HTTP method call on the `AsyncInvoker` instance. The following code snippet illustrates how you can implement `InvocationCallback` for a GET method type. The `InvocationCallback::completed()` method is called upon the successful completion of a request. The `InvocationCallback::failed()` method is called upon the failure of a request for any reason:

```
//Other imports are omitted for brevity
import javax.ws.rs.client.InvocationCallback;

String BASE_URI =
    "http://localhost:8080/hr-services/webresources";
```

```
final Client client =
     javax.ws.rs.client.ClientBuilder.newClient();
WebTarget webTarget =
    client.target(BASE_URI).path("hr").path("departments");
AsyncInvoker asyncInvoker = webTarget.
    request(javax.ws.rs.core.MediaType.APPLICATION_JSON).async();
Future<List<Department>> entity = asyncInvoker.get(
    new InvocationCallback<List<Department>>() {
    @Override
    public void completed(List<Department> response) {
        //Call back on request completion
        //You can process the result here, if required
        client.close();
    }

    @Override
    public void failed(Throwable throwable) {
        //Call back on request failure
        //Handle the exception
        //log(...) method definition is not shown here
        log(throwable);
    }
});
```

In synchronous web services, the client connection is accepted and processed in a single I/O thread by a server. In asynchronous web services, the container accepts the client connection in a thread and then dispatches the actual processing of the request to a different thread so that it can release the thread used for client connection. In the previous section, we saw the usage of `AsyncInvoker.get(..)` to asynchronously consume the RESTful service. In this case, although the calling request thread is released by the server, the client keeps waiting until the business logic execution is finished by the server calling the `resume` method of the injected `AsyncResponse` object. Behind the scenes, the underlying I/O thread from the client side continues to block until it gets a response from the server or a timeout occurs.

Server-sent events

The preceding sections have introduced you to synchronous and asynchronous patterns of web service interaction. The JAX-RS 2.1 API introduces support for the publish-subscribe pattern with the inclusion of server-sent events. Server-sent events (SSEs) are a specification originally introduced as part of HTML5 by the W3C. It provides a way to establish a one-way channel from a server to a client. The connection is long running; it is reused for multiple events sent from the server, yet it is still based on the HTTP protocol. Clients request the opening of an SSE connection by using the special media type `text/event-stream` in the Accept header.

 The publish-subscribe pattern involves two key actors, publisher and subscribers, connected via a communication channel. One or more subscribers register for the event with the publisher, and the publisher publishes the corresponding event to all the registered subscribers.

The following are the key JAX-RS APIs defined for the realization of SSE under the `javax.ws.rs.sse` package:

Interface	Description
`SseEvent`	Base Server-Sent Event definition. The basic attributes of an event are ID, name, and comment. There are two types of `SseEvent`: • `InboundSseEvent` is used on the client side for accepting Server-Sent Events. • `OutboundSseEvent` is used on the server side when creating and sending an event to a client. `OutboundSseEvent.Builder` is used for creating `OutboundSseEvent`.
`Sse`	Used on the server side to create an event.
`SseEventSource`	This is the client for reading and processing incoming Server-Sent Events.
`SseEventSink`	This is the events stream used to publish the event to the client.
`SseBroadCaster`	Applications may need to send events to multiple clients simultaneously. This action is called broadcasting in JAX-RS. Multiple `SseEventSink` can be registered (or subscribed) on a single `SseBroadcaster`.

The following sequence diagram depicts the realization of SSE using the previously mentioned JAX-RS APIs. In the next chapter, we will see an example of SSE implementation using the Jersey framework:

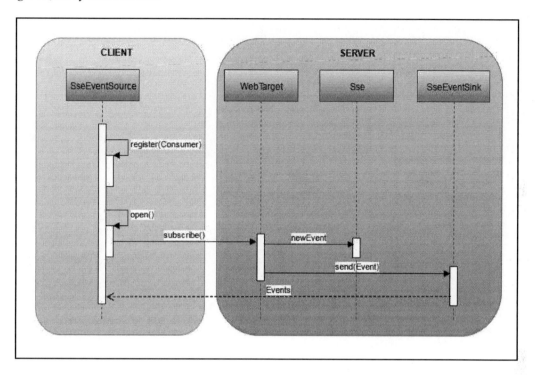

Managing an HTTP cache in a RESTful web service

Reading resources over the web is always a challenging process in terms of time and network latency. As a result, when you build a web application or web service, the ability to cache and reuse previously retrieved resources is a critical aspect of optimizing for performance. The HTTP/1.1 protocol specification provides a number of features to facilitate the caching of network resources.

In this section, we will discuss the native support in the HTTP protocol for managing the cache of the resources retrieved from the server. Similarly, we will see how the JAX-RS framework APIs embrace the HTTP caching features for managing the cache of the results returned by the RESTful web services.

Using the Expires header to control the validity of the HTTP cache

You can use the `Expires` HTTP header field to let all entities involved in the request-response chain know when a resource has expired. The `Expires` HTTP header was defined as part of the HTTP/1.0 specification. You can specify the date and time in the `Expires` header, after which the resource fetched from the server is considered stale.

The following code snippet shows how you can add the `Expires` HTTP header to the resource returned by the method:

```
@GET
@Path("departments/{id}/holidays")
@Produces(MediaType.APPLICATION_JSON)
public Response getHolidayListForCurrentYear(@PathParam("id")
    Short deptId) {
    //Reads the list of holidays
    List<Date> holidayList = getHolidayListForDepartment(deptId);
    //Build response
    Response.ResponseBuilder response = Response.ok(holidayList).
        type(MediaType.APPLICATION_JSON);
    //Set the expiry for response resource
    //This example sets validity as
    //Dec 31 of the current year
    int currentYear = getCurrentYear();
    Calendar expirationDate = new GregorianCalendar
        (currentYear,12, 31);
    response.expires(expirationDate.getTime());
    return response.build();
}
```

Here is the sample response header generated by the preceding method for the GET departments/10/holidays HTTP/1.1 request:

```
Server: GlassFish Server Open Source Edition 4.1
Expires: Sat, 31 Dec 2015 00:00:00 GMT
Content-Type: application/json
Date: Mon, 02 Mar 2015 05:24:58 GMT
Content-Length: 20
```

`Expires` headers are good for the following uses:

- Making static resources returned by the server, such as images, cacheable.
- Controlling the caching of a resource returned by servers that changes only at specific intervals. For instance, a list of public holidays for an organization for a specific year, which does not usually change within a year.

Using Cache-Control directives to manage the HTTP cache

The `Cache-Control` header was defined as part of HTTP/1.1 and offers more options than the `Expires` HTTP header. This header is used for specifying the directives that must be obeyed by all caching mechanisms involved in HTTP communication. These directives indicate who can do the caching of a resource returned by the server, how the caching is done, and for how long the resource can be cached.

 The `Expires` header is recommended for static resources such as images. The `Cache-Control` header is useful when you need more control over how caching is done.

Here is a list of useful `Cache-Control` directives:

- `private`: This directive indicates only those clients who originally requested the resource (for example, browser). This directive can do the caching and no other entity in the request-response chain (for example, proxy) is expected to do the caching.
- `public`: This marks a response as cacheable and caching can be done by any entity in the request-response chain.
- `no-cache`: This directive tells the client (for example, browser or proxies) that it should validate with the server before serving the resource from the cache. The validation can be done with the server by sending a request with the appropriate header fields, such as `If-Modified-Since`, `If-Unmodified-Since`, `If-Match`, and `If-None-Match`.
- `no-store`: This directive indicates that a response can be cached (for example, in-memory), but should not be stored on a permanent storage (for example, disk).

- `no-transform`: This directive means that the resource should not be modified by any entity in the request-response chain. This directive is used for avoiding loss of data while transforming a response from one format to another by intermediate entities.
- `max-age`: This value (measured in seconds) indicates how long the cached resource will be considered fresh. After this, the cached content needs to be validated with the server while serving the next request.
- `s-maxage`: This directive is similar to the `max-age` directive, except that it only applies to shared (for example, proxy) caches, not for the client who originated the request.
- `must-revalidate`: This directive tells all caches that they must follow the freshness information set by the server while generating the resource. Note that the HTTP protocol allows caches to serve stale resources under special conditions. By specifying the `must-revalidate` directive in the header of a response, you are telling all caches not to use any stale resource from the cache and validate the expired cache resources with the server before serving the request.
- `proxy-revalidate`: This directive is similar to the `must-revalidate` header item, except that it only applies to the proxy caches (not for the client that originally requested the resource).

A detailed discussion of the `Cache-Control` directives in HTTP/1.1 is available at `http://www.w3.org/Protocols/rfc2616/rfc2616-sec14.html`.

JAX-RS allows you to specify the `Cache-Control` directives on the `javax.ws.rs.core.Response` object returned by your REST resource method via the `javax.ws.rs.core.CacheControl` class. The `CacheControl` class exposes methods for accessing all possible `Cache-Control` directives.

The following code snippet illustrates the use of the `CacheControl` class for specifying cache expiry directives on the response object (the `Department` object) returned by the resource class method:

```
//Other imports are omitted for brevity
import javax.ws.rs.core.CacheControl;
import javax.ws.rs.core.MediaType;
import javax.ws.rs.core.Response;
import javax.ws.rs.core.Response.ResponseBuilder;

@GET
```

```
@Path("departments/{id}")
@Produces(MediaType.APPLICATION_JSON)
public Response findDepartmentById(@PathParam("id") Short deptId)
    {

    Department department = findDepartmentEntityById(deptId);
    //Specifies max-age and private directive for the response
    CacheControl cc = new CacheControl();
    //Cache is valid for a day (86400 sec)
    cc.setMaxAge(86400);
    cc.setPrivate(true);

    ResponseBuilder builder = Response.ok(myBook);
    //set the CacheControl object and build Response
    builder.cacheControl(cc);
    return builder.build();
}
```

Here is the sample response header generated by the preceding method for the GET
departments/10 HTTP/1.1 request:

```
Server: GlassFish Server Open Source Edition 4.1
Cache-Control: private, no-transform, max-age=86400
Content-Type: application/json
Date: Mon, 02 Mar 2015 05:56:29 GMT
Content-Length: 82
```

Conditional request processing with the Last-Modified HTTP response header

The Last-Modified header field value in HTTP is often used for validating the cached
response contents. The Last-Modified entity-header field indicates the date and time at
which the entity present in the response body was last modified. A client can use the Last-
Modified header field value in combination with the If-Modified-Since or If-
Unmodified-Since request headers to perform conditional requests.

The following example illustrates the use of the `Last-Modified` HTTP header field in the JAX-RS application. The `Last-Modified` field contains the date when the resource was last changed. When a client requests the same resource next time, it sends the `If-Modified-Since` header field, with the value set to the date and time at which the resource was last updated on the server. On the server, you can call `javax.ws.rs.core.Request::evaluatePreconditions()` to check whether the resource has been modified in between the requests. This method evaluates request preconditions on the basis of the passed-in value. If this method returns `null`, the resource is out of date and needs to be sent back in the response. Otherwise, this method returns the `304 Not Modified` HTTP status code to the client. Here is the code snippet for this example:

```
//Other imports are removed for brevity
import javax.ws.rs.core.Request;
import javax.ws.rs.core.Context;
import javax.ws.rs.core.Response.ResponseBuilder;


@GET
@Path("departments/{id}")
@Produces(MediaType.APPLICATION_JSON)
public Response
    findDepartmentWithCacheValidationWithLastModifiedDate(
        @PathParam("id") Short id, @Context Request request) {

    //Reads the latest Department object from DB
    Department department = entityManager.find(Department.class,
        id);
    //Gets the last modified date
    Date latModifiedDate = department.getModifiedDate();
    //Evaluates request preconditions on the basis
    //of the passed-in value.
    //evaluatePreconditions() return null If-Modified-Since
    //check succeeds. This implies that resource is modified
    ResponseBuilder builder =
        request.evaluatePreconditions(latModifiedDate);

    //cached resource did change; send new one
    if (builder == null) {
        builder = Response.ok(department);
        builder.lastModified(latModifiedDate);

    }
    return builder.build();

}
```

To learn more about the `javax.ws.rs.core.Request::evaluatePreconditions()` method, read the API documentation available at `https://jax-rs-spec.java.net/nonav/2.0/apidocs/javax/ws/rs/core/Request.html`.

Conditional request processing with the ETag HTTP response header

Sometimes, you may find that the precision of the HTTP date object (precision in seconds) is not granular enough to decide the freshness of the cache. You can use **Entity tags (ETag)** present in the HTTP response header field for such scenarios. ETag is part of HTTP/1.1 and provides a way of incorporating caching into HTTP. This tag can be used for comparing the validity of a cached object on the client side with the original object on the server.

When a server returns a response to a client, it attaches an opaque identifier in the ETag HTTP header present in the response. This identifier represents the state of the resource entity returned in response to the client's request. If the resource identified by the URI changes over time, a new identifier is assigned to ETag. When the client makes a request for a resource, it attaches the last received ETag header for the same resource (if any) as the value for the `If-None-Match` or `If-Match` HTTP header field in the request. The server uses this identifier for validating the cached representation of the resource. If the state of the requested resource has not been changed, the server responds with a `304 Not Modified` status code, which instructs the client to use a copy of the resource from its local cache.

At the bottom level, ETag is different from the `Client-Cache` and `Expires` HTTP headers discussed in the previous sections. The ETag header does not have any information that the client can use to determine whether or not to make a request for a specific resource again in the future. However, when the server reads the ETag header from the client request, it can determine whether to send the resource (HTTP status code: `200 OK`) or tell the client to just use the local copy (STTP status code: `304 Not Modified`). You can treat ETag as a checksum for a resource that semantically changes when the content changes.

To learn more about ETag, visit the following page:
`http://tools.ietf.org/html/rfc7232#section-2.3`.

The following code snippet shows the use of the JAX-RS APIs for building and validating ETag on the server. In this example, the client uses the `If-None-Match` header field to attach ETag to the request:

```
@GET
@Path("departments/{id}")
@Produces(MediaType.APPLICATION_JSON)
public Response findDepartmentWithCacheValidationWithEtag(
    @PathParam("id") Short deptId, @Context Request request) {

        //Reads latest department object from server
        Department department = findDepartmentEntity(deptId);
        //Builds ETag for department resource
        EntityTag etag = new
            EntityTag(Integer.toString(department.hashCode()));

        //Checks whether client-cached resource has changed
        //by checking ETag value present in request with value
        //generated on server
        //If changed, sends new resource with new ETag
        ResponseBuilder builder =
            request.evaluatePreconditions(etag);
        if (builder == null) {
            builder = Response.ok(department);
            builder.tag(etag);
        }
    }

    return builder.build();
}
```

Here is the sample response header generated by the preceding method for the GET departments/10 HTTP/1.1 request:

```
Server: GlassFish Server Open Source Edition 4.1
ETag: "03cb35ca667706c68c0aad4cb04c7a211"
Content-Type: application/json
Date: Mon, 02 Mar 2015 05:30:11 GMT
Content-Length: 82
```

Conditional data update in RESTful web services

In the previous two sections, we learned how to leverage HTTP caching features to optimize read operations (the HTTP GET type) in RESTful web APIs. In this section, we will discuss how to leverage these features during the entity updates in these APIs (the HTTP POST or PUT request types). Conditional updates help you to avoid performing modifications on the stale representation of resources, thereby avoiding the overwriting of changes performed by other users of the system on the same resource. You can perform conditional updates by using either of the following approaches:

- **Comparing the last modified date of the resource**: When a client sends a modified resource to the server via the PUT or POST method, the request also carries the If-Modified-Since HTTP header field with the value set to the last modified date of the resource. The server can evaluate the If-Modified-Since header field to see whether it matches with the time stamp on the resource residing on the server.

- **Comparing Etag of the resource**: If the modified date is not precise enough to decide the freshness of the resource, you can use ETag. In this case, the PUT or POST request from the client carries the If-None-Match header field with the value set to that of the ETag header sent by the server when the resource was last retrieved. The server can evaluate the value of the If-None-Match header field present in the HTTP request header to see whether it matches with the current ETag of the resource on the server.

If the validation check fails for the preceding two cases, the server will return an error response code of 412 (precondition failed). The client can take appropriate action on the basis of the status code received as part of the response. If all checks go through, the update succeeds on the server. The following code snippet illustrates how you can use the last modified date or the ETag header present in the request for performing the conditional updates on a resource:

```
@PUT
@Path("etag/departments/{id}")
@Consumes(MediaType.APPLICATION_JSON)
public Response edit(@PathParam("id") Short deptId,
    @Context Request request, Department entity) {

    //Reads latest Department object from DB and generates ETag
    Department detEntityInDB = finDepartmentEntity(deptId);
    //You can use a better algorithm for getting ETag in real life
    EntityTag etag = new
        EntityTag(Integer.toString(detEntityInDB.hashCode()));
```

```
//Evaluates request preconditions on the basis of the passed-in value.
//A client may pass either ETag or last modified date
//in the request.
// evaluatePreconditions() returns null if the
//preconditions are met or a ResponseBuilder is set with
//the appropriate status if the preconditions are not met.
Response.ResponseBuilder builder =
    request.evaluatePreconditions(
        detEntityInDB.getModifiedDate(), etag);
// Client is not up to date (send back 412)
if (builder != null) {
    return builder.status(
        Response.Status.PRECONDITION_FAILED).build();
}
updateDepartmentEntity(entity);

EntityTag newEtag = new
    EntityTag(Integer.toString(entity.hashCode()));
builder = Response.noContent();
builder.lastModified(entity.getModifiedDate());
builder.tag(newEtag);
return builder.build();
}
```

The ETag and Last-Modified entity tags in the HTTP header can be used for reducing the network usage of the REST APIs by introducing the conditional retrieval of the resources on the server. You may also find it useful for concurrency control for the REST APIs by introducing conditional updates on the server.

Understanding filters and interceptors in JAX-RS

The default request-response model offered in the JAX-RS implementation fits well for many common use cases. However, at times, you may look at extending the default request-response model. For instance, you may need such extension capabilities while adding support for the custom authentication, customized caching of responses, encoding request content, and so on, without polluting the application code. JAX-RS allows you to do this by adding your own interceptors and filters for both the REST requests and responses, as appropriate.

Typically, filters are used for processing the request-response headers, whereas interceptors are concerned with the marshaling and unmarshaling of the HTTP message bodies. Filters and interceptors can be set on both the client and the server. Let's learn more about these offerings in this section.

Modifying request and response parameters with JAX-RS filters

The JAX-RS APIs offer distinct filters for both the client and the server. Let's take a quick look at the JAX-RS filter APIs in this section.

Implementing server-side request message filters

You can build a request filter for the server by implementing the `javax.ws.rs.container.ContainerRequestFilter` interface. This filter intercepts the REST API calls and runs before the request invokes the REST resource. You will find this useful for performing authorization checks, auditing requests, or manipulating the request header parameters before invoking the REST API implementation.

The `ContainerRequestFilters` implementation falls into two categories on the basis of the stage in the request processing cycle that the filters are executed at:

- **Postmatching**: These filters are executed after identifying the matching Java class resource method for processing the incoming HTTP request (the REST API call). The `ContainerRequestFilters` implementations, by default, are postmatching (unless you designate them as `@PreMatching`).
- **Prematching**: These filters are executed before identifying the matching resource class for a REST API call. Prematching `ContainerRequestFilters` are designated with the `@javax.ws.rs.container.PreMatching` annotation.

Postmatching server-side request message filters

These postmatching filters are applied only after a matching Java class resource method has been identified to process the incoming request. As these filters are executed after the resource matching process, it is no longer possible to modify the request in order to influence the resource matching process.

Here is an example of a postmatching server-side request filter.
`AuthorizationRequestFilter`, shown in the following example, ensures that only users
with the `ADMIN` role can access the REST APIs used for configuring the system. The
configuration APIs are identified in this example by checking whether the request URI path
has the `/config/` part embedded in it:

```
//Other imports are omitted for brevity
import java.io.IOException;
import javax.ws.rs.container.ContainerRequestContext;
import javax.ws.rs.container.ContainerRequestFilter;
import javax.ws.rs.core.Response;
import javax.ws.rs.core.SecurityContext;
import javax.ws.rs.core.UriInfo;
import javax.ws.rs.ext.Provider;
@Provider
public class AuthorizationRequestFilter implements
    ContainerRequestFilter {
    @Override
    public void filter(ContainerRequestContext requestContext)
        throws IOException {
        //Get the URI for current request
        UriInfo uriInfo = requestContext.getUriInfo();
        String uri = uriInfo.getRequestUri().toString();
        int index = uri.indexOf("/config/");
        boolean isSettingsService = (index != -1);
        if (isSettingsService) {
            SecurityContext securityContext
                    = requestContext.getSecurityContext();
            if (securityContext == null
                || !securityContext.isUserInRole("ADMIN")) {

                requestContext.abortWith(Response
                    .status(Response.Status.UNAUTHORIZED)
                    .entity("Unauthorized access.")
                    .build());
            }
        }
    }
}
```

The `@javax.ws.rs.ext.Provider` annotation on the implementation of
a filter or an interceptor makes it discoverable by the JAX-RS runtime. You
do not need to do any extra configurations for integrating the filters or
interceptors.

Prematching server-side request message filters

You can designate `ContainerRequestFilters` as the prematching filter by annotating with the `@javax.ws.rs.container.PreMatching` annotation. The prematching filters are applied before the JAX-RS runtime identifies the matching Java class resource method. As this filter is executed before executing the resource matching process, you can use this type of filter to modify the HTTP request contents. Apparently, this can be used for influencing the request matching process, if required.

The following code snippet illustrates how you can use a prematching filter to modify the method type in the incoming HTTP request. This example modifies the method type from POST to PUT. As this is executed before identifying the Java resource method, the change in method type will influence the identification of the Java class resource method for executing the call:

```java
import java.io.IOException;
import javax.ws.rs.container.ContainerRequestContext;
import javax.ws.rs.container.ContainerRequestFilter;
import javax.ws.rs.ext.Provider;
import javax.ws.rs.container.PreMatching;

@Provider
@PreMatching
public class JAXRSContainerPrematchingRequestFilter implements
    ContainerRequestFilter  {
    @Override
    public void filter(ContainerRequestContext requestContext)
        throws IOException {
        //Modify the method type from POST to PUT
        if (requestContext.getMethod().equals("POST")) {
            requestContext.setMethod("PUT");
        }
    }
}
```

Implementing server-side response message filters

You can build a server-side response filter by implementing the `javax.ws.rs.container.ContainerResponseFilter` interface. This filter gets executed after the response is generated by the REST API. The response filters, in general, can be used to manipulate the response header parameters present in the response messages. The following example shows how you can use them to modify the response header.

When a REST web client is no longer on the same domain as the server that hosts the REST APIs, the REST response message header should have the **Cross Origin Resource Sharing (CORS)** header values set to the appropriate domain names, which are allowed to access the APIs. This example uses `ContainerResponseFilter` to modify the REST response headers to include the CORS header, thus making the REST APIs accessible from a different domain:

```
//Other imports are omitted for brevity
import javax.ws.rs.container.ContainerRequestContext;
import javax.ws.rs.container.ContainerResponseContext;
import javax.ws.rs.container.ContainerResponseFilter;
import javax.ws.rs.ext.Provider;
import java.io.IOException;

@Provider
public class CORSFilter implements ContainerResponseFilter {

    @Override
    public void filter(ContainerRequestContext requestContext,
        ContainerResponseContext cres) throws IOException {
        //Specify CORS headers: * represents allow all values
        cres.getHeaders().add("Access-Control-Allow-Origin", "*");
        cres.getHeaders().add("Access-Control-Allow-Headers",
            "*");
        cres.getHeaders().add("Access-Control-Allow-Credentials",
            "true");
        cres.getHeaders().add("Access-Control-Allow-Methods",
            "GET, POST, PUT, DELETE, OPTIONS, HEAD");
        cres.getHeaders().add("Access-Control-Max-Age",
            "1209600");
    }
}
```

Implementing client-side request message filters

JAX-RS lets you build a client-side request filter for REST API calls by implementing the `javax.ws.rs.client.ClientRequestFilter` interface. This filter is used for intercepting the REST API calls on the client itself.

A very common use case scenario where you may find these filters useful is for checking the accuracy of specific request parameters on the client itself. Even you can abort the call and return the error response object from these filters if the request parameter values are not properly specified.

The following code snippet illustrates how you can use ClientRequestFilter to ensure that all the requests carry the Client-Application header field, which you may use on the server for tracking all clients:

```
//Other imports are omitted for brevity
import javax.ws.rs.HttpMethod;
import javax.ws.rs.client.ClientRequestContext;
import javax.ws.rs.client.ClientRequestFilter;

@Provider
public class JAXRSClientRequestFilter implements
    ClientRequestFilter {
    @Override
    public void filter(ClientRequestContext requestContext)
        throws IOException {
        if(requestContext.getHeaders()
           .get("Client-Application") == null) {
               requestContext.abortWith(
                   Response.status(Response.Status.BAD_REQUEST)
                       .entity(
                          "Client-Application header is
                               required.")
                                  .build());
        }
    }
}
```

You can register the ClientRequestFilter interface to the client by calling the register() method on the javax.ws.rs.client.Client object. Note that the client object implements the javax.ws.rs.core.Configurable interface, and all the configurations that you see on Client are offered by the Configurable interface. The following code snippet shows how you can add JAXRSClientRequestFilter to the JAX-RS client implementation:

```
import javax.ws.rs.client.Client;
import javax.ws.rs.client.ClientBuilder;

Client client = ClientBuilder.newClient();
client.register(JSXRSClientRequestFilter.class);
```

Implementing client-side response message filters

You can build a client-side response filter by implementing the
javax.ws.rs.client.ClientResponseFilter interface. This filter is used for
manipulating the response message returned by the REST APIs.

The following code snippet shows the use of JAXRSClientResponseFilter to check the
response received from the server and then log the error (if any) for audit purposes:

```
//Other imports are omitted for brevity
import javax.ws.rs.client.ClientRequestContext;
import javax.ws.rs.client.ClientResponseContext;
import javax.ws.rs.client.ClientResponseFilter;

public class JAXRSClientResponseFilter implements
    ClientResponseFilter {

    @Override
    public void filter(ClientRequestContext reqContext,
        ClientResponseContext respContext) throws IOException {
        if (respContext.getStatus() == 200) {
            return;
        }else{
            logError(respContext);
        }
    }

    private void logError(ClientResponseContext respContext) {
        //Code for logging error goes here.
    }
}
```

You can register the ClientResponseFilter interface to the JAX RS client by calling the
register() method on the javax.ws.rs.client.Client object. An example is given
here:

```
import javax.ws.rs.client.Client;
import javax.ws.rs.client.ClientBuilder;

Client client = ClientBuilder.newClient();
client.register(JAXRSClientResponseFilter.class);
```

Modifying request and response message bodies with JAX-RS interceptors

JAX-RS provides the request and response interceptors to manipulate entities or message bodies by intercepting the input and output streams, respectively. In this section, we will learn the request and response interceptors offered by JAX-RS. You can use the interceptors on both the client and the server.

 Unlike JAX-RS filters, interceptors do not have separate contracts for the client and the server.

Implementing request message body interceptors

You can use the `javax.ws.rs.ext.ReaderInterceptor` interface to intercept and manipulate the incoming message body.

The following example illustrates how you can implement `ReaderInterceptor` to intercept the incoming message in order to unzip the zipped body content:

```
//Other imports are omitted for brevity
import java.util.zip.GZIPInputStream;
import javax.ws.rs.WebApplicationException;
import javax.ws.rs.ext.Provider;
import javax.ws.rs.ext.ReaderInterceptor;
import javax.ws.rs.ext.ReaderInterceptorContext;

@Provider
public class JAXRSReaderInterceptor implements ReaderInterceptor {

    @Override
    public Object aroundReadFrom(ReaderInterceptorContext context)
        throws IOException, WebApplicationException {
        List<String> header = context.getHeaders()
            .get("Content-Encoding");
        // decompress gzip stream only
        if (header != null && header.contains("gzip")) {

            InputStream originalInputStream =
            context.getInputStream();
            context.setInputStream(new
            GZIPInputStream(originalInputStream));
        }
```

```
            return context.proceed();

        }
    }
```

You follow the same interface contract (ReaderInterceptor) for building the read interceptors for client-side use as well. You can register the ReaderInterceptor interface to the JAX-RS client by calling the register() method on the javax.ws.rs.client.Client object.

Implementing response message body interceptors

You may use the javax.ws.rs.ext.JAXRSWriterInterceptor interface to intercept and manipulate the outgoing message body. The following example illustrates the use of WriterInterceptor to compress the response body content:

```
//Other imports are omitted for brevity
import java.util.zip.GZIPOutputStream;
import javax.ws.rs.WebApplicationException;
import javax.ws.rs.core.MultivaluedMap;
import javax.ws.rs.ext.Provider;
import javax.ws.rs.ext.WriterInterceptor;
import javax.ws.rs.ext.WriterInterceptorContext;

@Provider
public class JAXRSWriterInterceptor implements WriterInterceptor {
    @Override
    public void aroundWriteTo(WriterInterceptorContext context)
        throws IOException,
        WebApplicationException {
        MultivaluedMap<String, Object> headers =
            context.getHeaders();
        headers.add("Content-Encoding", "gzip");
        OutputStream outputStream =
            context.getOutputStream();
        context.setOutputStream(new
            GZIPOutputStream(outputStream));
        context.proceed();
    }
}
```

You will use the same interface contract for building the write interceptors for the client side use as well. You can register the WriterInterceptor interface to the JAX-RS client by calling the register() method on the javax.ws.rs.client.Client object.

Managing the order of execution for filters and interceptors

It is perfectly legal to have multiple filters or interceptors added for a REST client or server. In such a case, you might want to control the order in which they are executed at runtime. JAX-RS allows you to manage the order of execution by adding the `@javax.annotation.Priority` annotation on the filter or the interceptor class. The `Priority` values should be non-negative. You can use standard constants defined in the `javax.ws.rs.Priorities` class to set the priorities. An example is given here:

```
@Provider
@Priority(Priorities.HEADER_DECORATOR)
public class JAXRSReaderInterceptor implements ReaderInterceptor {
    //Interceptor implementation goes here
}
```

Interceptors and filters are sorted on the basis of their priority in ascending order. While processing a request, the request filter with the lowest priority will be executed first and followed by the next one in the sequence. While processing a response, filters are executed in reverse order. In other words, the response filter with the highest priority will be executed first, followed by the next highest one in the sequence.

Selectively applying filters and interceptors on REST resources by using @NameBinding

The `@javax.ws.rs.NameBinding` annotation is used for creating the name-binding annotation for filters and interceptors. Later, developers can selectively apply the name-binding annotation on the desired REST resource classes or methods.

For example, consider the following name-binding annotation, `RequestLogger`:

```
@NameBinding
@Retention(RetentionPolicy.RUNTIME)
@Target({ElementType.METHOD,ElementType.TYPE})
public @interface RequestLogger {
}
```

You can use the preceding name-binding annotation, `RequestLogger`, to decorate the desired filters and interceptors, as shown here:

```
//imports are removed for brevity
@RequestLogger
public class RequestLoggerFilter implements ContainerRequestFilter {
    @Override
    public void filter(ContainerRequestContext requestContext)
        throws IOException {
    //Implementation body is not shown in this
    //example for brevity
    }
}
```

Note that the preceding filter is not annotated with the `@Provider` annotation, and therefore it will not be applied globally on all resources.

As the last step, you can apply the name-binding annotation to the resource class or method to which the name-bound JAX-RS provider(s) should be bound to. In the following code snippet, we apply the `@RequestLogger` name-binding annotation to the `findDepartment()` method. At runtime, the framework will identify all filters and interceptors decorated with `@RequestLogger` and will apply all of them to this method:

```
//imports are omitted for brevity
@Stateless
@Path("hr")
public class HRService {
    @GET
    @Path("departments/{id}")
    @Produces(MediaType.APPLICATION_JSON)
    @RequestLogger
    public Department findDepartment(@PathParam("id")  Short id) {

        findDepartmentsEntity(id);
        return department;
    }
}
```

The `@NameBinding` annotation really helps you to selectively apply JAX-RS providers to REST resources. However, you need to choose the resource methods to which the name-binding annotation should be applied while developing the API. What if you want to apply the filters or interceptors to the REST resources dynamically on the basis of some business conditions? JAX-RS offers the `javax.ws.rs.container.DynamicFeature` metaprovider for such use cases. Let's discuss this feature in the next section.

Dynamically applying filters and interceptors on REST resources using DynamicFeature

The `javax.ws.rs.container.DynamicFeature` contract is used by the JAX-RS runtime to register providers, such as interceptors and filters, to a particular resource class or method during application deployment.

The following code snippet shows how you can build the `DynamicFeature` provider. This example applies `RequestLoggerFilter` to resource methods annotated with `@RequestLogger`.

```
import javax.ws.rs.container.DynamicFeature;
import javax.ws.rs.container.ResourceInfo;
import javax.ws.rs.core.FeatureContext;
import javax.ws.rs.ext.Provider;

@Provider
public class DynamicFeatureRegister implements DynamicFeature {
    @Override
    public void configure(ResourceInfo resourceInfo,
        FeatureContext context) {
        //This simple example adds RequestLoggerFilter to methods
        //annotated with @ RequestLogger
        if (resourceInfo.getResourceMethod().isAnnotationPresent
            (RequestLogger.class)) {
            context.register(RequestLoggerFilter.class);
        }
    }
}
```

The `DynamicFeature` interface is executed at deployment time for each resource method. You can register filters or interceptors on the desired resource class or method in the `DynamicFeature` implementation.

Understanding the JAX-RS resource life cycle

Before winding up this chapter, let's take a quick look at the life cycle of the JAX-RS components on the server when a client makes a RESTful web API call. This discussion would be a good summary of the topics that we learned so far on JAX-RS.

The following diagram depicts the sequence of actions taking place on the server when a client invokes the JAX-RS RESTful web service:

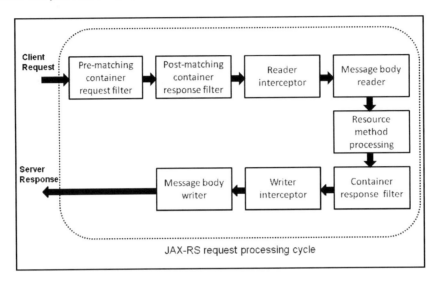

For an incoming REST API call, the container identifies the Java servlet configured for handling the REST API calls by parsing the URI, and then delegates the request to the designated servlet. The servlet initializes the JAX-RS runtime and kicks off the RESTful web service request processing cycle for the REST API call in the following sequence:

1. The runtime executes prematching filters (`ContainerRequestFilter` with the `@Prematching` annotation), which happens before resolving the resource method. The prematching filters are useful if you want to influence resource method resolution. The next step is to identify the resource method for serving the request.

2. After the resolution of the resource method, postmatching filters are executed (filters without `@Prematching`). Postmatching filters are useful for performing an authentication check or for performing a basic sanity check on the request parameters.

3. After executing all filters, the JAX-RS runtime invokes `ReaderInterceptor`. The reader interceptors are useful for manipulating the inbound request stream. A common use case may be to unzip the compressed stream before converting it into Java objects.

4. The next phase in the cycle is to convert the inbound stream into the Java object representation. This is done by matching the `MessageBodyReader` provider identified by the runtime.

5. After taking the incoming request through the configured filters, interceptors, and message body readers, the JAX-RS runtime invokes the resource class method identified for serving the request. If you have any Bean Validation annotation configured on the method parameters, it will get executed at this stage:

    1. If the validation fails and results in `ConstraintViolationException`, the runtime skips the execution of the method and identifies `ExceptionMapper` to handle the exception. The exception mapper generates the HTTP response content for the exception.

    2. Upon successful validation, the resource method is executed. If the resource method throws some exception, the framework invokes the matching `ExceptionMapper` to generate the HTTP response body for the exception.

6. The runtime takes the response content through the following stages before sending it to the client. The runtime executes `ContainerResponseFilter`, which can be used for adding the desired response header, such as cache parameters and content type.

7. The runtime executes `WriterInterceptors` for the response content. The interceptor class can hold logic for manipulating the response before sending it to the client, such as zipping the response body.

8. As the next step, the runtime invokes the appropriate `MessageBodyWriter`, which writes the Java type to an HTTP message to send it over HTTP. `MessageBodyWriter` can optionally amend or add the HTTP response headers. For instance, `200 OK` is added to the response header if the method execution went well and returned an object. If the method is void, `204 No Content` is set.

9. Once the response is ready, the container passes the response back to the client.

Note that the default scope of the root resource classes is a request. This means that a new instance of a root resource class is created for serving the next request.

Summary

In this chapter, we explored the advanced offerings in the JAX-RS framework. In particular, we discussed subresources and subresource locators, validations, exception handling, JAX-RS entity providers, asynchronous RESTful web services and interceptors, and filters for JAX-RS applications. We concluded this chapter by discussing the life cycle of all JAX-RS components that we have learned about so far.

In the next chapter, we will learn about the Jersey and RESTEasy framework extensions in detail.

5
Introducing JAX-RS Implementation Framework Extensions

In the last two chapters, we discussed the standard JAX-RS APIs for building RESTful web APIs. JAX-RS is a specification for RESTful web services with Java, not a product. In the previous chapters, we gave an overview of popular JAX-RS implementations, such as Jersey, Apache CXF, RESTEasy, Restlet, and so on. Also, we have been using Jersey for running the JAX-RS samples that we built in the previous chapters.

As you may know, Jersey is one of the many reference implementations available in the market today for the JAX-RS specification. In reality, the Jersey framework is more than just a JAX-RS reference implementation. It offers additional features and utilities to further simplify RESTful services and client development. In this chapter, we will discuss some of the most useful extension APIs provided by the Jersey and RESTEasy frameworks, which are not part of the JAX-RS standard.

We will cover the following topics in this chapter:

- Dynamically configuring JAX-RS resources during deployment
- Modifying JAX-RS resources during deployment using ModelProcessor
- Building HATEOAS APIs
- Reading and writing large binary objects using Jersey APIs
- Generating chunked output using Jersey APIs
- Supporting server-sent events (SSE) in RESTful web services
- Understanding Jersey server-side configuration properties

- Monitoring RESTful web services using Jersey APIs
- RESTEasy framework extensions

All the examples that you see in this chapter use the latest versions of the Jersey (`https://jersey.github.io/download.html`) and RESTEasy (`http://resteasy.jboss.org/downloads`) releases.

Jersey framework extensions

Let's start our discussions on Jersey with a baby step. If you want to use any Jersey-specific feature in an application, then you will have to add a dependency to the appropriate Jersey libraries. For instance, to use a Jersey configuration class such as `org.glassfish.jersey.server.ResourceConfig` in your application, you need to depend on the `jersey-container-servlet` JAR. If the consuming application uses Maven for building the source, then specifying a dependency to the `jersey-container-servlet` JAR in the **Project Object Model (POM)** file may look like the following:

```
<dependency>
    <groupId>org.glassfish.jersey.containers</groupId>
  <!-- module -->
    <artifactId>jersey-container-servlet</artifactId>

  <!-2.26: latest release version -->
    <version>2.26</version>
    <!-- container(GlassFish) provides dependency
         for this example -->
    <scope>provided</scope>
</dependency>
```

An application that uses Jersey and depends on Jersey modules is, in turn, required to also include in the application dependencies the set of third-party modules that the Jersey modules depend on. Jersey is designed as a pluggable component architecture, and different applications can therefore require different sets of Jersey modules. This also means that the set of external Jersey dependencies required to be included in the application dependencies may vary in each application, based on the Jersey modules that are being used by the application. A list of the core Jersey modules and their dependencies is available at `https://jersey.github.io/documentation/latest/modules-and-dependencies.html`.

Dynamically configuring JAX-RS resources during deployment

You have learned multiple resource configurations and packaging models for JAX-RS applications in the previous chapter under the *A quick look at the packaging of JAX-RS applications* section. A common approach is to subclass `javax.ws.rs.core.Application` and configure the RESTful resources by overriding the appropriate methods.

The Jersey framework eases the configuration of resources via a custom class, `org.glassfish.jersey.server.ResourceConfig`, which extends the JAX-RS core class, `javax.ws.rs.core.Application`. We have used the `Application` class in the previous chapter for configuring a vanilla JAX-RS application. The `ResourceConfig` class offers many extra configuration features on top of the standard JAX-RS `Application` class. With the `ResourceConfig` class, you can define the JAX-RS resources via an array of class names; you can even specify the package names where you have defined the JAX-RS component. During deployment, Jersey will automatically discover and register all the components found in the packages that you set.

What if you want to define a JAX-RS resource during deployment? Apart from static resource class definitions, Jersey allows you to define and configure the JAX-RS components during the deployment of the application. The following is an example that illustrates this idea.

In this example, we will build a REST API resource during deployment to return the server information. We will expose this API only to selective customer deployments, managed via an application configuration parameter. The following code snippet illustrates how you can do this with the Jersey APIs. While deploying the application, the `ApplicationConfig` class that you see in the code snippet will read the context parameter's `system.info.allow` entry from `web.xml`. If this flag is configured to return `true`, then `ApplicationConfig` will build a REST resource method during the deployment in order to return the system information for the REST API, with `GET /server/info HTTP/1.1` as the path URI:

```
//Other imports are omitted for brevity
import org.glassfish.jersey.process.Inflector;
import org.glassfish.jersey.server.ResourceConfig;
import org.glassfish.jersey.server.model.Resource;
import org.glassfish.jersey.server.model.ResourceMethod;
import org.glassfish.jersey.filter.LoggingFilter;
import org.glassfish.jersey.media.multipart.MultiPartFeature;

@Provider
```

```
@javax.ws.rs.ApplicationPath("webresources")
public class ApplicationConfig extends ResourceConfig {
    private String configSysInfoParam = "true";

    @Context
    public void setServletContext(ServletContext context) {
        //Read the context param
        if(context != null)
          configSysInfoParam =
context.getInitParameter("system.info.allow");
    }
     public ApplicationConfig() {
         // Package names that will be used
         //to scan for components.
        packages("com.packtpub.rest.ch5");
        boolean allowViewServerInfo =
            (configSysInfoParam == null) ?
             false : Boolean.valueOf(configSysInfoParam);
        //if param 'system.info.allow=true',register REST Resources
        if (allowViewServerInfo) {
            addResources();
        }
    }
    //Add resource to return server information during deployment
    private void addResources()
    {
        //Omitted for brevity
    }
}
```

The sample response content generated by the newly added resource for the GET
/server/info HTTP/1.1 REST API call may look like the following:

```
{"hostName":"localhost","processor":"Intel","serverName":"XXX","threads":33
4235235,"userSessions":123233}
```

Let's briefly discuss some of the core APIs used in this example. The
org.glassfish.jersey.server.model.Resource.Builder instance that you will
obtain by calling Resource.builder() has many useful builder methods for generating a
complete REST resource dynamically. Some of the important methods in
Resource.Builder that need your attention are as follows:

- Resource.Builder::path(String path): This method defines the path for
  the resource that you build. The client can use this URI path to invoke the
  resource.

- `Resource.Builder::addMethod(String httpMethod)`: This method adds a new HTTP method model to the resource. The `httpMethod` parameter defines specific HTTP request types (such as GET, POST, and PUT) to which this method responds to. This call returns an instance of `org.glassfish.jersey.server.model.ResourceMethod.Builder`, which can later be used for building the body for the method.
- You can dynamically implement the method for handling the REST call by invoking `handledBy(Class<? extends Inflector> inflectorClass)` on `ResourceMethod.Builder`.
- `ResourceConfig::registerResources(Resource... resources)`: This method registers newly created resource models in `ResourceConfig`.

A quick look at the static resource configurations

In the earlier `ApplicationConfig` class, you will also notice a call to the `ResourceConfig::packages(String... packages)` method with an array of packages as the parameter. This tells the runtime to scan the input packages for discovering the JAX-RS components (which include REST resources and provider components) used in the application. You can also use the `ResourceConfig::register()` method to register an individual JAX-RS component as appropriate.

> To learn more about the APIs exposed in the `ResourceConfig` class, visit the API documentation at `https://jersey.github.io/apidocs/latest/jersey/index.html`.

Modifying JAX-RS resources during deployment using ModelProcessor

Sometimes, you may want to modify the existing JAX-RS resources during deployment to meet the specific business conditions set by customers. For instance, consider a scenario where you want to add additional APIs to return the JSON schema, which describes the content structure for all the REST resources that your application exposes. Furthermore, there may be scenarios where you may want to change the entire resource method implementation itself to meet the requirements of some of the customers. In this section, you will learn how to address such use case requirements with the Jersey framework.

The Jersey framework allows you to modify or enhance the JAX-RS resources during deployment by registering your own JAX-RS resource model processor providers. Let's take a closer look at this feature.

What is the Jersey model processor and how it works?

When you deploy a JAX-RS application into a Jersey-based container, the Jersey runtime generates the `org.glassfish.jersey.server.mode.ResourceModel` instance to store all the root REST resources registered in the application. Jersey allows you to enhance the generated resource model via the `org.glassfish.jersey.server.model.ModelProcessor` providers. You can build your own model processor providers by implementing the `ModelProcessor` interface. This implementation can have the logic to enhance the current resource model by adding additional methods or resources. For instance, you can build a model processor to inject support for the `HTTP OPTION` method on every REST resource during deployment.

A brief look at the ModelProcessor interface

The `ModelProcessor` interface has the following methods:

- `processResourceModel(ResourceModel, Configuration)`: This method is invoked during deployment, right after parsing all the registered root resources. The `ResourceModel` parameter to this method comprises all the registered root resources. This method can have the logic to modify the REST resources before publishing them for use.
- `processSubResource(ResourceModel, Configuration)`: This method is meant for processing the subresource model. Remember that when a request is handled by a subresource, the subresource class instance that handles the requests will be resolved only during runtime. Therefore, the `processSubResource()` method is invoked only at runtime (not during deployment), when the framework can resolve the subresource class type. The `ResourceModel` parameter for this method contains only one subresource model that is returned by the subresource locator.

> If you need a quick brush up on subresources, refer to the *Understanding subresources and subresource locators in JAX-RS* section, in Chapter 4, *Advanced Features in the JAX-RS APIs.*

Let's look at an example to understand how to use the model processor APIs provided by Jersey to add additional HTTP methods to all the registered top-level JAX-RS resources. This example uses a custom model processor implementation to add an additional HTTP GET method on all the registered resources to return the latest version of the resource for the URI temple /version request path:

```
//Other imports are omitted for brevity
import org.glassfish.jersey.process.Inflector;
import org.glassfish.jersey.server.model.ModelProcessor;
import org.glassfish.jersey.server.model.Resource;
import org.glassfish.jersey.server.model.ResourceModel;

@Provider
public class VersionsModelProcessor implements ModelProcessor {

    @Override
    public ResourceModel processResourceModel(ResourceModel
        resourceModel, Configuration configuration) {

    // Get the resource model and enhance resource with latest version
info
        ResourceModel.Builder newResourceModelBuilder = new
            ResourceModel.Builder(false);
        for (final Resource resource :
                resourceModel.getResources()){
            // For each resource, create a new builder
            final Resource.Builder resourceBuilder =
                Resource.builder(resource);
            // Add a new child resource
            resourceBuilder.addChildResource("version")
                .addMethod(HttpMethod.GET)
                .handledBy(
                    new Inflector<ContainerRequestContext,
                        String>(){
                        @Override
                        public String apply(
                            ContainerRequestContext cr) {
                                return "version : 1.0" ; //add latest
version
                        }
                }).produces(MediaType.TEXT_PLAIN)
                    .extended(true);
```

```
                newResourceModelBuilder.addResource(resourceBuilder.build());
        }

        final ResourceModel newResourceModel = new
ResourceModelBuilder.build();
            return newResourceModel;
        }

    @Override
    public ResourceModel processSubResource(ResourceModel
        subResourceModel, Configuration configuration) {
        return subResourceModel;
    }
}
```

The preceding model processor example modifies all the registered resources during deployment by adding a child resource to each root resource. The child resource added via the model processor is configured to respond to the `version` query from the client. For example, a RESTful web API call to read the version of the department resource, `GET /departments/version HTTP/1.1`, will now return the following result: `version : 1.0`.

In the last two sections, we talked about runtime configurations and resource enhancement APIs offered by the Jersey framework for a RESTful application. The next section is a bit different in nature. In the coming section, you will learn about using hypermedia links in the REST resource representation.

Building Hypermedia As The Engine Of Application State (HATEOAS) APIs

We briefly covered this topic in Chapter 1, *Introducing the REST Architectural Style,* under the *Hypermedia as the Engine of Application State (HATEOAS)* section.

Before we get into the details of the JAX-RS and Jersey offerings, let's take a step back to understand the need for HATEOAS APIs. When exposing operations to be performed on an entity via RESTful services, one of the key things that gets undermined is exposing the entity relationships to the consumer of the service. The flow on impact is that the consumer ends up hardcoding the logic in the client application.

Let's take the case of an online shopping cart application. Is it wise to allow the creation of an order without any products added to the basket or any payments done? Autonomously implementing an order, product, or payments entity service without considering the relationship is obviously not a good design. The realization of entity linking while developing RESTful services is made possible using the HATEOAS constraint. Also, this gives a representation of the state of the application, with the choice of the next possible actions based on the state of the entity. Since the next possible actions are commonly represented as the endpoint for a service or link, you must include all the possible links in the API responses when you build a HATEOAS-compliant API.

Please be warned that there is no universally accepted format for representing links between two resources in JSON. Various API vendors or enterprises use different formats, depending upon the API guidelines that they follow.

Choosing where to place the links is based on the REST API guidelines that you follow for your application. We will discuss this topic in detail in `Chapter 8`, *RESTful API Design Guidelines*.

Some of the formats in practice are listed here:

- Web Linking (`http://tools.ietf.org/html/rfc5988`)
- **Hypertext Application Language (HAL)**
- JavaScript Object Notation for Linked Data (`http://json-ld.org`)

The link APIs offered by both JAX-RS and Jersey are flexible enough to meet the requirements of many of the common formats.

Programmatically building entity body links using JAX-RS APIs

Before getting into the declarative offerings from the Jersey framework to build HATEOAS APIs, let's see what is there in the JAX-RS API specification for solving this use case. JAX-RS 2.1 has the basic API support for representing hypermedia links with resources.

Let's take an example to understand the APIs provided by JAX-RS for building resource links. Consider the following REST resource class method, which returns a list of department resources:

```
//Rest of the code is omitted for brevity
@GET
@Path("departments")
@Produces(MediaType.APPLICATION_JSON)
public List<Department> findAllDeprtments(){
  //Finds all departments from database
  List<Department> departments = findAllDepartmentEntities();
  return departments;
}
```

Let's see how we can add hypermedia links for accessing employee resources in each department resource representation returned by the preceding method. This link can be traversed by a client to read the employees for a department. To add a link, you use the `javax.ws.rs.core.Link` API. The entity provider components that come with the JAX-RS implementation will automatically convert the links to the appropriate media type representation at runtime:

```
//Other imports are omitted for brevity
import javax.ws.rs.core.Link;
import javax.xml.bind.annotation.adapters.XmlAdapter;
@XmlRootElement
public class Department {

    private Short departmentId;
    private String departmentName;
    private Integer managerId;
    private Short locationId;

    Link employeesLink;
    @XmlElement(name = "link")
    @XmlJavaTypeAdapter(XmlAdapter.class)
    public Link getEmployeesLink() {
        employeesLink = Link.fromUri("{id}/employees")
                .rel("employees").build(departmentId);
        return employeesLink;
    }
  //Rest of the getters and setters are omitted for brevity

}
```

Here is a quick overview of the APIs used in this example:

- In the preceding code snippet, the `Link.fromUri()` method call creates a new hypermedia link builder object, which is an instance of `javax.ws.rs.core.Link.Builder`. This `Builder` instance is used for building hypermedia links.
- The `rel()` method on the `Builder` instance lets you set the name for the `link` field present in the resource. This example sets the link relation as `employees`.
- You can also set certain attributes on a link object, such as the media type, title, or parameter, by calling the respective methods, such as `type()`, `title()`, or `param()`, defined on the `Builder` instance.
- The final `build()` method results in building the hypermedia link with the supplied values. In this example, the `build()` method will replace the param `{id}` template present in the URI, with the supplied `departmentId` parameter.

Here is the sample JSON representation generated for the `Department` resource that we discussed in this example:

```
[{"departmentId":300,"departmentName":"Administration",
"link":{"href":"300/employees","rel":"employees"},
"locationId":1700,"managerId":200} ...]
```

Programmatically building header links using JAX-RS APIs

The JAX-RS APIs allow you to add links to the HTTP header content as well. In the following code snippet, a link to the access manager for a department resource is added to the HTTP response header:

```
//Rest of the code is omitted for brevity
@GET
@Path("{id}")
@Produces(MediaType.APPLICATION_JSON)
public Response find(@PathParam("id") Short id) {

  Department deptEntity = findDepartmentEntity(id);
   //Add links to header
  return
    Response.ok()
       .links(getLinks(deptEntity.getManagerId()))
       .entity(deptEntity).build();
```

```
}
//Get the link object representing URI for manager
private Link[] getLinks(int departmentId) {
  Link managerLink = Link.fromUri("{id}/employees")
      .rel("manager").build(departmentId);
  return new Link[]{managerLink};
}
```

The following is the sample response generated by the preceding resource method implementation for the GET /departments/60 HTTP/1.1 request:

```
Header
Server: GlassFish Server
Link: <103/employees>; rel="manager"
Content-Type: application/json
Date: Sun, 29 Mar 2015 11:12:26 GMT
Content-Length: 124
Body
{
departmentId: 60
departmentName: "IT"
locationId: 1400
managerId: 103
}
```

Declaratively building links using Jersey annotations

In the previous section, we saw the offerings in JAX-RS APIs for programmatically building hypermedia links for the REST resources. Jersey simplifies this task further with its annotation-driven API model. In this session, we will take a quick look at the Jersey annotations for building HATEOAS APIs.

Specifying the dependency to use Jersey declarative linking

The first step to use Jersey declarative linking features is to add a dependency to the jersey-declarative-linking JAR. If you use Maven for building a source, then the dependency to jersey-declarative-linking in pom.xml will look like the following:

```
<dependency>
      <groupId>org.glassfish.jersey.ext</groupId>
```

```
        <artifactId>jersey-declarative-linking</artifactId>
        <!-- Choose the right version -->
        <version>RELEASE</version>
    </dependency>
```

Enabling the Jersey declarative linking feature for the application

Once you have the appropriate dependency set up, the next step is to enable the declarative linking feature by registering the `org.glassfish.jersey.linking.DeclarativeLinkingFeature` class with the application. You can do this via the `org.glassfish.jersey.server.ResourceConfig` class, as shown in the following code snippet:

```
//Other imports are omitted for brevity
import org.glassfish.jersey.server.ResourceConfig;
import org.glassfish.jersey.linking.DeclarativeLinkingFeature;
@Provider
@javax.ws.rs.ApplicationPath("webresources")
public class ApplicationConfig extends ResourceConfig {
  public ApplicationConfig() {
    // Register a class of JAX-RS component
    register(DeclarativeLinkingFeature.class);
    //Package that needs to be scanned for other resource
    packages("com.packtpub.rest.ch5.service");
  }
}
```

Declaratively adding links to the resource representation

We are now ready with all the necessary measures for using the Jersey declarative hyperlink feature. Let's get started on using the Jersey annotation in a recourse class to declaratively generate links in the resource representation generated at runtime.

Take a look at the following `Department` resource class. This class is almost the same as the one that we discussed a while ago in the *Programmatically building entity body links using JAX-RS APIs* section. One difference that you may find in the `Department` resource class used in this section is the presence of the `@org.glassfish.jersey.linking.InjectLink` annotation. This is used for generating hypermedia links in the resource representation and can be used on fields of the String or URI type. The following code snippet uses `InjectLink` for generating hypermedia links for accessing employee resources:

```
//Other imports are removed for brevity
import org.glassfish.jersey.linking.Binding;
import org.glassfish.jersey.linking.InjectLink;
import org.glassfish.jersey.linking.InjectLink.Style;
import javax.xml.bind.annotation.adapters.XmlAdapter;
@XmlRootElement
public class Department {

    private Short departmentId;
    private String departmentName;
    private Integer managerId;
    private Short locationId;

    @InjectLink(
            value = "{id}/employees",
            style = Style.RELATIVE_PATH,
            bindings = @Binding(name = "id",
            value = "${instance.departmentId}"),
            rel = "employees"
    )
    @XmlJavaTypeAdapter(XmlAdapter.class)
    @XmlElement(name = "link")
    Link link;
    //getters and setters for the properties are omitted for brevity
}
```

The entity providers offered by Jersey will take care of generating the appropriate representation for the preceding class when returned in response to a REST API call at runtime. For instance, when the preceding resource class is used with the `public List<Department> findAllDeprtments()` methods that we discussed in the *Programmatically building entity body links using JAX-RS APIs* section, the runtime will generate the appropriate hypermedia links as shown here (without you doing any extra coding, except using appropriate hyperlink annotations):

```
[{"link":{"href":"300/employees","rel":"employees"},"departmentId":300,"dep
artmentName":"Administration","locationId":1700,"managerId":200}, ...]
```

Let's take a look at the `@InjectLink` annotation to understand the usage better:

```
@InjectLink(
                  value = "{id}/employees",
                  style = Style.RELATIVE_PATH,
                  bindings = {@Binding(name = "id",
                  value = "${instance.departmentId}")},
                  rel = "employees"
)
@XmlJavaTypeAdapter(XmlAdapter.class)
@XmlElement(name = "link")
Link link;

private Short departmentId;
```

Here is a quick summary of the important elements that you can use in the `@InjectLink` annotation:

- `value`: This element specifies a URI template that will be used to build the injected URI. The URI template may contain parameters referring to properties in the current object and **Expression Language** (EL) expressions. For instance, the `${instance.departmentId}` EL expression refers to `departmentId` in the current object. The EL expression that you use here can refer to three types of implicit objects:
    - **Instance**: This represents the instance of the class that contains the annotated field.
    - **Entity**: This represents the entity class instance returned by the resource method. It is typically used in defining link headers.
    - **Resource**: This represents the resource class instance that returns the entity.

- `resource`: This element specifies a resource class whose `@Path` URI template will be used to build the injected URI.
- `bindings`: This element specifies the runtime binding for embedded URI template parameters. For instance, `bindings = @Binding(name = "id", value = "${instance.departmentId}")` indicates that the template parameter `id` is bound to the EL, `${instance.departmentId}`, and `value` for `id` can be resolved from the EL that it is bound to.
- `condition`: This element specifies a Boolean EL expression whose value determines whether a `Link` value can be injected into the resource.
- `style`: This defines the style of the URI to inject, such as the relative path or the absolute path.
- `rel`: This specifies the relationship with the target resource.
- `type`: This specifies the media type for the referenced resource content, for example, `application/json`.
- `hreflang`: This indicates the language for the referenced resource, for example, `hreflang="en"`.

See the API doc to learn about all the elements available with `@InjectLink`: `https://jersey.github.io/apidocs/latest/jersey/org/glassfish/jersey/linking/InjectLink.html`.

Grouping multiple links using @InjectLinks

You can use the `@org.glassfish.jersey.linking.InjectLinks` annotation to group multiple hypermedia links as an array and inject it to the `List` or `Link[]` property present in the resource representation class. Here is an example:

```
@InjectLinks({
    @InjectLink(
        value = "{id}/employees",
        style = Style.RELATIVE_PATH,
        bindings = @Binding(name = "id", value =
                        "${instance.departmentId}"),
        rel = "employees"
    ),
    @InjectLink(
        value = "{id}/employees/{managerId}",
        style = Style.RELATIVE_PATH,
        bindings = {
            @Binding(name = "id", value =
```

```
                    "${instance.departmentId}"),
                @Binding(name = "managerId", value =
                    "${instance.managerId}")},
            rel = "manager"
    )})
@XmlJavaTypeAdapter(LinkAdaptor.class)
@XmlElement(name = "links")
List<Link> links;
```

The sample resource link produced by the preceding definition may look like the following:

```
"links":[{"href":"300/employees","rel":"employees"},
        {"href":"300/employees/200","rel":"manager"}]
```

Declaratively building HTTP link headers using @InjectLinks

RFC 5988 mentions about defining Links in a HTTP header using the Link Header field. Adding links to a header is useful for capturing the metadata of a resource, for example, license information, policy information, and so on. To declaratively add the Link Header field, you can use @InjectLinks to add HTTP link headers as well. Here is an example:

```
@InjectLinks({
  @InjectLink(
    value = "{id}/employees/{managerId}",
    style = Style.RELATIVE_PATH,
    bindings = {
      @Binding(name = "id", value =
        "${instance.departmentId}"),
      @Binding(name = "managerId", value =
        "${instance.managerId}")},
    rel = "manager"
  )})@XmlRootElement
public class DepartmentRepresentation {
....
}
```

This generates the following link header at runtime:

```
Link: <300/employees/24170>; rel="manager"
```

Reading and writing large binary objects using Jersey APIs

When you work on enterprise-grade business applications, you may often want to build RESTful web APIs for reading and writing large binary objects, such as images, documents, and various types of media files. Unfortunately, the JAX-RS API does not have standardized APIs for dealing with large binary files. In this section, we will see offerings from the Jersey framework to store and retrieve images files. These APIs are generic in nature and can be used with any large binary file.

Building RESTful web services for storing images

Let's build a REST API to store the image sent by the client. We will start with the client and then move on to the server-side implementation.

This example uses an HTML client to upload images to the REST API. When you make a POST request to the server, you have to encode the data that forms the body of the request. You can use the multipart/form-data encoding to deal with a large binary object uploaded via <input type="file">. The client-side HTML code may look like the following:

```html
<html>
  <head>
   <title>File upload</title>
   <meta charset="UTF-8">
  </head>
  <body>
   <form action="employees/100/image"
     method="post" enctype="multipart/form-data">
     Choose photo for employee# 100 :
     <input type="file" name="empImgFile" />
     <br>
     <input type="submit" value="Upload Image" />
   </form>
  </body>
</html>
```

This HTML client uploads images for an employee identified by id=100. The RESTful web API for storing images is located at the employees/100/image URI. The client code for uploading an image to the RESTful web API is in place now.

As the next step, we will build a RESTful web API that accepts an uploaded image and stores it in a database. Jersey makes it simple by offering many binding annotations for method parameters to extract the desired value from the request body. For instance, it offers the @org.glassfish.jersey.media.multipart.FormDataParam annotation, which can be used for binding the named body parts of a multipart/form-data request body to a method parameter or a class member variable, as appropriate. We will use this annotation in conjunction with the request content encoded with multipart/form-data for consuming forms that contain files, non-ASCII data, and binary data. Jersey allows you to inject @FormDataParam onto the following parameter types:

- *Any type of parameter for which a message body reader is available*: The following example binds an input stream present in the first named body part, empImageFile, with an inputStream object: @FormDataParam("empImgFile") InputStream inputStream.

- org.glassfish.jersey.media.multipart.FormDataBodyPart: This object can be used for reading the value of a parameter that represents the first named body part present in the request body. You can also use List or Collection of FormDataBodyPart to read the values of multiple body parts with the same name. An example is @FormDataParam("p1") List<FormDataBodyPart> values.

- org.glassfish.jersey.media.multipart.FormDataContentDisposition : This represents the form-data content disposition header in the incoming payload. You can use it for retrieving details about the uploaded file, such as its name and size.

When you use @FormDataParam on a field, the entity provider will inject content from the incoming message body to the annotated fields, as appropriate.

The following code snippet demonstrates how you can use `@FormDataParam` for building a REST API that reads an image uploaded by a client. Note that the name parameter set for `@FormDataParam(...)` must match with the file input component present in the request payload. In this example, we name the input file component `empImgFile` in the HTML, `<input type="file" name="empImgFile" />`. You must use the same name as the parameter for `@FormDataParam("empImgFile")` to read the uploaded file content present in the payload posted to the server. This example uses JPA to persist the data:

```java
//Other imports are not shown for brevity
import org.glassfish.jersey.media.multipart.
         FormDataContentDisposition;
import org.glassfish.jersey.media.multipart.FormDataParam;
@Stateless
@Path("employees")
public class EmployeeResource {
    //Name of the persistence unit from persistence.xml
    @PersistenceContext(unitName = "EMP_PU")
    private EntityManager entityManager;

    @POST
    @Path("{empId}/image")
    @Consumes(MediaType.MULTIPART_FORM_DATA)
    public void uploadImage(@Context HttpServletRequest request,
        @FormDataParam("empImgFile") InputStream in,
        @FormDataParam("empImgFile") FormDataContentDisposition
        fileDetail,
        @PathParam("empId") Integer empId) throws Exception {

        try(ByteArrayOutputStream bos = new ByteArrayOutputStream())
        {
            int size = request.getContentLength();
            byte[] buffer = new byte[size];
            int len=0;
            while ((len = in.read(buffer, 0, 10240)) != -1) {
              bos.write(buffer, 0, len);
            }
            byte[] imgBytes = bos.toByteArray();
            //Pass the image to underlying entity
            //to persist the content
            EmployeeImage empImg = findEmployeeImageEntity(empId);
            empImg.setImage(imgBytes);
            entityManager.merge(empImg);
        }
    }
//Other methods are not shown for brevity
}
```

Before ending this section on REST support for handling binary files, let's take a quick look at the code snippet for reading binary files (or images) as well.

Building RESTful web service for reading images

The following method reads the binary representation of an image from the database and streams the content by using the `javax.ws.rs.core.StreamingOutput` class. The method is annotated with `@Produces(MediaType.APPLICATION_OCTET_STREAM)` to indicate that the response is in a binary form:

```
//Other imports are omitted for brevity
import javax.ws.rs.core.StreamingOutput;

@GET
@Path("/{empId}/image")
@Produces(MediaType.APPLICATION_OCTET_STREAM)
public Response getImage(final @PathParam("empId") Integer id) throws
Exception {

   StreamingOutput outputImage = new StreamingOutput() {
      @Override
      Public void write(OutputStream output)
          throws IOException {
      EmployeeImage empImg = findEmployeeImageEntity(id);
      byte[] buf = empImg.getImage();
      output.write(buf);
      output.flush();
        }
   };
   ResponseBuilder response = Response.ok((Object) outputImage);
   response.header("Content-Disposition", "inline;filename=image.jpeg");
   return response.build();
}
```

You can use the preceding RESTful web API directly with the `<img>` component present in the HTML page, as shown in the following HTML snippet. The `employees/100/image` URI points to the RESTful web API that we built for reading the image content:

```
<img alt="Employee image" src="employees/100/image" id="id"/>
```

Generating a chunked output using Jersey APIs

A chunked response means that instead of waiting for the entire result, the results are split into chunks (partial results) and sent one after the other. Sending a response in chunks is useful for a RESTful web API if the resource returned by the API is huge in size.

With Jersey, you can use the `org.glassfish.jersey.server.ChunkedOutput` class as the return type to send the response to a client in chunks. The chunked output content can be any data type for which `MessageBodyWriter<T>` (entity provider) is available.

When you specify `ChunkedOutput` as the return type for a REST resource method, it tells the runtime that the response will be chunked and sent one by one to the client. Seeing `ChunkedOutput` as the return type for a method, Jersey will switch to the asynchronous processing mode while processing this method at runtime, without you having to explicitly use `AsyncResponse` in the method signature. Furthermore, when the response content is generated for this method, Jersey will set `Transfer-Encoding: chunked` in the response header. The chunked transfer encoding allows the server to maintain an HTTP-persistent connection for sending the result to the client in a series of chunks, as and when they become available.

The following example shows how you can use `ChunkedOutput` to return a large amount of data:

```
//Other imports are omitted for brevity
import org.eclipse.persistence.queries.CursoredStream;
import org.glassfish.jersey.server.ChunkedOutput;

@Stateless
@Path("employees")
public class EmployeeResource {
  //A thread manager that manages a long-running job
    private final ExecutorService executorService =
      Executors.newCachedThreadPool();
  @GET
  @Path("chunk")
  @Produces({MediaType.APPLICATION_JSON})
  public ChunkedOutput<List<Employee>> findAllInChunk() {
      final ChunkedOutput<List<Employee>> output = new
        ChunkedOutput<List<Employee>>() {
          };
       //Execute the thread
      executorService.execute(new
        LargeCollectionResponseType(output));
```

```
        // Returns chunked output set by
        // LargeCollectionResponseType thread class
        return output;
}


//This thread class reads employee records from database
//in batches. This thread is used to back up asynchronous
//processing of the chunked output.

class LargeCollectionResponseType implements Runnable {

    ChunkedOutput output;
    EntityManager entityManagerLocal = null;
    //Stream class used to deal
    //with large collections
    CursoredStream cursoredStream = null;
    //Page size used for reading records from DB
    final int PAGE_SIZE = 50;

    LargeCollectionResponseType(ChunkedOutput output) {
        this.output = output;
        //Get the entity manager instance
        EntityManagerFactory emf =
            Persistence.createEntityManagerFactory("EMP_PU");
        entityManagerLocal = emf.createEntityManager();
        //Get employee query
        //Employee entity definition is not shown for brevity
        Query empQuery = entityManagerLocal.
            createNamedQuery("Employee.findAll");
        //AScrollableCursor is enabled using query hint
        //This hint allows the client to scroll through
        //the results page by page
        empQuery.setHint("eclipselink.cursor", true);
        cursoredStream = (CursoredStream)
            empQuery.getSingleResult();
    }

    public void run() {
        try {
            boolean hasMore = true;
            do {
                //Scroll through the results page by page
                List<Employee> chunk = (List<Employee>)
                    getNextBatch(cursoredStream, PAGE_SIZE);
                hasMore = (chunk != null && chunk.size() > 0);
                if (hasMore) {
                    //Write current chunk to ChunkedOutput
                    output.write(chunk);
```

```
                        }
                    } while (hasMore);
            } catch (IOException e) {
                    // IOException thrown when writing the
                    // chunks of response: Should be handled
                    e.printStackTrace();
            } finally {
                    try {
                        output.close();
                    } catch (IOException ioe) {
                        ioe.printStackTrace();
                    }

            }
        }


        //CursoredStream is used to deal with large
        //collections returned from TOPLink queries
        //more efficiently
        private List<Employee> getNextBatch(CursoredStream
            cursoredStream, int pagesize) {
            List emps = null;
            if (!cursoredStream.atEnd()) {
                emps = cursoredStream.next(pagesize);
            }
            return emps;
        }
//Rest of the code goes here
}
```

Here is a quick summary of this example:

- This example uses a JPA entity to read an employee record from the database.
  The employee entity definition is not listed in the code snippet in order to save
  space. We use `org.eclipse.persistence.queries.CursoredStream` to read
  records in batches from the database. Under the cover, `CursoredStream` wraps a
  database result set cursor to provide a stream on the resulting selected objects.
- This example defines the `ChunkedOutput<List<Employee>>`
  `findAllInChunk()` method to return the employee collection in a series of
  chunks.

- Jersey will process the resource method that returns `ChunkedOutput` asynchronously. This is the reason why this example uses a worker thread to read records from the database. The read operation makes use of the `org.eclipse.persistence.queries.CursoredStream` class from `EclipseLink` (which is the JPA provider for this example) to wrap a database result set cursor to provide a stream on the resulting selected objects.
- While returning a response to the client, Jersey will add the `Transfer-Encoding: chunked` response header for the `ChunkedOutput` return type. The client now knows that the response is going to be chunked, so it reads each chunk of the response separately, processes it, and waits for more chunks to arrive at the same connection. This allows the server to maintain an HTTP-persistent connection for sending the series of chunks to clients. Once everything is done, the server closes the connection.

Jersey client API for reading chunked input

To read the chunked input on the client, Jersey offers the `org.glassfish.jersey.client.ChunkedInput<T>` class. Here is a client example that reads the employee list in chunks, as returned by the server:

```
//Other imports omitted for brevity
import org.glassfish.jersey.media.sse.EventInput;
import javax.ws.rs.client.ClientBuilder;

String BASE_URI = "http://localhost:8080/hr-app/api";
Client client = ClientBuilder.newClient();
Response response = client.target().path("employees")
   .path("chunk").request().get();
ChunkedInput<List<Employee>> chunks = response
    .readEntity(new GenericType<ChunkedInput<List<Employee>>>(){});
List<Employee> chunk;
while ((chunk = chunks.read()) != null) {
  //Code to process List<Employee> received in chunks goes here
}
//Close the client after use
client.close();
```

Having discussed chunked output and input, we now will move on to another exciting feature offered by the Jersey framework, which allows the RESTful web APIs to push notifications to clients.

Supporting server-sent events in RESTful web services

The **Server-sent event (SSE)** is a mechanism where a client (browser) receives automatic updates from a server via a long-living HTTP connection that was established when the client contacted the server for the first time. The SSE client subscribes to a stream of updates generated by a server, and whenever a new event occurs, a notification is sent to the client via the existing HTTP connection. The connection is then left open until the server has some data to send. In this section, we will discuss how the SSE technology can be used in a REST API to send continuous updates to the client.

 Server-sent events use a single, unidirectional, persistent connection between the client and the server. This is suited for the one-way publish-subscribe model, whenever the server pushes updates to the clients.

In a typical HTTP client-server communication model, the client opens the connection and sends a request to the server. The server then responds back with the result and closes the connection. With SSE, the server leaves the connection open even after sending the first response back to the client. This connection will be left open as long as the server wants and can be used for sending notifications to all the connected clients.

Let's see how we can implement SSE in RESTful web services by using Jersey APIs. The following are the core Jersey classes that you may want to use while building SSE-enabled RESTful resources:

- `org.glassfish.jersey.media.sse.SseBroadcaster`: This is a utility class, used for broadcasting SSE to multiple subscribers. Each subscriber is represented by an `EventOutput` instance, which is explained next.
- `org.glassfish.jersey.media.sse.EventOutput`: One instance of this class corresponds with exactly one HTTP connection. When a client subscribes to SSEs by calling the designated REST API method, the server (Jersey application) generates `EventOutput` and returns it to the caller. When `EventOutput` is returned from the resource method, the underlying HTTP connection will be left open for later use by the server. The server can use this HTTP connection to broadcast messages whenever needed.

Let's build a simple example to learn how to enable SSE support in RESTful web services.

The first step is to add the required dependencies for SSE (the `jersey-media-sse` JAR) to the project. If you use Maven for building your source, then the dependency to `jersey-media-sse` may look like the following:

```
<dependency>
  <groupId>org.glassfish.jersey.media</groupId>
  <artifactId>jersey-media-sse</artifactId>
   <!-specify right version -->
  <version>RELEASE</version>
  <type>jar</type>

   <!-- container(GlassFish) provides dependency
         for this example -->
  <scope>provided</scope>
</dependency>
```

The Jersey runtime will automatically discover and register the Jersey SSE module if it is found in the application class path. You do not need to do anything explicitly in order to enable this feature.

In the following example, we will use an SSE event mechanism to notify the subscribed clients whenever the department resource gets modified on the server.

Let's take a closer look at the implementation to understand how SSE is leveraged in this example via the Jersey APIs:

Let's understand the image in detail:

1. The client subscribes to SSEs by calling the `manageSSEEvents(...)` RESTful web service method, which is accessible via the following URI: GET `departments/events HTTP/1.1`.

2. When clients subscribe to events, we add them to the `SseBroadcaster` instance.

3. Later, when the event needs to be broadcast, we ask `SseBroadcaster` to broadcast the events to all the subscribed parties.

4. This example uses a singleton resource class. The reason why we use a singleton resource class is primarily to make sure that API calls, which need access to `SseBroadcaster`, use the same `SseBroadcaster` instance. You can improve this example by adding proper thread synchronization blocks.

5. Later, when a client updates a department resource, this example will create an `OutboundEvent` instance and broadcast it to all the listeners via the `SseBroadcaster` instance discussed in *Step 1*. The `OutboundEvent` object holds the relevant message about the modifications made on the department.

6. Let's see how the client deals with the SSE client. An SSE client keeps track of the most recently received event identifier. If the connection fails, the client will attempt to reconnect and send a special `Last-Event-ID` HTTP header containing the event ID. This header can be used as a synchronization mechanism between the client and the server in the event of a temporary connection failure. The following method `manageSSEEvents` accepts the `Last-Event-ID` sent by the client and replays all the missed events: `public EventOutput manageSSEEvents( @HeaderParam(SseFeature.LAST_EVENT_ID_HEADER) @DefaultValue("-1") int lastEventId)`.

7. When the client closes a connection and does not respond within the reconnect delay window, then the broadcaster identifies the corresponding `EventOutput` and releases it along with all the resources associated with it.

8. Alternatively, the server can close all the open connections by invoking the `closeAll()` method on the `SseBroadcaster` object.

The following is the code snippet used for building an SSE-enabled RESTful web API discussed in this example:

```
//Other imports are omitted for brevity
import org.glassfish.jersey.media.sse.EventOutput;
import org.glassfish.jersey.media.sse.OutboundEvent;
import org.glassfish.jersey.media.sse.SseBroadcaster;
import org.glassfish.jersey.media.sse.SseFeature;

@Path("departments/events")
```

```
@Singleton
public class SSEEnabledDeptResource {

    @PersistenceContext(unitName = "SSE_PU")
    private EntityManager entityManager;

    private static ArrayList<String> modifiedDepts = new
        ArrayList<String>();
    private static final SseBroadcaster broadcaster = new
        SseBroadcaster();
    // Client subscribes to SSEs by calling
    // this RESTful web service method.
    @GET
    @Produces(SseFeature.SERVER_SENT_EVENTS)
    public EventOutput manageSSEEvents(
        @HeaderParam(SseFeature.LAST_EVENT_ID_HEADER)
        @DefaultValue("-1") int lastEventId) {

        EventOutput eventOutput = new EventOutput();
        if (lastEventId > 0) {
            replayMissedUpdates(lastEventId, eventOutput);
        }
        if (!broadcaster.add(eventOutput)) {
            // Let's try to force a 5-s delayed client
            // reconnect attempt
            throw new ServiceUnavailableException(5L);
        }
        return eventOutput;
    }

  private void replayMissedUpdates(final int lastEventId,
      final EventOutput eventOutput) {
    try {
      for (int i = lastEventId;
                    i < modifiedDepts.size(); i++) {
        eventOutput.write(createItemEvent(i,
                        modifiedDepts.get(i)));
      }
    } catch (IOException ex) {
      throw new InternalServerErrorException
                    ("Error replaying missed events", ex);
    }
  }

  //This method generates an SSE whenever any client
  //invokes it to modify the department resource
  //identified by path parameter
  @PUT
```

```
@Path("{id}")
@Consumes(MediaType.APPLICATION_JSON)
public void edit(@PathParam("id") Short id,
    Department entity) {
    entityManager.merge(entity);
    final int modifiedListIndex = modifiedDepts.size() + 1;
    broadcaster.broadcast(createItemEvent
        (modifiedListIndex, entity.getDepartmentName()));
    modifiedDepts.add(entity.getDepartmentName());
}
private OutboundEvent createItemEvent(final int eventId,
    final String name) {
  return
     new OutboundEvent.Builder()
    .id(String.valueOf(eventId))
    .data(String.class, name).build();
}
}
```

Remember that an SSE is unidirectional by nature and is appropriate for a publish-subscribe communication model. Here are some advantages of using SSEs:

- With an SEE, a message is transported over the popular HTTP instead of a custom protocol. This keeps both the server and the client simple and easy to work on.
- HTTP has a built-in support for reconnection and event-id used in an SSE.
- SSE is a simple and lightweight protocol.

Understanding the Jersey server-side configuration properties

Each application is different and must be tuned separately. Things that work for one application do not necessarily work for another. Keeping this point in mind, Jersey offers various server-side configuration properties to optimize the runtime performance of RESTful web services. The following table lists some of the core properties that you may find useful while tuning RESTful web APIs.

 To view the complete list of configuration properties offered by Jersey, visit the following Appendix page in the Jersey User Guide:
https://jersey.github.io/documentation/latest/appendix-properties.html

Here are a few major configuration properties with a detailed explanation for each:

Configuration Property	Description
`jersey.config.server.subresource.cache.size`	This property takes an integer value that defines the cache size for subresource locator models. The default value is 64. Caching of subresource locator models is useful for avoiding the repeated generation of subresource models while processing the request. The runtime identifies the cached subresource with the RESTful web API URI and the input parameter values.
`jersey.config.server.subresource.cache.age`	This property takes an integer value that defines the maximum age (in seconds) for cached subresource locator models. This is not enabled by default. This is useful for reducing the memory footprint when your application is idle.
`jersey.config.server.subresource.cache.jersey.resource.enabled`	This property takes a `true` or `false` value. If it is set to `true`, then Jersey will cache resources in addition to caching subresource locator classes and instances (which are cached by default). To leverage this feature, your resource method needs to return the same resource instances for the same input parameters. This is not enabled by default.

You can configure these properties either by extending the
`org.glassfish.jersey.server.ResourceConfig` class or by using `init-param` in
`web.xml` as follows:

- Configuring server-side properties by extending `ResourceConfig`:

```
@Provider
@javax.ws.rs.ApplicationPath("webresources")
public class ApplicationConfig extends ResourceConfig {

    public ApplicationConfig(@Context ServletContext
        context) {
        //Specify server-side configuration properties
        property(ServerProperties
            .SUBRESOURCE_LOCATOR_CACHE_SIZE, 1000);
        property(ServerProperties
            .SUBRESOURCE_LOCATOR_CACHE_AGE, 60 * 10);
    }
}
```

- Specifying configuration properties in `web.xml`:

```
<web-app ...>
    <servlet>
        <servlet-name>
            JerseyRestApplicationServlet
        </servlet-name>
        <servlet-class>
            org.glassfish.jersey.servlet.ServletContainer
        </servlet-class>
        <init-param>
            <param-name>
                jersey.config.server.subresource.cache.size
            </param-name>
            <param-value>1000</param-value>
        </init-param>
    <init-param>
            <param-name>
                jersey.config.server.subresource.cache.age
            </param-name>
            <param-value>600</param-value>
        </init-param>
    </servlet>
</web-app>
```

Monitoring RESTful web services using Jersey APIs

Jersey lets you register various event listeners to monitor the state of your JAX-RS application. Here are the two core listener interfaces that you may need to be aware of:

- `org.glassfish.jersey.server.monitoring.ApplicationEventListener` : This is a Jersey-specific provider component that listens to application events such as the initialization of the application, the start and stop of the application, and so on. The implementation class can be registered as any standard JAX-RS provider.
- `org.glassfish.jersey.server.monitoring.RequestEventListener`: The implementation of the interface will be called for request events when they occur. This is not a JAX-RS provider; an instance of `RequestEventListener` must be returned from `ApplicationEventListener::onRequest(RequestEvent)`.

The following sample code illustrates the usage of `ApplicationEventListener` to log the application event states and invoke `RequestEventListener`:

```
package com.packtpub.rest.ch5.service.monitor;

import java.util.logging.Logger;
import javax.ws.rs.ext.Provider;
import org.glassfish.jersey.server.monitoring.ApplicationEvent;
import org.glassfish.jersey.server.monitoring.ApplicationEventListener;
import org.glassfish.jersey.server.monitoring.RequestEvent;
import org.glassfish.jersey.server.monitoring.RequestEventListener;

@Provider
public class ApplicationEventListenerImpl implements
ApplicationEventListener {
private static final Logger logger =
Logger.getLogger(ApplicationEventListenerImpl.class.getName());
    private int requestCount = 0;

    @Override
    public void onEvent(ApplicationEvent ae) {
        logger.info("ApplicationEventListenerImpl::onEvent");

        //Check the application event type and log the status
        switch (ae.getType()) {
            case INITIALIZATION_START:
                logger.info("INITIALIZATION_START");
                break;
```

```
            case INITIALIZATION_APP_FINISHED:
                logger.info("INITIALIZATION_APP_FINISHED");
                break;
            case INITIALIZATION_FINISHED:
                logger.info("INITIALIZATION_FINISHED");
                break;
            case RELOAD_FINISHED:
                logger.info("RELOAD_FINISHED");
                break;
            case DESTROY_FINISHED:
                logger.info("DESTROY_FINISHED");
        }
    }

    @Override
    public RequestEventListener onRequest(RequestEvent re) {
        //Increment the Request Counter for each request
        requestCount++;
        logger.fine("ApplicationEventListenerImpl::onRequest");
        return new RequestEventListenerImpl(requestCount);
    }
}
```

The following sample code illustrates the usage of `RequestEventListener` to log the processing of each request:

```
package com.packtpub.rest.ch5.service.monitor;

import java.util.logging.Level;
import java.util.logging.Logger;
import org.glassfish.jersey.server.monitoring.RequestEvent;
import org.glassfish.jersey.server.monitoring.RequestEventListener;

public class RequestEventListenerImpl implements RequestEventListener {

private static final Logger logger =
Logger.getLogger(RequestEventListenerImpl.class.getName());

 private int requestNumber;

 public RequestEventListenerImpl(int id)
 {
 this.requestNumber = id;
 }

 @Override
 /*
 * For each request event log the request being and end time
```

```
  */
 public void onEvent(RequestEvent event) {
     logger.info("RequestEventListenerImpl::onEvent");
     switch (event.getType()) {
       case RESOURCE_METHOD_START:
           logger.log(Level.INFO, "Resource method {0} started for
request {1}",
              new Object[]{event.getUriInfo().getMatchedResourceMethod()
         .getHttpMethod(), requestNumber});
        break;
        case FINISHED:
         logger.log(Level.INFO, "Request {0} finished. ", requestNumber);
         break;
     }
   }
 }
```

Given ahead is the output of processing the REST API request via
`ApplicationEventListener` **and** `RequestEventListener`:

```
Program Output:

Info: ApplicationEventListenerImpl::onEvent
Info: INITIALIZATION_START
Info: ApplicationEventListenerImpl::onEvent
Info: INITIALIZATION_APP_FINISHED
Info: ApplicationEventListenerImpl::onEvent
Info: INITIALIZATION_FINISHED
Info: ApplicationEventListenerImpl::onEvent
Info: DESTROY_FINISHED
Info: RequestEventListenerImpl::onEvent
Info: Resource /rest-chapter5-advfeatures/webresources/server/info method
GET started for request 1
Info: Request 1 finished.
```

Jersey also comes with the `MonitoringStatistics` JMX bean to collect the application
state, which can be enabled by setting the following configuration property:
`jersey.config.server.monitoring.statistics.mbeans.enabled=true`

To learn more about the monitoring framework in Jersey, visit the
following chapter in the Jersey User Guide:
`https://jersey.github.io/documentation/latest/monitoring_`
`tracing.html`

RESTEasy framework extensions

RESTEasy is another popular implementation of the JAX-RS specification available under the ASL (Apache) 2.0 license, which can run in any Servlet container. RESTEasy also comes with additional features on top of the plain JAX-RS functionalities.

To seamlessly integrate the RESTEasy features, the following Maven dependencies must be configured in the project in `pom.xml` under the `dependencies` element, as shown ahead:

```xml
<!-- RESTEasy Core APIs-->
<dependency>
    <groupId>org.jboss.resteasy</groupId>
    <artifactId>resteasy-jaxrs</artifactId>
    <version>RELEASE</version>
 </dependency>
 <dependency>
    <groupId>org.jboss.resteasy</groupId>
    <artifactId>resteasy-jaxb-provider</artifactId>
    <version>RELEASE</version>
 </dependency>

<!-- RESTEasy Client APIs-->
 <dependency>
    <groupId>org.jboss.resteasy</groupId>
    <artifactId>resteasy-client</artifactId>
    <version>RELEASE</version>
 </dependency>
 <dependency>
    <groupId>org.jboss.resteasy</groupId>
    <artifactId>resteasy-jackson-provider</artifactId>
    <version>RELEASE</version>
 </dependency>

<!-- RESTEasy Cache APIs-->
 <dependency>
    <groupId>org.jboss.resteasy</groupId>
    <artifactId>resteasy-cache-core</artifactId>
    <version>RELEASE</version>
 </dependency>
```

In the following sections, let's take a look at some of the useful features provided by the RESTEasy framework

Caching using RESTEasy

REST APIs are being used for a majority of B2B interactions, and often, they are constrained by the strict performance obligations to deliver the agreed quality of service. Though network-level caching may be helpful to improve throughput, it does not fully address performance needs. In cases where the underlying state of the data is not prone to frequent changes, such as static data, and there is a significant load on the system, it becomes advantageous to use caching to improve the response time. To facilitate the implementation of caching for RESTful services, RESTEasy comes with the following features:

- Cache-control annotations for server-side caching
- Client-side caching
- Multipart content handling

Cache-control annotations

RESTEasy provides the `@Cache` and `@NoCache` annotations, following the JAX-RS specifications, with the `@GET` annotation for controlling the cache. These annotations can be applied at class and method levels.

The `@NoCache` annotation is used to specify when caching is not required; hence, the server needs to respond back with a fresh response for every request.

The `@Cache` annotation is used when the caching of a response is required. Given ahead is a brief list of attributes used to control the caching behavior. Take some time to refer to the previous chapter, which talks in detail about each of these attributes.

- `maxAge`: This indicates the maximum time the response message will remain in the cache.
- `sMaxAge`: This is the same as `maxAge`, but it applies for a proxy cache.
- `noStore`: This is used to avoid caching sensitive information set to `true`.
- `mustRevalidate`: If this is `true`, it revalidates the cache content and serves the fresh response.
- `proxyRevalidate`: This is the same as `mustRevalidate`, but it applies for a proxy cache.
- `isPrivate`: If this is `true`, the response messages will be cached for a single user only and will not be shared. If `false`, it means that the response messages can be cached by any cache.

Given ahead is the application of cache-control annotations for caching the response of the `findDepartment` function of `DepartmentService`:

```
//The response of findDepartment method will be cached for the specified
maxAge //duration and user will get the response from cache for same
department id //request until the cache expires.

@GET
@Path("{id}")
@Produces(MediaType.APPLICATION_JSON)
@Cache(maxAge=2000,mustRevalidate = false,noStore = true, proxyRevalidate
= false, sMaxAge = 2000)
public Departments findDepartment(@PathParam("id") Short id) {
return entityManager.find(Departments.class, id);
}
```

In the preceding code snippet, when the client invokes the `findDepartment` function, the server will respond back with the response from the cache if it exists; otherwise, it will execute the function and return the response. In the latter case, the response will be cached as per the caching definition and will be used to serve future requests.

To set up the server-side cache, you must register an instance of `org.jboss.resteasy.plugins.cache.server.ServerCacheFeature` via your application's `getSingletons()` or `getClasses()` method. The underlying cache is Infinispan. By default, RESTEasy will create an Infinispan cache for you.

Client-side caching

With server-side caching, the client will still have to hit the target resource. When the bandwidth is a constraint and there is a requirement to save network-round trips, it makes sense to enable caching at the client side when the consuming system has enough resources required for caching. The `HTTP 1.1` protocol specification defines the guidelines around client-side caching with control parameters such as cache-control headers to decide about caching the server response and the cache-expiry mechanisms.

Following the HTTP specification, RESTEasy provides the `BrowserCacheFeature` API for implementing client-side caching, as shown ahead:

```
//Enabling Client-Side Caching
public DepartmentServiceClient(){
    webTarget = (ResteasyWebTarget)
ClientBuilder.newClient().target(BASE_URI);
```

```
//Step1: Construct an instance of RESTEasy LightweightBrowserCache
   LightweightBrowserCache cache = new LightweightBrowserCache();
//Step2: Default 2 MB of data is the max size, override as relevant
   cache.setMaxBytes(20);
//Step3: Apply the BrowserCacheFeature to the target resource to enable
caching
   BrowserCacheFeature cacheFeature = new BrowserCacheFeature();
   cacheFeature.setCache(cache);
   webTarget.register(cacheFeature);
}
```

GZIP compression/decompression

With a lot of mobile applications being used in the market, it becomes essential to enable faster transmission of large chunks of data over a network. RESTEasy provides the GZIP compression/decompression feature. When the response body is plain text, it can be easily compressed on the server side and then decompressed on the client side. RESTEasy accomplishes this with the @GZIP annotation applied at the method level, as shown ahead:

```
/**
 * Returns list of departments
 *
 */
@GET
@Produces(MediaType.APPLICATION_JSON)
@GZIP
public List<Departments> findAllDepartments() {
//Find all departments from the data store and return compressed response
javax.persistence.criteria.CriteriaQuery cq =
entityManager.getCriteriaBuilder().createQuery();
 cq.select(cq.from(Departments.class));
 List<Departments> departments =
entityManager.createQuery(cq).getResultList();
 return departments;
}
```

The @GZIP annotation of RESTEasy takes care of compressing the response message body and similarly when a server receives a request with content-encoding equal to GZIP then the request message body is decompressed automatically.

Multipart content handling

RESTEasy provides abstraction of multipart content handling with the multipart data provider plugin. This plugin enables you to easily parse the uploaded content submitted via HTML forms. To use the plugin, include the following Maven dependencies in the POM file:

```
<dependency>
    <groupId>org.jboss.resteasy</groupId>
    <artifactId>resteasy-multipart-provider</artifactId>
    <version>RELEASE</version>
</dependency>
```

Let's try with the simple use case of an employee uploading/downloading his/her profile picture. For this use case, we will create a simple HTML form for the employee to upload his/her profile picture, as shown ahead:

```
<html>
<body>
<h1>Upload Employee Profile Picture</h1>

  <form action="webresources/employee/addimage" method="post"
enctype="multipart/form-data">
     <p>
    Employee Id : <input type="text" name="employeeId" size="50" />
     </p>
     <p>
    Select Profile Image : <input type="file" name="profilePicture"
size="50" />
     </p>
     <p>
    Description : <input type="text" name="imageDesc" size="50" />
     </p>
     <input type="submit" value="Upload Image" />
  </form>

</body>
</html>
```

Please make sure that the form attribute, enctype, is specified as multipart/form-data. Once the user submits the form, the request is submitted to the EmployeeImageResoure class's addImage operation. The org.jboss.resteasy.plugins.providers.multipart.MultipartFormDataInput argument of the addImage operation will be used to read the submitted form contents. Similarly, to download the image, the user can use the getProfilePicture operation, which wraps the image file in the response using the javax.ws.rs.core.Response.ResponseBuilder class, as shown ahead:

```java
/**
 * This class used to upload or download an employee profile picture
 *
 */
@Path("employee")
@Stateless
public class EmployeeImageResource {

    @PersistenceContext(unitName = "com.packtpub_rest-chapter5-resteasy-
service_war_1.0-SNAPSHOTPU")
    private EntityManager entityManager;
    private static final Logger logger =
Logger.getLogger(EmployeeImageResource.class.getName());

    @GET
    @Path("/image/{id}")
    @Produces("image/png")
    /*
     * Download the employee profile picture for the given employee id
     */
    public Response getProfilePicture(@PathParam("id") Short empId) {

        try {

            //Step-1: Fetch the employee profile picture from datastore
            EmployeeImage profile = entityManager.find(EmployeeImage.class,
empId);

            //Ste-2:
            String fileName = empId + "-image.png";
            File imageFile = new File(fileName);
            try (FileOutputStream imageFOS = new
FileOutputStream(imageFile)) {
                imageFOS.write(profile.getEmployeePic());
                imageFOS.flush();
            }

            ResponseBuilder responseBuilder = Response.ok((Object)
```

```
imageFile);
            responseBuilder.header("Content-Disposition", "attachment;
filename=\"" + fileName + "\"");
            return responseBuilder.build();
        } catch (IOException e) {
            logger.log(Level.SEVERE, "Error Fetching Employee Profile
Picture", e);
            return
Response.status(Status.INTERNAL_SERVER_ERROR).entity("Error Fetching
Employee Profile Picture").build();
        }

    }

    @POST
    @Consumes("multipart/form-data")
    @Path("/addimage")
    /*
    * Upload the employee profile picture for the given employee id
    */
    public Response addImage(MultipartFormDataInput form) {

        try {
            //Step-1: Read the Form Contents
            Map<String, List<InputPart>> formContents =
form.getFormDataMap();
            List<InputPart> imagePart = formContents.get("profilePicture");

            if (imagePart == null) {
                return Response.status(400).entity("Invalid Content
Uploaded").build();
            }
            byte[] profilePic = null;

            for (InputPart inputPart : imagePart) {

                profilePic =
IOUtils.toByteArray(inputPart.getBody(InputStream.class, null));
            }
            //Step-2: Validate the presence of mandatory content and
            //if invalid content reply as Bad Data Request
            if (profilePic == null || profilePic.length<1 ||
formContents.get("employeeId") == null) {
                return Response.status(Status.BAD_REQUEST).entity("Invalid
Content Uploaded").build();
            }

            String empId =
```

```
formContents.get("employeeId").get(0).getBodyAsString();
            String desc = "";
            if (formContents.get("imageDesc") != null
                    && formContents.get("imageDesc").get(0) != null) {
                desc =
formContents.get("imageDesc").get(0).getBodyAsString();
            }

            //Step-3:Persist the uploaded image to datastore
            EmployeeImage empImgEntity = new EmployeeImage(
                    Short.parseShort(empId),
                    profilePic, desc);
            entityManager.persist(empImgEntity);

            return Response.status(Status.CREATED).entity("Saved Employee
Profile Picture").build();

        } catch (IOException | NumberFormatException e) {
            logger.log(Level.SEVERE, "Error Saving Employee Profile
Picture", e);
            return
Response.status(Status.INTERNAL_SERVER_ERROR).entity("Error Saving Employee
Profile Picture").build();

        }

    }

}
```

Summary

In this chapter, we covered some very useful extensions offered by the Jersey and RESTEasy frameworks. These features are really useful to address specific use cases that you may see very often in real-life REST API development. Remember that all the features that we discussed in this chapter are not part of the JAX-RS standard (unless otherwise stated). It is always best practice to go with the standard and minimal use of extensions to avoid vendor lock-in. Therefore, if your application really needs some vendor-specific offering, consider all the aspects and then take a decision.

By now, you must have a good understanding of the JAX-RS APIs and reference implementation extensions. In the next chapter, you will learn how to secure RESTful web services.

6
Securing RESTful Web Services

As RESTful web services use the HTTP transport protocol for communication, they are equally vulnerable to security risks observed with web applications. Often, the development of RESTful web services is focused on the functional requirements, and the security requirements get overlooked. As a best practice, a RESTful web service must be designed considering the security requirements to ensure that it is made bulletproof from security threats or attacks.

In this chapter, you will learn the different ways of securing RESTful web services from a development standpoint, and you will learn the applicable best practices. The following topics are discussed in this chapter:

- HTTP basic authentication
- HTTP digest authentication
- JWT authentication
- Securing RESTful web services with OAuth
- Authorizing the RESTful web service accesses
- Input validation
- Best practices for securing RESTful services

Securing and authenticating web services

Security on the internet takes many forms. In the context of RESTful web services and this book, we are only interested in two forms of security—securing access to web services and accessing web services on behalf of the allowed users.

What we accomplish with securing web services is the calculated control of resources. Even though most web services are publicly available, we still need to control the data access and traffic throughput. We can do both by restricting the access through subscription accounts. For example, the API access can be limited based on the number of queries a registered user could execute daily. Similarly, many other API vendors restrict the access of their APIs.

Security has two essential elements:

- **Authentication**: This involves verifying the identity of the user who is trying to access the application or web service. This is typically performed by obtaining the login credentials and validating them against the user details configured on the server.
- **Authorization**: This involves verifying what an authenticated user is permitted to do in the application or service.

In this chapter, we will take a look at the various approaches for authenticating and authorizing RESTful web services. We will start with the simplest mechanism among all of them.

HTTP basic authentication

Basic HTTP authentication works by sending the Base64-encoded username and password as a pair in the HTTP authorization header. The username and password must be sent for every HTTP request made by the client. A typical HTTP basic authentication transaction can be depicted with the following sequence diagram. In this example, the client is trying to access a protected RESTful web service endpoint (/webresources/departments) to retrieve the department details:

The preceding diagram represents an entire transaction. A client begins by requesting the URI, /webresources/departments. Because the resource is secured using HTTP basic authentication and the client does not provide the required authorization credentials, the server replies with a 401 HTTP response. The client receives the response, scans through it, and prepares a new request with the necessary data needed to authenticate the user. The new request from the client will contain the authorization header set to a Base64-encoded value of column-delimited username and password string, <username>:<password>. This time, the server will verify the credentials and reply with the requested resource.

As you have seen earlier, client requests can be generated from any application that can create HTTP connections, including web browsers. Web browsers typically cache the credentials so that the users do not have to type in their login credentials for every secured resource request. This is viewed as a deficiency of the protocol, since unauthorized access can take place with cached credentials, and there is no way for a web service to differentiate authorized requests from the unauthorized ones. Also, the login credentials can be easily deciphered as they are Base64-encoded. However, the intent of Base64 is not to secure the name-value pair but to uniformly encode the characters when transferred over HTTP. Because of these reasons, it is not recommended to use basic HTTP authentication for any application accessed over the internet. In general, we solve this potential security hole by using HTTPS (transport layer security) instead of HTTP, which we will discuss later in this chapter.

Building JAX-RS clients with basic authentication

A normal client-server transaction can follow two scenarios of basic authentication. On one hand, a client submits a request to the server without any authentication credentials (as depicted in the previous sequence diagram). On the other hand, a client submits a request to the server with the authentication credentials. Let's take a closer look at these two scenarios.

When a client submits a request without the authentication credentials, the server responds back stating unauthorized access with an HTTP error code of **401**. If the request is executed from a web browser, users see the ubiquitous **Authentication Required** browser popup, as shown here:

Users can then supply the valid credentials to complete the request. Note that the web browser keeps track of the 401 response and is charged with sending the proper authentication credentials back with the original URI. This makes the transaction seamless for the users. Now, had we been using a client rather than a web browser, we would have needed to programmatically intercept the 401 response and then provide the valid credentials to complete the original request.

The second scenario that comes up while using HTTP basic authentication is when we do not wait for a server's 401 response but provide the authentication credentials at the beginning itself. As we said, we provide the credentials in the HTTP header authorization. The APIs for setting the HTTP headers vary with the client frameworks that you use. The following JAX-RS client example uses the `javax.ws.rs.client.ClientRequestFilter` implementation to associate the HTTP header authorization with each request. If you need a quick brush up on `ClientRequestFilter`, refer to the *Modifying request and response parameters with JAX-RS filters* section, in `Chapter 4`, *Advanced Features in the JAX-RS API*:

```
//Other imports are removed for brevity
import java.util.Base64;
import javax.ws.rs.client.ClientRequestContext;
import javax.ws.rs.client.ClientRequestFilter;
import javax.ws.rs.core.MultivaluedMap;
import javax.ws.rs.ext.Provider;

@Provider
public class ClientAuthenticationFilter implements
    ClientRequestFilter {
    private static final Logger logger =
        Logger.getLogger(ClientAuthenticationFilter.class.getName());
    private final String user;
    private final String password;

    public ClientAuthenticationFilter(String user,
        String password) {
```

```
            this.user = user;
            this.password = password;
    }


    //The filter() method is called before a request has been
    //dispatched to a client transport layer.
    //This method is used in this example for attaching user
    //name-password token with authorization header
    public void filter(ClientRequestContext requestContext) throws
        IOException {
        MultivaluedMap<String, Object> headers =
            requestContext.getHeaders();
        final String basicAuthentication =
            getBasicAuthentication();
        headers.add("Authorization", basicAuthentication);
      for (String header : headers.keySet()) {
            logger.log(Level.INFO, "Authentication Header:{0}-{1}",
                new Object[]{header,headers.get(header)});
        }
    }
    //Return BASE64 encoded username and password
    private String getBasicAuthentication() {
        String token = this.user + ":" + this.password;
        try {
            byte[] encoded =
                Base64.getEncoder().encode(
                    token.getBytes("UTF-8"));
            return "BASIC " + new String(encoded);
        } catch (UnsupportedEncodingException ex) {
            throw new IllegalArgumentException(
                "Cannot encode with UTF-8", ex);
        }
    }
}
```

The next step is to register the preceding filter implementation with the JAX-RS client code that makes the REST API call. The following code snippet illustrates how to accomplish this step. This example invokes a protected RESTful web service URI, /hr/departments, to fetch the departments in an enterprise. The client sets the HTTP basic authentication header via ClientAuthenticationFilter:

```
//JAX-RS REST client generated for REST resource:HRService
//to demonstrate usage of ClientAuthenticationFilter
public class HRServiceBasicAuthClient {
    private WebTarget webTarget;
    private Client client;
    //Port#15647 can vary based on the http listener port of the server
```

```
    private static final String BASE_URI = "http://localhost:15647/rest-
                      chapter6-service/webresources";
    private static final Logger logger =
          Logger.getLogger(HRServiceBasicAuthClient.class.getName());

    public HRServiceBasicAuthClient() {
      client = javax.ws.rs.client.ClientBuilder.newClient();
        webTarget = client.target(BASE_URI).path("hr").path("departments");
      //Pass the credentials to Auth Filter
      ClientAuthenticationFilter filter = new
                  ClientAuthenticationFilter("hr", "hr");
      webTarget.register(filter);
    }

    public <T> T findAll(GenericType<T> responseType) throws
        ClientErrorException {

        return
  webTarget.request(javax.ws.rs.core.MediaType.APPLICATION_JSON).
          get(responseType);
    }

    public void disconnect() {
        client.close();
    }

     public static void main(String arg[]) {

        HRServiceBasicAuthClient hrServiceClient =
                                     new HRServiceBasicAuthClient();
        List<Department> depts = hrServiceClient.findAll(
                new GenericType<List<Department>>() { });
        logger.log(Level.INFO, depts.toString());
        hrServiceClient.disconnect();
    }


}
```

The output of preceding program is as follows:

```
com.packtpub.rest.ch6.filter.ClientAuthenticationFilter filter
INFO: Authentication Header:Accept-[application/json]
com.packtpub.rest.ch6.filter.ClientAuthenticationFilter filter
INFO: Authentication Header:Authorization-[BASIC dGVzdDE6dGVzdDE=]
com.packtpub.rest.ch6.client.HRServiceBasicAuthClient main
INFO: [com.packtpub.rest.ch6.model.Department[ departmentId=10 ],
com.packtpub.rest.ch6.model.Department[ departmentId=20 ],
com.packtpub.rest.ch6.model.Department[ departmentId=30 ],
```

```
com.packtpub.rest.ch6.model.Department[ departmentId=40 ],
com.packtpub.rest.ch6.model.Department[ departmentId=50 ],
com.packtpub.rest.ch6.model.Department[ departmentId=60 ],
com.packtpub.rest.ch6.model.Department[ departmentId=70 ],
com.packtpub.rest.ch6.model.Department[ departmentId=80 ],
com.packtpub.rest.ch6.model.Department[ departmentId=90 ],
com.packtpub.rest.ch6.model.Department[ departmentId=100 ],
com.packtpub.rest.ch6.model.Department[ departmentId=110 ],
com.packtpub.rest.ch6.model.Department[ departmentId=120 ],
com.packtpub.rest.ch6.model.Department[ departmentId=130 ],
com.packtpub.rest.ch6.model.Department[ departmentId=140 ],
com.packtpub.rest.ch6.model.Department[ departmentId=150 ],
com.packtpub.rest.ch6.model.Department[ departmentId=160 ],
com.packtpub.rest.ch6.model.Department[ departmentId=170 ],
com.packtpub.rest.ch6.model.Department[ departmentId=180 ],
com.packtpub.rest.ch6.model.Department[ departmentId=190 ],
com.packtpub.rest.ch6.model.Department[ departmentId=200 ],
com.packtpub.rest.ch6.model.Department[ departmentId=210 ],
com.packtpub.rest.ch6.model.Department[ departmentId=220 ],
com.packtpub.rest.ch6.model.Department[ departmentId=230 ],
com.packtpub.rest.ch6.model.Department[ departmentId=240 ],
com.packtpub.rest.ch6.model.Department[ departmentId=250 ],
com.packtpub.rest.ch6.model.Department[ departmentId=260 ],
com.packtpub.rest.ch6.model.Department[ departmentId=270 ]]
```

The JAX-RS client runtime invokes all the registered filters before the request has been dispatched to the transport layer. In this example, `ClientAuthenticationFilter` adds the HTTP authentication header to each request made by the client. Because we are sending the authentication credentials in the first invocation itself, we do not expect a `401` response from the server, and the API call will proceed as any other request.

For the other HTTP request types, such as `POST`, `PUT`, and `DELETE`, the client request process cycle follows the same pattern as shown earlier. The client runtime sets the credentials and proceeds with the request and consumption of the response. Finally, every request type must include the authentication credentials, or else we will have to programmatically handle the server's `401` response. If the client knows the type of authentication required by the target API in advance, it makes sense to attach the necessary authentication content with the very first request itself, which will help you in avoiding an extra round trip that would otherwise be required for authentication.

For more details on HTTP basic authentication, see the page at `http://www.ietf.org/rfc/rfc2617.txt`.

In the next section, we will learn how to secure a JAX-RS RESTful web service application deployed on a server, such as the GlassFish server.

Securing JAX-RS services with basic authentication

In this section, we'll cover how to configure a JAX-RS application to challenge the clients for valid authentication credentials.

The basic authentication configuration depends on the web container being used. Throughout this book, we have used the GlassFish server for every application that required a Java web container; therefore, this example also assumes GlassFish as the target server for running the RESTful web APIs. We'll only look at the basic authentication configuration for the latest version of GlassFish (version 4.x).

The problem to solve is restricting the access for RESTful web services by creating a set of users for a specific security realm. A security realm is a mechanism used for protecting application resources. It gives you the ability to protect a resource by defining the security constraints and user roles for granting or restricting access. Let's see how the security realms are defined in the GlassFish server for securing the deployed resources.

Configuring the basic authentication

You can secure the deployed resources in the web server via basic authentication by making the appropriate security entries in the `web.xml` descriptor file and also in the container (vendor)-specific deployment descriptor file (`glassfish-web.xml`, in this example).

Let's say we want to use basic authentication for one of the JAX-RS sample web service applications that we built in the previous chapters.

The first step is to update the web descriptor web.xml file to look as follows. Note that web.xml is found in the WEB-INF folder of your web application; you should generate a new one if it is found to be missing:

```xml
<?xml version="1.0" encoding="UTF-8"?>
<web-app ...>
    <security-constraint>
        <web-resource-collection>
            <web-resource-name>
                Protected resource
            </web-resource-name>
            <url-pattern>/*</url-pattern>
            <http-method>GET</http-method>
        </web-resource-collection>

        <auth-constraint>
            <!-- role name that authorized users belongs to-->
            <role-name>APIUser</role-name>
        </auth-constraint>
        <!-- /added -->
        <!-- Use it only if you use https -->
        <user-data-constraint>
            <transport-guarantee>
              CONFIDENTIAL
            </transport-guarantee>
        </user-data-constraint>
    </security-constraint>
    <login-config>
        <auth-method>BASIC</auth-method>
        <!-- realm name used in GlassFish -->
        <realm-name>file</realm-name>
    </login-config>
    <security-role>
        <role-name>APIUser</role-name>
    </security-role>
</web-app>
```

Here is a quick summary of the core elements that you saw in the preceding web.xml file:

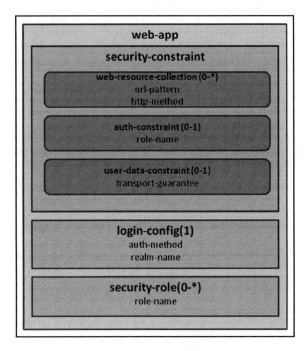

- The <security-constraint> element in web.xml is used to secure a collection of resources by restricting the access to them with the appropriate URL mapping:
  - The <web-resource-collection> subelement describes the protected resources in the application, which are identified via URL patterns and HTTP methods.
  - The subelement, <auth-constraint>, defines the user roles that are authorized to access constrained resources.
  - The subelement, <user-data-constraint>, defines how the data is protected in the transmission channel. It takes the following values: CONFIDENTIAL, INTEGRAL, or NONE. CONFIDENTIAL and INTEGRAL are treated in the same way by the Java EE container, and these values imply the use of the **Transport Layer Security (TLS)** (HTTPS) to all incoming requests matching the URL patterns present in <web-resource-collection>.

- The element, `<login-config>`, defines the login configurations used in the application:

  - The subelement, `<realm-name>`, refers to a collection of security information checked for authenticating the user when a secured page (resource) is accessed at runtime. The realm name that you enter should match with the security realm that you configured on the server.
  - The subelement, `<auth-method>`, defines the authorization method used in the application. The possible values are as follows:

    - `BASIC`: This is the HTTP basic authentication that we discussed a while ago.
    - `DIGEST`: This is the same as HTTP basic authentication, except that instead of a password, the client sends a cryptographic hash of user credentials along with the username.
    - `FORM`: This uses an HTML form for login, with field names that match the specific convention. For instance, `j_username` and `j_password` are used as names for the username and password fields respectively.
    - `CLIENT-CERT`: This uses a client digital certificate or other custom tokens in order to authenticate a user.

- The element, `<security-role>`, defines all the security roles used in the application.

Let's get back to the configurations for basic authentication that we were discussing. The `web.xml` file that we used for this example is read by the web server to infer that the web application uses basic authentication and that any URI access must be authenticated for the role name, `APIUser`. This means that to access the URI, `http://hostname:port/rest-chapter6-service/webresources/hr/departments`, the user should belong to the `APIUser` role.

We have not yet finished the configuration entries for the web application. The following step is to map the role that we specified in `web.xml` (`APIUser`) to the user groups that we will define on the server. This configuration is done on the vendor-specific deployment descriptor, `glassfish-web.xml`:

```xml
<?xml version="1.0" encoding="UTF-8"?>
<glassfish-web-app error-url="">
    <!-- Other entries go here -->
    <security-role-mapping>
        <!-- maps "Users" group to APIUser -->
        <role-name>APIUser</role-name>
        <group-name>Users</group-name>
    </security-role-mapping>
</glassfish-web-app>
```

While configuring the security realm on the server, we should map the actual users of the application to the user groups as appropriate. This is explained in the next section. Though the basic concepts of the security configuration remain the same across various Java EE servers, the actual steps may vary. This example takes GlassFish as a server and explains the security configurations in the next section.

Defining groups and users in the GlassFish server

GlassFish allows you to define users for the application using the concept of realms. As we mentioned in the previous section, a security realm can be treated as a mechanism that allows us to define users and groups. GlassFish offers various credential realms, including FileRealm, JDBCRealm, JNDIRealm, LDAPRealm, and so on. In this example, we will use an existing FileRealm that comes with GlassFish by default. Here are the steps for adding users and groups to the FileRealm in GlassFish:

1. Start the GlassFish server. If you are new to the GlassFish server, take a look at the tutorial at `https://javaee.github.io/glassfish/doc/4.0/quick-start-guide.pdf`.
2. Log in as the administrator to **Admin interface**.

2. Navigate to **Configurations** | **server-config** | **Security** | **Realms** | **File**. In this example, we use a file to store the user information. In a real-life scenario, you may use LDAP or RDBMS:

4. Click on the **Manage User** button at the top of the page:

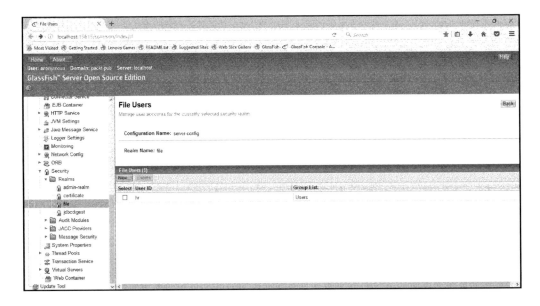

5. On the **File Users** page, click on **New**, add a user, and give a password. Set the appropriate **Group List** value. In web.xml, we have configured **Users** as a group, so specify the same name as a value for **Group List**, for this example:

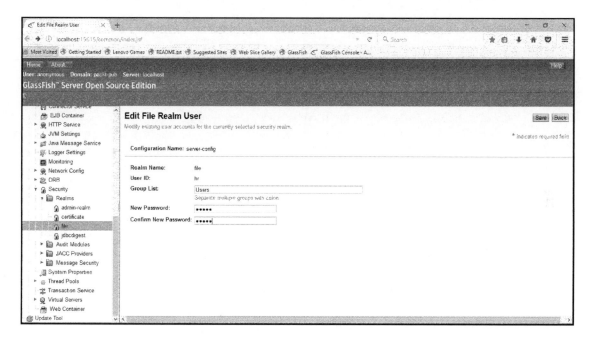

6. Click on **OK** to save the changes.

Now, you can deploy the secured RESTful web service application into the server. The client can use the username and password that we configured in this section for accessing the RESTful web APIs.

The basic authentication methods described here have a fundamental security hole. It sends the credentials as clear text in every HTTP request. Therefore, we need a mechanism to ensure that the credentials cannot be spoofed during a transaction. The solution is to use the **Secure Socket Layer (SSL)** or **Transport Layer Security (TLS)** protocol.

SSL is the standard for securing data transfer over the internet. HTTP over SSL (HTTPS) is used to secure connections between the internet browser client and server. The HTTPS protocol uses certificates to ensure secure communications between the client and server. The latest version of the SSL standard is called TLS.

TLS/SSL is a well-understood web protocol, and because the RESTful web services we implemented in the previous chapters are nothing more than the server components, all we need to do is configure GlassFish to use the TLS/SSL; therefore, every request and response message between the clients and servers, assuming the TLS/SSL has been configured properly, will now be encrypted.

Just remember that once the TLS/SSL has been turned on, the requests will be HTTPS requests; this means that URIs take the form of `https://<REST-RESOURCE-URI>` (note the `https` prefix in the address).

> For the sake of brevity, we have not covered how to configure TLS/SSL in this book. The GlassFish server administration guide covers this topic in *Chapter 14, Administering Internet Connectivity*. You can download the administration guide from `https://javaee.github.io/glassfish/doc/4.0/administration-guide.pdf`.
>
> To learn how to set up the SSL configuration on the Jersey client, take a look at *Section 5.9, Securing a Client* in the *Jersey 2.26 User Guide*. The link to the documentation is `https://jersey.github.io/documentation/latest/index.html`.

HTTP digest authentication

To overcome the challenge with using clear text login credentials in HTTP basic authentication, the cryptographic hash of the login credentials are used for HTTP digest authentication. The client sends a one-way cryptographic hash of the username, password, and a few other security-related fields using the MD5 message-digest hash algorithm. When the server receives the request, it regenerates the hashed value for all the fields used by the client to generate the hash and compare it with the one present in the request. If the hashes match, the request is treated as authenticated and valid. To follow the steps of configuring the digest authentication realm in the GlassFish server, refer to *Chapter 2, Administering User Security in GlassFish Security Guide*.

If the client application uses the Jersey framework implementation, then the API to invoke the RESTful web services secured via the HTTP digest authentication looks like the following code snippet:

```
//Rest of the imports are removed for brevity
import org.glassfish.jersey.client.authentication.
    HTTP_AUTHENTICATION_DIGEST_USERNAME;
import org.glassfish.jersey.client.authentication.
```

```
    HTTP_AUTHENTICATION_DIGEST_PASSWORD;

//Client code goes here
final String RESOURCE_URI =
    "http://localhost:8080/hrapp/departments";
Client client = javax.ws.rs.client.ClientBuilder.newClient();
//Provide the username and password, and invoke method
Response response = client.target(RESOURCE_URI).request()
  .property(HTTP_AUTHENTICATION_DIGEST_USERNAME, "<Username>")
  .property(HTTP_AUTHENTICATION_DIGEST_PASSWORD, "<Password>")
  .get();
```

JWT authentication

With HTTP being a stateless protocol, following HTTP authentication means that the client has to be authenticated with its credentials for every request. For stateful applications, this becomes an issue, as the user will be prompted to log in for every action they perform. For example, once the user logs in via a shopping cart application, he/she may proceed with choosing the selected items and checking out until he/she is done with the shopping. To handle such scenarios, the legacy solution was to implement session-based authentication, which uses server sessions to maintain the authenticated state of a client.

In session-based authentication, after the authentication of the user, a session ID is created by the server and sent in the HTTP response using cookies, and the same is passed along with every subsequent request to the server. So, until the user logs out of the application or the session expires, the client can continue to use the application. The same is illustrated in the following diagram:

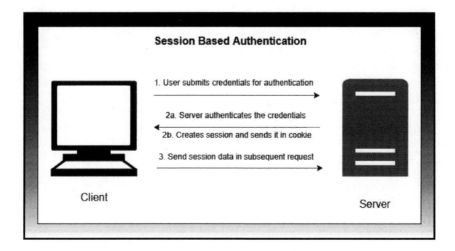

The preceding pattern may work well with monolithic applications but not for hybrid applications, wherein different functionalities in an application will be implemented as separate services and deployed in their own container. Modern single-page web applications or mobile applications will have to interact with multiple backend services hosted on different servers to fetch the data. For example, the user home page may have to display the weather forecast based on the location and a stock ticker based on the trading account held by the user. In this case, as the weather forecast and the stock ticker service may be hosted on different servers, sharing the session cookie will not be possible.

What is the solution for hybrid applications if the session-based authentication fails?

Let me give a clue. Session-based authentication can be considered analogous to legacy lockers. Think about opening the main door of a house using keys and getting access to the house. In this case, anyone with the relevant keys for the main door lock can log in to the house. Hmm!

Digital transformation helps to address the aforementioned security concern. The solution is digitizing the legacy keys with electronic keys and the access grants customized specific to the user. For example, take the case of an employee ID card. Before issuing the employee ID card, the details are verified first and then the employee ID card is granted with access to an organization's common floor or a specific department and prohibited access to the other departments or secure data centers. Also the access granted is timebound and can be revoked when required. The best part of digital keys is that they can be used across multiple locations. **JSON Web Token (JWT)** is similar in concept to digital keys; it follows a token-based authentication approach. In token-based authentication, the user supplies the credentials to acquire a token with a predefined validity from the Auth Server, and the token can be used further to access the resources as per the claims of the user:

JSON Web Token (JWT) overview

JWT is self-contained and secured compared to the session ID, as it is digitally signed. JWT consists of the following building blocks:

- **Header**: This contains the token type and hashing algorithm
- **Body**: This contains the reserved or custom claims, which serves the user verification details
- **Signature**: This contains the cryptographic signature made out of the encoded data and private key

Here is a graphical representation of the JWT:

For more details on JWT, refer to the JWT specifications at `https://tools.ietf.org/html/rfc7519`.

The RFC 7523 (`https://tools.ietf.org/html/rfc7523`) specification details the usage of JWT for OAuth2.0 client authentication and authorization grants. OAuth2.0 will be covered in the subsequent sections.

Using JWT to secure RESTful services

We will now see how to secure RESTful services using JWT. Let's take the HR service developed in the previous chapter for this purpose. For illustration purposes, we will be abstracting the authentication as part of `HRService`. In a real-life scenario, the authentication service will be deployed in a separate server. The authentication function will validate the user credentials and respond back with the JWT token for valid users; otherwise, it sends an unauthorized status in response, as follows:

```
/**
* Performs authentication of the user and generates JWT Token
*
* @return JWT Token in the Response
*/
@POST
@Path("/login")
@Consumes(APPLICATION_FORM_URLENCODED)
public Response authenticateUser(@FormParam("login") String login,
                                 @FormParam("password") String
password) {
    try {
        // TO-DO Authenticate the user using the credentials provided
        //for brevity authenticaton of credentials is not included.
        //Also as best practice authentication service will be hosted
on
        //dedicated auth server.
        // Issue a token for the user
        String token =
JWTAuthHelper.issueToken(login,uriInfo.getAbsolutePath().toString());
        // Return the token in the response HTTP Authorization Header
        return Response.ok().header(AUTHORIZATION, "Bearer " +
token).build();
    } catch (Exception e) {
        return Response.status(UNAUTHORIZED).build();
    }
}
```

Once the JWT token is sent to the client, the client uses the token to invoke business functions, such as `findDepartment`:

```
//Step-1: Submit the login credential to fetch the JWT token
String token = hrServiceClient.getToken("xxxxxx", "yyyyyy");

logger.log(Level.INFO, "Obtained Token:{0}", token);

//Step-2: Find the department using the valid token
if (token != null && !"".equals(token.trim())) {
    Department dept =
hrServiceClient.findDepartMent(Department.class, "10", token);
    if(dept != null)
        logger.log(Level.INFO, dept.toString());
}
```

How does the `findDepartment` function know that the supplied token is valid? This is accomplished using a custom `ContainerRequestFilter` filter called the `JWTAuthValidationFilter` class:

```
@Provider
@JWTTokenRequired
@Priority(Priorities.AUTHENTICATION)
public class JWTAuthValidationFilter implements ContainerRequestFilter {

    private static final Logger logger =
Logger.getLogger(JWTAuthValidationFilter.class.getName());
    @Override
    public void filter(ContainerRequestContext requestContext) throws
IOException {
        //Step-1: Get the HTTP Authorization header from the request
        String authorizationHeader =
requestContext.getHeaderString(HttpHeaders.AUTHORIZATION);
        logger.log(Level.INFO, "Authorization Header : {0}",
authorizationHeader);

        //Step-2: Check if the Authorization header contains the Token
        if (authorizationHeader == null ||
!authorizationHeader.startsWith("Bearer ")) {
            logger.log(Level.SEVERE, "Invalid Authorization Header : {0}",
authorizationHeader);
            throw new NotAuthorizedException("Authorization header is
missing");
        }

        //Step-3: Extract the token from the Authorization header
        String token =
```

```
authorizationHeader.substring("Bearer".length()).trim();

        //Step-4: Validate the token. If invalid, set UNAUTHORIZED response
status
        if(!JWTAuthHelper.isValidToken(token)) {
requestContext.abortWith(Response.status(Response.Status.UNAUTHORIZED).buil
d());
        }
    }
}
```

This class will be bound to `JWTTokenRequired` so that the `JWTTokenRequired` annotation can be used relevantly to secure the `findDepartment` function, as follows:

```
/**
 * Get the department details of the specified department only
 * when valid authentication token was provided.
 *
 * @return Department
 */
@GET
@Path("departments/{id}")
@Produces(MediaType.APPLICATION_JSON)
@JWTTokenRequired
public Department findDepartment(@PathParam("id") @Min(value = 0,
message = "Department Id must be a positive value") Short id, @Context
Request request) {

        Department department = entityManager.find(Department.class, id);
        return department;
}
```

Let's wrap up the overall interaction with the following sequence diagram to get an end-to-end view:

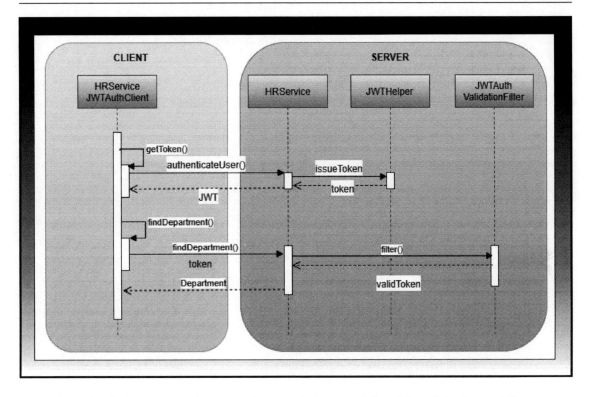

Now, let's check the program's output by supplying a valid and invalid token while invoking the findDepartment function of HRService. With a valid token, the corresponding department details are fetched, while the invalid token results in an HTTP 401 Unauthorized error message:

Program Output:
com.packtpub.rest.ch6.client.HRServiceJWTAuthClient main
INFO: Obtained Token:Bearer
eyJhbGciOiJIUzUxMiJ9.eyJzdWIiOiJ4eHh4eHgiLCJpc3MiOiJodHRwOi8vbG9jYWxob3N0Oj
E1NjQ3L3Jlc3QtY2hhcHRlcjYtand0c2VydmljZS93ZWJyZXNvdXJjZXMvaHIvbG9naW4iLCJpY
XQiOjE1MDM3NzIwNjEsImV4cCI6MTUwMzc3Mjk2MX0.9pUgOkC39yzDGmM9FCtB9tmqA1Wutbhe
KCd94fRkpe_ePC2hvZ3DB50bPOvFvg4eac1NYs30pSWLm9pjm-Mv_g
com.packtpub.rest.ch6.client.HRServiceJWTAuthClient main
INFO: Outcome using valid token:Bearer
eyJhbGciOiJIUzUxMiJ9.eyJzdWIiOiJ4eHh4eHgiLCJpc3MiOiJodHRwOi8vbG9jYWxob3N0Oj
E1NjQ3L3Jlc3QtY2hhcHRlcjYtand0c2VydmljZS93ZWJyZXNvdXJjZXMvaHIvbG9naW4iLCJpY
XQiOjE1MDM3NzIwNjEsImV4cCI6MTUwMzc3Mjk2MX0.9pUgOkC39yzDGmM9FCtB9tmqA1Wutbhe
KCd94fRkpe_ePC2hvZ3DB50bPOvFvg4eac1NYs30pSWLm9pjm-Mv_g
com.packtpub.rest.ch6.client.HRServiceJWTAuthClient main
INFO: com.packtpub.rest.ch4.model.Department[departmentId=10]
com.packtpub.rest.ch6.client.HRServiceJWTAuthClient main

```
INFO: Outcome using invalid token:t@´—à%O˜v+nî...SYg¯µ$%...9cZ
com.packtpub.rest.ch6.client.HRServiceJWTAuthClient main
SEVERE: HTTP 401 Unauthorized
```

In the preceding example, the JWT library is used to issue and verify the JWT token. The following maven dependencies must be included to build the project:

```
<!--Begin : Added for JWT -->
<dependency>
            <groupId>io.jsonwebtoken</groupId>
            <artifactId>jjwt</artifactId>
            <version>0.7.0</version>
</dependency>
<dependency>
            <groupId>com.fasterxml.jackson.core</groupId>
            <artifactId>jackson-databind</artifactId>
            <version>2.8.2</version>
</dependency>
<!-- End : Added for JWT -->
```

The complete source code for this example is available on the Packt website. You can download the example from the Packt website link that we mentioned at the beginning of this book, in the *Preface* section. In the downloaded source code, see the `rest-chapter6-jwt` project.

Securing RESTful web services with OAuth

OAuth is an open standard for authorization, used by many enterprises and service providers to protect their resources. OAuth solves a different security problem from what HTTP basic authentication has been used for. The OAuth protocol allows client applications to access protected resources on behalf of the resource owner (typically, the application user).

If we look at the history of this protocol, OAuth version 1.0 was published as RFC 5849 in 2010. Later, the next evolution of OAuth, version 2.0, was published as RFC 6749 in 2012. Note that these two versions are different in their implementations and do not have many things in common. In this section, we will explore what the OAuth protocol and its details are. We will also discuss accessing OAuth-protected RESTful web APIs from a RESTful web service client.

Understanding the OAuth 1.0 protocol

The OAuth protocol specifies a process for resource owners to authorize third-party applications to access their server resources without sharing their credentials.

Consider a scenario where Jane (the user of an application) wants to let an application access her private data, which is stored in a third-party service provider. Before OAuth 1.0 or other similar open source protocols, such as Google AuthSub and FlickrAuth, if Jane wanted to let a consumer service use her data stored on some third-party service provider, she would need to give her user credentials to the consumer service to access data from the third-party service via appropriate service calls. Instead of Jane passing her login information to multiple consumer applications, OAuth 1.0 solves this problem by letting the consumer applications request authorization from the service provider on Jane's behalf. Jane does not divulge her login information; authorization is granted from the service provider, where both her data and credentials are stored. The consumer application (or consumer service) only receives an authorization token that can be used to access data from the service provider. Note that the user (Jane) has full control of the transaction and can invalidate the authorization token at any time during the signup process, or even after the two services have been used together.

The typical example used to explain OAuth 1.0 is that of a service provider that stores pictures on the web (let's call the service StorageInc) and a fictional consumer service that is a picture printing service (let's call the service PrintInc). On its own, PrintInc is a full-blown web service, but it does not offer picture storage; its business is only printing pictures. For convenience, PrintInc has created a web service that lets its users download their pictures from StorageInc for printing.

This is what happens when a user (the resource owner) decides to use PrintInc (the client application) to print his/her images stored in StorageInc (the service provider):

1. The user creates an account in PrintInc. Let's call the user Jane, to keep things simple.
2. PrintInc asks whether Jane wants to use her pictures stored in StorageInc and presents a link to get the authorization to download her pictures (the protected resources). Jane is the resource owner here.
3. Jane decides to let PrintInc connect to StorageInc on her behalf and clicks on the authorization link.

4. Both PrintInc and StorageInc have implemented the OAuth protocol, so StorageInc asks Jane whether she wants to let PrintInc use her pictures. If she says yes, then StorageInc asks Jane to provide her username and password. Note, however, that her credentials are being used at StorageInc's site and PrintInc has no knowledge of her credentials.

5. Once Jane provides her credentials, StorageInc passes PrintInc an authorization token, which is stored as a part of Jane's account on PrintInc.

6. Now, we are back at PrintInc's web application, and Jane can now print any of her pictures stored in StorageInc's web service.

7. Finally, every time Jane wants to print more pictures, all she needs to do is come back to PrintInc's website and download her pictures from StorageInc without providing the username and password again, as she has already authorized these two web services to exchange data on her behalf.

The preceding example clearly portrays the authorization flow in OAuth 1.0 protocol. Before getting deeper into OAuth 1.0, here is a brief overview of the common terminologies and roles that we saw in this example:

- **Client (consumer)**: This refers to an application (service) that tries to access a protected resource on behalf of the resource owner and with the resource owner's consent. A client can be a business service, mobile, web, or desktop application. In the previous example, PrintInc is the client application.

- **Server (service provider)**: This refers to an HTTP server that understands the OAuth protocol. It accepts and responds to the requests authenticated with the OAuth protocol from various client applications (consumers). If you relate this with the previous example, StorageInc is the service provider.

- **Protected resource**: Protected resources are resources hosted on servers (the service providers) that are access-restricted. The server validates all incoming requests and grants access to the resource, as appropriate.

- **Resource owner**: This refers to an entity capable of granting access to a protected resource. Mostly, it refers to an end user who owns the protected resource. In the previous example, Jane is the resource owner.

- **Consumer key and secret (client credentials)**: These two strings are used to identify and authenticate the client application (the consumer) making the request.

- **Request token (temporary credentials)**: This is a temporary credential provided by the server when the resource owner authorizes the client application to use the resource. As the next step, the client will send this request token to the server to get authorized. On successful authorization, the server returns an access token. The access token is explained next.

- **Access token (token credentials)**: The server returns an access token to the client when the client submits the temporary credentials obtained from the server during the resource grant approval by the user. The access token is a string that identifies a client that requests for protected resources. Once the access token is obtained, the client passes it along with each resource request to the server. The server can then verify the identity of the client by checking this access token.

The following sequence diagram shows the interactions between the various parties involved in the OAuth 1.0 protocol:

You can get more information about the OAuth 1.0 protocol at http://tools.ietf.org/html/rfc5849, which is their official website.

Building the OAuth 1.0 client using Jersey APIs

Let's build a simple client to understand the API usage for accessing the OAuth 1.0 protected resource. Note that the JAX-RS specification does not have standardized APIs for the OAuth client yet. This example uses the Jersey API to build the OAuth 1.0 client.

 The complete source code for this example is available on the Packt website. You can download the example from the Packt website link that is mentioned at the beginning of this book, in the *Preface* section. In the downloaded source code, see the `rest-chapter6-oauth1-client` project.

You should start by specifying the dependency to the `oauth1-client` JAR file in the client application. If you use Maven to build the client, the dependency entry in `pom.xml` may look as follows:

```
<dependency>
    <groupId>org.glassfish.jersey.security</groupId>
    <artifactId>oauth1-client</artifactId>
    <!-- specify appropriate version(2.26-b09) -->
    <version>${jersey.version}</version>
</dependency>
```

Here are the detailed steps for accessing the OAuth 1.0 protected resource:

1. OAuth 1.0 includes a consumer key and a matching consumer secret that together authenticate the client application to the service provider. You may want to obtain these credentials from the respective service provider for use in the client code. The `org.glassfish.jersey.client.oauth1.OAuth1ClientSupport` class is the starter class to build the support for OAuth 1.0 into the Jersey client. The `OAuth1Builder` object obtained from `OAuth1ClientSupport` can be used to build `OAuth1AuthorizationFlow` by calling the `authorizationFlow()` method. The `authorizationFlow()` method takes the following endpoints (these values can be obtained from the service provider):
   - **Request token URI**: This is the URI of the endpoint on the authorization server, where the request token can be obtained
   - **Access token URI**: This is the URI of the endpoint on the authorization server, where the access token can be obtained
   - **Authorization URI**: This is the URI of the endpoint on the authorization server to which the user (the resource owner) should be redirected in order to grant access to this application (our consumer)

2. The following code snippet illustrates the previously discussed step. This example tries to access the Twitter API protected with OAuth 1.0:

```
//Other imports are not shown for brevity
import javax.ws.rs.client.Client;
import javax.ws.rs.client.ClientBuilder;
import javax.ws.rs.core.Feature;
import org.glassfish.jersey.client.oauth1.ConsumerCredentials;
import org.glassfish.jersey.client.oauth1.OAuth1AuthorizationFlow;
import org.glassfish.jersey.client.oauth1.OAuth1ClientSupport;

// Read consumer key/secret from API provider
// You should obtain these keys from appropriate
// service provider (e.g. Twitter)
final String CONSUMER_KEY = "xxxxxxxx";
final String CONSUMER_SECRET =  "xxxxxxx";
// ConsumerCredentials stores client secret as
// byte array to improve security.
final ConsumerCredentials consumerCredentials = new
    ConsumerCredentials( CONSUMER_KEY,  CONSUMER_SECRET);
//Build the OAuth1AuthorizationFlow by supplying URI for
//reading request token, access token and authorize token
//This client reads Tweets on behalf of the end user
final OAuth1AuthorizationFlow oauth1AuthoriznFlow =
    OAuth1ClientSupport.builder(consumerCredentials)
        .authorizationFlow(
            "https://api.twitter.com/oauth/request_token",
            "https://api.twitter.com/oauth/access_token",
            "https://api.twitter.com/oauth/authorize")
            .build();
```

3. Once you have the `org.glassfish.jersey.client.oauth1.OAuth1AuthorizationFlow` instance ready, you can kick off the authorization process. To start the authorization process, call the `start()` method on the `OAuth1AuthorizationFlow` instance. Under the cover, the `start()` method makes a request to the request token URI and gets the request token that will be used for the authorization process. The method returns the authorization URI as a string:

```
//Get authorization URI
String authorizationUri = oauth1AuthoriznFlow
    .start();
```

4. The next step in the authorization flow is to redirect the user to the authorization URI returned by the `start()` method. If the client is a web application, you can use servlet APIs or JAX-RS APIs to implement the redirection.

5. After successful authorization, the authorization server redirects the user back to the URI specified by `OAuth1Builder.FlowBuilder::callbackUri(String)` and also provides `oauth_verifier` as a query parameter in the callback URI. The client should extract this parameter from the request and finish the authorization flow by calling the `finish(verifier)` method. The `finish()` method will internally request the access token from the authorization server and return it:

```
//Get the access token and finish the authorization flow
AccessToken accessToken = oauth1AuthoriznFlow.finish(verifier);
```

 OAuth 1.0 works by ensuring that both the client and server share an OAuth token and a consumer secret. The client must generate a signature on every request (or REST API call) by encrypting a bunch of unique information using the consumer secret. The server must generate the same signature, and only grant access if both the signatures match.

6. The OAuth client application used in this example will use the access token obtained from the `AccessToken` instance together with the client secret from the `org.glassfish.jersey.client.oauth1.ConsumerCredentials` object to perform OAuth-authenticated requests to the service provider. Remember that we have created the `ConsumerCredentials` instance at the beginning of this example as a part of the `OAuth1AuthorizationFlow` initialization by passing the consumer key and secret.

7. The `OAuth1` filter feature obtained by calling `getOAuth1Feature()` on the `OAuth1AuthorizationFlow` object can be used to configure client instances to perform authenticated requests to the server. This filter feature will prepare all the requests from the client compatible to OAuth 1.0. The following code snippet illustrates the use of the OAuth filter feature to access the protected resources from the service provider:

```
//See the code snippet at the beginning of this section
//to know how we created oauth1AuthoriznFlow object
Feature filterFeature = oauth1AuthoriznFlow.getOAuth1Feature();
//create a new Jersey client and register filter
//feature that will add OAuth signatures and  access token
Client client = ClientBuilder.newBuilder()
        .register(filterFeature)
        .build();
```

```
// Protected REST API URI that application wants to access:
//https://<service-provider>/<resource>"
//This example access following twitter API
final String PROTECTED_RESOURCE_URI =
    "https://api.twitter.com/1.1/statuses/home_timeline.json";

  // make requests to protected resources
  final Response response =
        client.target(PROTECTED_RESOURCE_URI).request().get();
if (response.getStatus() != 200) {
  String errorEntity = null;
  if (response.hasEntity()) {
    errorEntity = response.readEntity(String.class);
  }
  throw new RuntimeException(
      "Request to protected resource was not successful");
}else{
    //Code for processing the response goes here
     String result = response.readEntity(String.class);
  }
```

After having understood the OAuth 1.0 protocol and its usage, let's move on to the OAuth 2.0 protocol. The next section discusses this topic in detail.

Understanding the OAuth 2.0 protocol

OAuth 2.0 is the latest release of the OAuth protocol, mainly focused on simplifying the client-side development. Note that OAuth 2.0 is a completely new protocol, and this release is not backwards-compatible with OAuth 1.0. It offers specific authorization flows for web applications, desktop applications, mobile phones, and living room devices. The following are some of the major improvements in OAuth 2.0, as compared to the previous release:

- **The complexity involved in signing each request**: OAuth 1.0 mandates that the client must generate a signature on every API call to the server resource using the token secret. On the receiving end, the server must regenerate the same signature, and the client will be given access only if both the signatures match. OAuth 2.0 requires neither the client nor the server to generate any signature for securing the messages. Security is enforced via the use of TLS/SSL (HTTPS) for all communication.

- **Addressing non-browser client applications**: Many features of OAuth 1.0 are designed by considering the way a web client application interacts with the inbound and outbound messages. This has proven to be inefficient while using it with non-browser clients such as on-device mobile applications. OAuth 2.0 addresses this issue by accommodating more authorization flows suitable for specific client needs that do not use any web UI, such as on-device (native) mobile applications or API services. This makes the protocol very flexible.
- **The separation of roles**: OAuth 2.0 clearly defines the roles for all parties involved in the communication, such as the client, resource owner, resource server, and authorization server. The specification is clear on which parts of the protocol are expected to be implemented by the resource owner, authorization server, and resource server.
- **The short-lived access token**: Unlike in the previous version, the access token in OAuth 2.0 can contain an expiration time, which improves the security and reduces the chances of illegal access.
- **The refresh token**: OAuth 2.0 offers a refresh token that can be used for getting a new access token on the expiry of the current one, without going through the entire authorization process again.

Before we get into the details of OAuth 2.0, let's take a quick look at how OAuth 2.0 defines roles for each party involved in the authorization process. Though you might have seen similar roles while discussing OAuth 1.0 in last section, it does not clearly define which part of the protocol is expected to be implemented by each one:

- **The resource owner**: This refers to an entity capable of granting access to a protected resource. In a real-life scenario, this can be an end user who owns the resource.
- **The resource server**: This hosts the protected resources. The resource server validates and authorizes the incoming requests for the protected resource by contacting the authorization server.
- **The client (consumer)**: This refers to an application that tries to access protected resources on behalf of the resource owner. It can be a business service, mobile, web, or desktop application.
- **Authorization server**: This, as the name suggests, is responsible for authorizing the client that needs access to a resource. After successful authentication, the access token is issued to the client by the authorization server. In a real-life scenario, the authorization server may be either the same as the resource server or a separate entity altogether. The OAuth 2.0 specification does not really enforce anything on this part.

It would be interesting to learn how these entities talk with each other to complete the authorization flow. The following is a quick summary of the authorization flow in a typical OAuth 2.0 implementation:

Let's understand the diagram in more detail:

1. The client application requests authorization to access the protected resources from the resource owner (user). The client can either directly make the authorization request to the resource owner or via the authorization server by redirecting the resource owner to the authorization server endpoint.

2. The resource owner authenticates and authorizes the resource access request from the client application and returns the authorization grant to the client. The authorization grant type returned by the resource owner depends on the type of client application that tries to access the OAuth protected resource. Note that the OAuth 2.0 protocol defines four types of grants in order to authorize access to protected resources. To learn more about grant types, please take a look at the *Understanding the grant types in OAuth 2.0* section.

3. The client application requests an access token from the authorization server by passing the authorization grant along with other details for authentication, such as the client ID, client secret, and grant type.

4. On successful authentication, the authorization server issues an access token (and, optionally, a refresh token) to the client application.

5. The client application requests the protected resource (RESTful web API) from the resource server by presenting the access token for authentication.

6. On successful authentication of the client request, the resource server returns the requested resource.

The sequence of interaction that we just discussed is of a very high level. Depending upon the grant type used by the client, the details of the interaction may change. The following section will help you understand the basics of grant types.

Understanding the grant types in OAuth 2.0

Grant types in the OAuth 2.0 protocol are, in essence, different ways to authorize access to protected resources using different security credentials (for each type). The OAuth 2.0 protocol defines four types of grants, as listed here; each can be used in different scenarios, as appropriate:

- **Authorization code**: This is obtained from the authentication server instead of directly requesting it from the resource owner. In this case, the client directs the resource owner to the authorization server, which returns the authorization code to the client. This is very similar to OAuth 1.0, except that the cryptographic signing of messages is not required in OAuth 2.0.
- **Implicit**: This grant is a simplified version of the authorization code grant type flow. In the implicit grant flow, the client is issued an access token directly as the result of the resource owner's authorization. This is less secure, as the client is not authenticated. This is commonly used for client-side devices, such as mobile, where the client credentials cannot be stored securely.
- **Resource owner password credentials**: The resource owner's credentials, such as username and password, are used by the client for directly obtaining the access token during the authorization flow. The access code is used thereafter for accessing resources. This grant type is only used with trusted client applications. This is suitable for legacy applications that use the HTTP basic authentication to incrementally transition to OAuth 2.0.
- **Client credentials**: These are used directly for getting access tokens. This grant type is used when the client is also the resource owner. This is commonly used for embedded services and backend applications, where the client has an account (direct access rights).

> A very detailed discussion of the authorization flow for each grant type in OAuth 2.0 is not in the scope of this book. You can learn more about OAuth 2.0 at https://tools.ietf.org/html/rfc6749.

Building the OAuth 2.0 client using Jersey APIs

Let's build a simple OAuth 2.0 client using Jersey APIs to understand the API usage pattern.

 The complete source code for this example is available on the Packt website. You can download the example from the Packt website link that we mentioned at the beginning of this book, in the *Preface* section. In the downloaded source code, take a look at the `rest-chapter6-oauth2-webclient` project.

To use the Jersey OAuth 2.0 client APIs in your application, you need to add a dependency to the `oauth2-client` JAR file. If you use Maven, the dependency entry in `pom.xml` may look as shown in the following lines:

```xml
<dependency>
  <groupId>org.glassfish.jersey.security</groupId>
  <artifactId>oauth2-client</artifactId>
  <!-- specify appropriate version(2.26-b09) -->
  <version>${jersey.version}</version>
</dependency>
```

 The Jersey framework (version 2.26.x), which is the latest release available at the time of writing this book, does not offer any server APIs for protecting services via the OAuth 2.0 protocol.

As OAuth 2.0 is not a strictly defined protocol, you may not find a generic client API solution that works with all the implementations of OAuth 2.0 (by different vendors). The `org.glassfish.jersey.client.oauth2.OAuth2ClientSupport` class is the main starting class for an OAuth 2.0 client. You will use this as the starting class for building the OAuth 2.0 authorization flow. The current release of the `OAuth2ClientSupport` class (version 2.26.x) provides dedicated methods for building the authorization grant flow for accessing the OAuth 2.0 protected RESTful web APIs from vendors such as Google and Facebook. The following are the steps for building a Jersey client for Google Tasks APIs:

1. To start with the authorization code grant flow, generate an instance of `org.glassfish.jersey.client.oauth2.ClientIdentifier` by passing the client ID and client secret obtained from the service provider (authorization server). This is usually obtained while registering the client with the server. This example accesses the Google Tasks API to read the tasks. Remember that the Jersey OAuth 2.0 client supports only the authorization code grant type, and so, this example also uses the same type.

> The following link will help you with details for accessing the OAuth 2.0 protected Google APIs:
>
> https://developers.google.com/identity/protocols/OAuth2.
>
> High-level steps for obtaining the client ID and client secret are available at https://support.google.com/cloud/answer/6158849?hl=en.

2. Once you have the `ClientIdentifier` instance ready, the next step is to start building the authorization code grant flow for accessing the Google Tasks API by calling the `googleFlowBuilder()` method. This method has the following signature:

```
OAuth2ClientSupport::googleFlowBuilder(
    ClientIdentifier clientIdentifier, String redirectURI,
    String scope)
```

3. This call returns the `org.glassfish.jersey.client.oauth2.OAuth2FlowGoogleBuilder` object that can be directly used to generate the authorization code grant flow defined by Google. Here is the quick summary of parameters for the `googleFlowBuilder` method:

   - `clientIdentifier`: This is the `ClientIdentifier` instance created using the client ID and client secret issued by the service provider.
   - `redirectURI`: This is the URI to which the user (the resource owner) should be redirected to after the user grants access to the consumer application. It will pass null if the application does not support redirection (for example, if it is not a web application).
   - `Scope`: This is the API to which access is requested (for example, Google Tasks).

4. To start the authorization flow, get an instance of `org.glassfish.jersey.client.oauth2.OAuth2CodeGrantFlow` by calling the `build()` method on `OAuth2FlowGoogleBuilder`. The `OAuth2CodeGrantFlow` instance is capable of authorizing the user using the *Authorization Code Grant Flow*. The following code snippet demonstrates the API usage for generating `OAuth2CodeGrantFlow` to access the Google Tasks API:

```
//Other imports are not shown for brevity
import org.glassfish.jersey.client.oauth2.OAuth2ClientSupport;
import org.glassfish.jersey.client.oauth2.OAuth2CodeGrantFlow;
```

```
import org.glassfish.jersey.client.oauth2.OAuth2FlowGoogleBuilder;
import org.glassfish.jersey.client.oauth2.ClientIdentifier;
import org.glassfish.jersey.client.oauth2.TokenResult;

final String CLIENT_ID =  "xxxxx";
final String CLIENT_SECRET = "xxxxxx";
//Protected ApI that needs to be accessed by client app
String SCOPE = "https://www.googleapis.com/auth/tasks.readonly";

//On successful authorization user
//is redirected to this URI
String redirectURI =
    "http://localhost:8080/hrapp/api/oauth2/authorize";

ClientIdentifier clientIdentifier = new
    ClientIdentifier(CLIENT_ID, CLIENT_SECRET);
final OAuth2CodeGrantFlow oauth2CodeGrantflow =
    OAuth2ClientSupport.googleFlowBuilder(
        clientIdentifier,  redirectURI, SCOPE)
            .prompt(OAuth2FlowGoogleBuilder.Prompt.CONSENT)
            .build();
```

5. The `OAuth2CodeGrantFlow` instance is ready for use by now. Let's start the authorization process. The `OAuth2CodeGrantFlow` object defines the OAuth 2.0 authorization code grant flow for the client. You can start the flow by calling the `start()` method:

```
//Get the authorization URI
String authorizationUri = oauth2CodeGrantflow.start();
```

This call triggers the authorization process and returns an authorization URI on which the user should give consent to our application to access the resources. The client application should redirect the user to the authorization URI. The resource owner should authorize the client application on the authorization URI to proceed further. On successful authorization, the authorization server automatically redirects the user back to the redirect URI specified while building `OAuth2CodeGrantFlow`. The authorization server also provides the code and state as a request query parameter for the redirect URI. The client application needs to extract the code and state parameters from the request to use them with the access token request. The state parameter is used for preventing cross-site request forgery. It is added to the redirect URI in the `start` method; the same parameter should be returned from the authorization response as a protection against CSRF attacks.

6. To finish the authorization process, call
`OAuth2CodeGrantFlow::finish(String code, String state)` by supplying the code and state returned by the authorization server on authorization. The method will internally request the access token from the authorization server and return the result as a `TokenResult` object. The `TokenResult` object contains the result of the authorization flow, including the access token.

7. Later, you can call `OAuth2CodeGrantFlow::getAuthorizedClient()` to get the JAX-RS client, which is configured to perform authorized requests to the service provider. The returned JAX-RS client has all the necessary information about the consumer credentials and access token that were received during the authorization process. You can directly use this client to access the protected resources. The following code snippet illustrates the usage of client APIs, as explained in steps 5-6:

```
//Step 5: code and state are returned by authorization server
TokenResult tokenResult = oauth2CodeGrantflow.finish(code, state);
//Step 6: Get the authorized client
Client client = oauth2CodeGrantflow.getAuthorizedClient();
String GOOGLE_TAKS_URI =
    "https://www.googleapis.com/tasks/v1/users/@me/lists";
//Prepare client to call Google Tasks API
WebTarget service = client.target(GOOGLE_TAKS_URI);
//Get the response object and work on it
Response response =  service.request().get();
if(response.getStatus() == 200){
//Code for processing response such as building
//Java model etc goes here
    String output = response.getEntity(String.class);
}
```

With this, we have finished the discussion on OAuth. In the next section, you will learn how to control access to RESTful resources via security APIs.

Building OAuth 2.0 compliant services

If you feel that the support for OAuth in the current Jersey release is not enough to meet your use cases, you can look into other OAuth implementations available in Java. Apache Oltu is one such popular OAuth protocol implementation available today. You can learn more about Apache Oltu at `https://oltu.apache.org`.

Note that the Jersey framework (version 2.26.x), which is the latest release available at the time of writing this book, does not offer any server API for protecting your RESTful web services via OAuth 2.0. However, with Oltu, you can easily create OAuth 2.0-compliant server endpoints. More details can be found at `https://cwiki.apache.org/confluence/display/OLTU/OAuth+2.0+Authorization+Server` .

Authorizing the RESTful web service accesses via the security APIs

The authorization process verifies whether the client requesting or initiating an action has the right to do so. In this section, we will see how to use the JAX-RS APIs for authorizing the incoming REST API calls from various clients.

Using SecurityContext APIs to control access

We started off this chapter by discussing how an application authenticates a user who is trying to access a secured resource. When a client accesses a secured resource, the server identifies and validates the requester, and on successful authentication, the requester is allowed to get inside the application. During this process, the underlying security framework generates a `javax.ws.rs.core.SecurityContext` object, which holds security-related information pertaining to the requester. The JAX-RS framework allows you to access the `SecurityContext` object in the code in order to retrieve security-related information pertaining to the current request.

Some of the frequently used methods exposed by `SecurityContext` are given as follows:

- `getAuthenticationScheme()`: This method returns the authentication scheme used for protecting resources, such as HTTP basic, HTTP digest, NTLM, and so on
- `getUserPrincipal()`: This method returns the logged-in username
- `isSecure()`: This returns `true` if the request is made through a secure channel (HTTPS)
- `isUserInRole(String role)`: This returns `true` if the logged-in user is in the role supplied as a parameter for this method

Please refer to the following API doc to learn more about
`SecurityContext`:
`http://docs.oracle.com/javaee/7/api/javax/ws/rs/core/SecurityCon`
`text.html`.

You can access `SecurityContext` in the JAX-RS resource methods and call the appropriate
APIs on it to perform the authorization of the requester. The following is an example
demonstrating the usage of `SecurityContext::isUserInRole(String)`. In this
example, the system information is returned to the caller but only if the requested user
(client) is in an admin role:

```java
//Other imports are not shown for brevity
import javax.ws.rs.core.Context;
import javax.ws.rs.core.MediaType;
import javax.ws.rs.core.Response;
import javax.ws.rs.core.SecurityContext;

@Path("system")
public class SystemResource {
    @GET
    @Path("info")
    public Response getSystemInfo(@Context SecurityContext
        securityContext) {
        String adminGroup = "admin";
        if (securityContext.isUserInRole(adminGroup)) {
            // getSystemInfo reads system info - not shown here
            SystemInfo sysInfo=getSystemInfo();
            return Response.ok(sysInfo,
                MediaType.APPLICATION_JSON).build();
        } else {
            return
                Response.status(Response.Status.FORBIDDEN).build();
        }
    }
}
```

Using the javax.annotation.security annotations to control access

The `javax.annotation.security` annotations available with Java EE simplify the coding effort for adding authentication and authorization checks for an application. The Jersey framework allows you to use the following `javax.annotation.security` annotations, on the JAX-RS resource class or methods, to control the access, based on the user role:

- `javax.annotation.security.DenyAl`: With this, no roles can invoke the annotated resource class or method
- `javax.annotation.security.PermitAll`: With this, all the security roles are allowed to invoke the annotated resource method(s)
- `javax.annotation.security.RolesAllowed`: This specifies the list of roles permitted to access the method(s) in an application

The security annotation support that we discussed in this section is brought into the RESTful web service resources via the Jersey framework, and you may not find it working in the same way with other implementations of JAX-RS.

To use the preceding annotations in your JAX-RS resource class or methods, you need to register the following dynamic feature provider offered by the Jersey framework: `org.glassfish.jersey.server.filter.RolesAllowedDynamicFeature`.

The following code snippet uses a subclass of `javax.ws.rs.core.Application` to register the `RolesAllowedDynamicFeature` provider:

```
//Other imports are removed for brevity
import org.glassfish.jersey.server.filter.RolesAllowedDynamicFeature;

@javax.ws.rs.ApplicationPath("webresources")
public class ApplicationConfig extends Application {
    @Override
    public Set<Class<?>> getClasses() {
        Set<Class<?>> resources = new java.util.HashSet<>();
        //Rest of the code goes here
        resources.add(RolesAllowedDynamicFeature.class);
        return resources;
    }
}
```

Let's see how to use the security annotation with a JAX-RS service to prevent unauthorized access. The following code snippet uses the `@RolesAllowed` security annotation to restrict access to the resource method. This example uses `@RolesAllowed("admin")` on the resource method to let only the users that have an admin role to access this API at runtime:

```
import javax.annotation.security.RolesAllowed;

@GET
@Path("security")
@RolesAllowed("admin")
public Response getSystemInfo() {
    // getSystemInfo reads system info
    //method definition is not shown here to save space
    SystemInfo sysInfo=getSystemInfo();
    return Response.ok(sysInfo,
        MediaType.APPLICATION_JSON).build();
}
```

Using Jersey's role-based entity data filtering

The entity-filtering feature offered by the Jersey framework allows you to conveniently filter out any non-relevant data from the response entity. To use this feature, create custom entity-filtering annotations based on `@org.glassfish.jersey.message.filtering.EntityFiltering` and apply them on model entity fields that you want to filter out conditionally. Later, while generating a response for the REST API call, runtime will match the entity filtering annotation present on the resource method with the annotation present on the entity fields and include only those matching fields in the response content.

 To learn more about entity filtering offerings in the Jersey framework, read the following section in the Jersey User Guide available at `https://jersey.github.io/documentation/latest/entity-filtering.html`.

The Jersey framework has extended this filtering feature to use with security annotations. You can filter out entities, or specific entity attributes, from the response body by using security annotations (`@PermitAll`, `@RolesAllowed`, and `@DenyAll`). Jersey offers this support via the `org.glassfish.jersey.message.filtering.SecurityEntityFilteringFeature` provider. Let's take an example that uses this feature to shape the response content, based on user roles.

The very first step is to add a dependency to the Jersey entity filtering JAR. If you use Maven, the dependency entry in pom.xml may look like the following:

```xml
<dependency>
  <groupId>org.glassfish.jersey.ext</groupId>
  <artifactId>jersey-entity-filtering</artifactId>
  <version>${jersey.version}</version>
</dependency>
```

The next step is to register the SecurityEntityFilteringFeature provider in the application. Here is an example:

```java
//Other imports are not shown for brevity
import org.glassfish.jersey.server.ResourceConfig;

@javax.ws.rs.ApplicationPath("webresources")
public class ApplicationConfig extends ResourceConfig {
    public ApplicationConfig() {
        register(org.glassfish.jersey.message.filtering.
            SecurityEntityFilteringFeature.class);
        //Rest of the code goes here
        register("com.packtpub.rest.ch6.security.resources");
        register(org.glassfish.jersey.server.filter.
            RolesAllowedDynamicFeature.class);
    }
}
```

Once you have configured the required things as discussed previously, the next step is to identify the field in the response entity object class definition that needs to be filtered out based on the user role. For instance, in the following example, you want to include the totalEmployees field of the Department entity in the response object only if the requesting user is in the administrator's or manager's role. You can achieve this by annotating the getTotalEmployees() method that returns totalEmployees with the @RolesAllowed({"manager", "admin"}) annotation, as shown in the following lines:

```java
//imports are omitted for brevity
@XmlRootElement
public class Department implements Serializable {
  private Short departmentId;
  private String departmentName;
  private Integer totalEmployees;
  private Integer managerId;

  @RolesAllowed({"manager", "admin"})
   public Integer getTotalEmployees() {
        return totalEmployees;
   }
```

```
    //All other getters and setters are not shown for brevity

}
```

The REST API method returning the discussed `Department` entity may look like the following:

```
@GET
@Path("departments/{id}")
@RolesAllowed({"users","manager","admin"})
@Produces("application/json")
public Department findDepartment(@PathParam("id") Short id) {
    Department dept= findDepartmentEntity(id);
    return dept;
}
```

At runtime, when a request for a department resource reaches the application (for example, `/departments/10`), the security entity filtering feature will check for user roles, and the `totalEmployees` attribute will be included in the entity response body only if the user role matches with the values given for the `@RolesAllowed` annotation that we had set in the `getTotalEmployees()` method in the `Department` model class.

For instance, with the previously described settings, when a normal user (*not* belonging to a manager's or admin's role) accesses the REST resource URI, `departments/300`, the `totalEmployees` attribute will not be rendered in the response entity body:

```
{"departmentId":300,"departmentName":"Administration",
"managerId":200}
```

Input validation

Input validation is the process of verifying the supplied data in the request against the contractual definition. Monitor the input validation failures, and to prevent the service quality degradation, consider restricting the access to consumers crossing the failure threshold limit. Developers leverage the JAX-RS 2.1 bean validation features to declaratively specify the validation constraints on an object model. If you need a quick brush up on bean validation support for the JAX-RS resource class, refer to the *Introducing validations in JAX-RS application* section in `Chapter 4`, *Advanced Features in the JAX-RS API*.

You can log the input validation failures for business-critical APIs. This may help you detect malformed and malicious inputs to the application.

Key considerations for securing RESTful services

In the previous sections, we covered in detail the various techniques for securing the RESTful services. Some of the best practices, apart from authentication and authorization, that are worth considering for securing RESTful services are listed as follows:

- A whitelist is a list of allowable actions on an entity; it is the reverse of blacklisting. It is important for a RESTful service to mention only the allowable action verbs such as GET/POST, so the other actions, even if triggered by the client, are denied.
- Validation of the URL is a must for RESTful services, as attackers tamper with the URL to perform injection attacks. Avoid encoding sensitive information in the URL.
- Ensure that the RESTful service definition includes the allowed content type.
- Ensure that the perimeter-level security is enabled using firewalls for enterprise services.
- The monitoring of the quality of service degradation helps to detect **Denial-Of-Service (DOS)**-type attacks.
- Not to undermine the security risks being overlooked from a coding perspective, use static code analysis tools such as Sonar to review the code for security vulnerabilities.

Summary

In this chapter, we covered the important topics of RESTful web service application development and security, albeit from a higher point of view than we did in the previous chapters. Because these topics require highly specialized knowledge, we only covered enough of them for you to be able to make pragmatic decisions during development. In all likelihood, the supporting environments for our web services will be managed by third-party vendors or internal IT departments.

In the next chapter, we will discuss various solutions for describing, producing, consuming, and visualizing RESTful web services.

7
Description and Discovery of RESTful Web Services

In the earlier days, many software solution providers did not really pay enough attention to documenting their RESTful web APIs, unlike web services, which used **Web Services Description Language (WSDL)**. However, many API vendors soon realized the need for a good API documentation solution in order to accelerate the adoption of their REST API services by customers, and to make it easier for businesses to understand the capabilities of the REST API. As a result, many REST API metadata standards have emerged in the recent past.

Today, you will find a variety of approaches to documenting RESTful web APIs. This chapter describes some of the popular solutions available today for describing, producing, consuming, and visualizing RESTful web services. This learning will definitely help you to quickly learn and use the other API documentation solutions available in the market.

The following solutions are covered in this chapter:

- Web Application Description Language
- RESTful API Modeling Language
- Swagger

The need for an interface contract

Having a well-documented interface contract enables design-time discovery. The API documentation for RESTful web services provides a standard, language-independent interface, which can be used by both humans and machines to discover the capabilities of APIs without accessing the source code. This chapter introduces a few of the various API documentation tools and options that you might choose from.

Let's start by discussing one of the earliest solutions for RESTful web API documentation—**Web Application Description Language (WADL)**.

Web Application Description Language

WADL is an XML description of HTTP-based web applications such as RESTful web services. WADL was submitted to the **World Wide Web Consortium (W3C)** by Sun in 2009 but has not been standardized yet.

Similar to WSDL used for describing SOAP web services, WADL models the resources provided by a RESTful web service with relationships between the resources. It also allows you to clearly represent the media types used for the request and response contents.

Overview of the WADL structure

The WADL schema that you use for building a WADL file is based on the WADL specification (`https://www.w3.org/Submission/wadl/`). Here is a quick overview of the WADL file content that describes the RESTful web APIs:

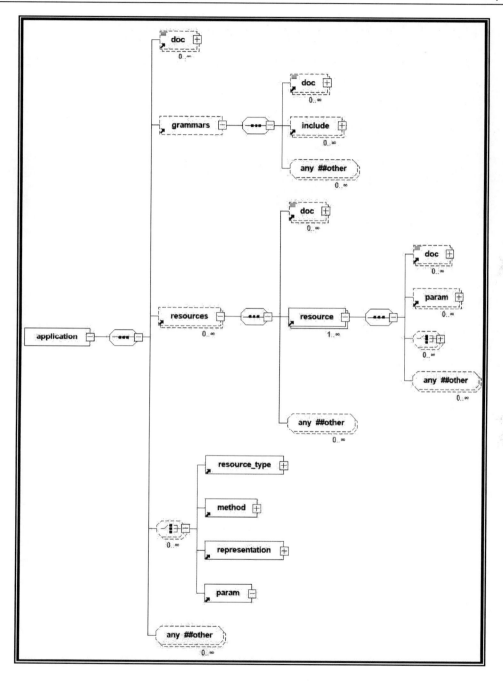

The top-level element in a WADL document is `application`. It contains global information about RESTful web services, such as links to the schema definition and documentation. Here is a quick summary of the elements that you'll see in WADL:

- `<resources>`: This element comes as wrapper for all the resources exposed by a RESTful web application. The `base` attribute for the resources identifies the base path of all the resources in the API.
- `<grammars>`: This element includes the definition of data formats using the `<include>` element, which references the data format with the `href` attribute.
- `<resource>`: This element appears as a child of the `<resources>` element. It is used for describing a set of resources, each identified by a URI. This element can optionally have `<param>` to describe the path parameters present in the request if any.
- `<method>`: A resource may have one or more `<method>` definitions. This element defines the HTTP methods, such as GET, POST, PUT, and DELETE, available to the resource with the relevant `request` and `response` elements. Note that the presence of this element in WADL represents a REST `resource` method in a RESTful web service.
- `<request>`: A `<method>` definition can optionally include this element, which describes an input to the `resource` method. A request can have one or more of the following elements as its child:
  - `<doc>`: This element is used for documenting the parameters
  - `<representation>`: This element specifies the internet media type for the payload present in the body of the request
  - `<param>`: This element specifies the query or header parameter present in the request

- `<response>`: This element specifies the result of invoking an HTTP method on a resource. The optional status code present in the response describes the list of the HTTP status codes associated with the response. A response can have one or more of the following elements as its child:
  - `<doc>`: This element is used for documenting the `<response>` header parameters
  - `<representation>`: This element describes the internet media type for the response content returned by the API
  - `<param>`: This element specifies the HTTP header parameters present in the response

To learn more about the WADL specification, visit
`http://www.w3.org/Submission/wadl`.

Let's take a look at a simple WADL example before proceeding further. See the following code snippet. This method returns a `Department` object for the department ID passed by the client:

```
@GET
@Path("{id}")
@Produces("application/json")
public Department findDepartment(@PathParam("id")
    Short id){
    //Method body is omitted for brevity
}
```

Wondering how the preceding REST API can be described in WADL? The following WADL code answers this question. You do not need to spend much time on understanding this WADL file structure at this point of time. We will discuss the generation of WADL from the JAX-RS resource class in detail later:

```
<application xmlns="http://wadl.dev.java.net/2009/02">
<doc xmlns:jersey="http://jersey.java.net/"
    jersey:generatedBy="Jersey: 2.10.4 2014-08-08 15:09:00"/>
<grammars/>
<resources base=
    "http://localhost:8080/hrapp/webresources/">
    <resource path="{id}">
        <param xmlns:xs="http://www.w3.org/2001/XMLSchema"
            name="id"
        style="template" type="xs:short"/>
            <method id="findDepartment" name="GET">
                <response>
                    <ns2:representation
                        xmlns:ns2=
                            "http://wadl.dev.java.net/2009/02"
                                xmlns=""
element="department"
                            mediaType="application/json"/>
                </response>
            </method>
        </resource>
    </resources>
</application>
```

Generating WADL from JAX-RS

The Jersey framework has a built-in support for generating the WADL file for your JAX-RS applications. In this section, we will discuss the Jersey support for generating the WADL file from the JAX-RS resource classes.

Consider the following JAX-RS web service implementation. The REST resource used in this example exposes the APIs for reading the list of departments, creating a department, and editing a department identified by the ID:

```
//Imports are removed for brevity
@Stateless
@Path("departments")
public class DepartmentResource{

    //Returns departments in the range specified via query params
    @GET
    @Produces("application/json")
    public List<Department> findAllDepartments(@QueryParam("from")
        Integer from, @QueryParam("to") Integer to) {
        return findAllDepartmentEntities(from, to);
    }

    //Creates department with data present in the request body
    @POST
    @Consumes("application/json")
    public void createDepartment(Department entity) {
        createDepartmentEntity(entity);
    }

    //Edits department with data present in the request body
    @PUT
    @Path("{id}")
    @Consumes("application/json")
    public void editDepartment(@PathParam("id") Short id,
        Department entity) {
        editDepartmentEntity(entity);
    }
    //Rest of the implementation is removed for brevity
}
```

The Department class used in this example will look like the following:

```
//Other imports are removed for brevity
import javax.xml.bind.annotation.XmlRootElement;
@XmlRootElement
public class Department implements Serializable {
```

```
    private Short departmentId;
    private String departmentName;
    private Integer managerId;
    private Short locationId;
//Getters and setters for the attributes are removed for brevity
}
```

The WADL generation feature is enabled in the Jersey framework by default. For instance, when you deploy the preceding JAX-RS application to a web server, the Jersey framework automatically generates a WADL file for all the JAX-RS resource classes present in the application. The generated WADL file is accessible via the following URI:
`http://<host>:<port>/<application-name>/<application-path>/application. wadl`

The URI for accessing WADL for this example is as follows:
`http://<host>:<port>/rest-chapter7-jaxrs2wadl/webresources/application. wadl`

The JAX-RS annotations present on the resource class decide how the APIs need to be represented in the WADL.

Every unique `@Path` value present in the resource class results in a new `<resource>` element in the generated WADL. Following this rule, this example adds the `findAllDepartments` and `createDepartment` methods as children to a common resource element, whereas the `editDepartment` method uses a path parameter, due to which this method is added as a child to a separate resource. In a nutshell, multiple `resource` methods with different HTTP methods but sharing the same `@Path` value will have the same parent `<resource>` element.

Here is the WADL file generated by the Jersey framework for the `DepartmentResource` resource shown in the preceding code:

```
<?xml version="1.0" encoding="UTF-8" standalone="yes"?>
<application xmlns="http://wadl.dev.java.net/2009/02">
    <doc xmlns:jersey="http://jersey.java.net/" jersey:generatedBy="Jersey:
2.21 2015-08-14 21:41:51"/>
    <doc xmlns:jersey="http://jersey.java.net/" jersey:hint="This is
simplified WADL with user and core resources only. To get full WADL with
extended resources use the query parameter detail. Link:
http://localhost:15647/rest-chapter7-jaxrs2wadl/webresources/application.wa
dl?detail=true"/>
    <grammars>
        <include href="application.wadl/xsd0.xsd">
            <doc title="Generated" xml:lang="en"/>
        </include>
    </grammars>
```

```
        <resources
base="http://localhost:15647/rest-chapter7-jaxrs2wadl/webresources/">
        <resource path="departments">
            <method id="createDepartment" name="POST">
                <request>
                    <ns2:representation
xmlns:ns2="http://wadl.dev.java.net/2009/02" xmlns="" element="department"
mediaType="application/json"/>
                </request>
            </method>
            <method id="findAllDepartments" name="GET">
                <request>
                    <param xmlns:xs="http://www.w3.org/2001/XMLSchema"
name="from" style="query" type="xs:int" default="1"/>
                    <param xmlns:xs="http://www.w3.org/2001/XMLSchema"
name="to" style="query" type="xs:int" default="100"/>
                </request>
                <response>
                    <ns2:representation
xmlns:ns2="http://wadl.dev.java.net/2009/02" xmlns="" element="department"
mediaType="application/json"/>
                </response>
            </method>
            <resource path="{id}">
                <param xmlns:xs="http://www.w3.org/2001/XMLSchema"
name="id" style="template" type="xs:short"/>
                <method id="findDepartment" name="GET">
                    <response>
                        <ns2:representation
xmlns:ns2="http://wadl.dev.java.net/2009/02" xmlns="" element="department"
mediaType="application/json"/>
                    </response>
                </method>
                <method id="editDepartment" name="PUT">
                    <request>
                        <ns2:representation
xmlns:ns2="http://wadl.dev.java.net/2009/02" xmlns="" element="department"
mediaType="application/json"/>
                    </request>
                </method>
            </resource>
        </resource>
    </resources>
</application>
```

If you want to disable the automatic generation of WADL in Jersey, configure `jersey.config.server.wadl.disableWadl` to `true`. This configuration parameter can be set in either of the following ways:

- By setting the `init-param` value, `jersey.config.server.wadl.disableWadl`, to `true` for the Jersey servlet (`org.glassfish.jersey.servlet.ServletContainer`) in `web.xml`
- By overriding `javax.ws.rs.core.Application::getProperties()` to return the map containing `jersey.config.server.wadl.disableWadl=true` as the property name and value

The default support for WADL in Jersey works for many use cases. However, it may fail to generate proper documentation in specific scenarios, as explained here:

- If the `resource` method returns the `javax.ws.rs.core.Response` object, Jersey will not be able to infer the HTTP response content and HTTP status codes returned by the method from the method signature
- Similarly, Jersey will not be able to identify the header parameters present in the `Response` object by just scanning through the method signature

The solution for the preceding scenario is to intercept the default WADL generation process and pass the necessary data about the return types. Jersey allows you to do so by extending `org.glassfish.jersey.server.wadl.config.WadlGeneratorConfig`.

Generating a Java client from WADL

You can generate the Java client for a WADL file by using the `wadl2java` tool. To download the ZIP file containing `wadl2java`, go to `https://github.com/javaee/wadl`.

After downloading the ZIP file, perform the following steps:

1. Extract the contents and set the path to the `bin` folder that contains the `wadl2java.bat` file (for example, `<wadl-dist-1.1.6>/bin`).
2. Set `JAVA_HOME` pointing to a valid JDK home folder.
3. Now, execute `wadl2java` as follows:

```
wadl2java -o outputDir -p package [-a] [-s jaxrs20] [-c
customization]  outputfile.wadl
```

Here is a brief description of the arguments used for `wadl2java`:

- `-o outputDir`: This argument specifies the target folder for storing the generated client source
- `-p package`: This argument specifies the Java package name for the generated client source
- `-a`: If you specify this parameter, each schema namespace name is mapped to a package and the element types for the namespace are generated in appropriate packages
- `-c customization`: This argument specifies the path or URL of a JAXB binding customization file
- `-s jaxrs20`: This argument specifies that the client code should be compatible with JAXRS2.0; the default value is `jersey1x`
- `outputfile.wadl`: Here, you can specify the path or the URL of the WADL file to process

The following example uses the `wadl2java` tool to generate the Java client for the WADL file located at
`http://<host>:<port>/rest-chapter7-jaxrs2wadl/webresources/application.wadl`:

```
wadl2java -o gen-src -p com.packtpub.demo.client -s jaxrs20
http://localhost:8080/rest-chapter7-jaxrs2wadl/webresources/application.wad
l
```

Market adoption of WADL

Many like WADL for its simplicity and tooling support. It is easy to read, understand, and implement.

However, the software industry has not yet considered it to be an actual standard for describing RESTful web APIs. Further, WADL does not cover authentication constructs for REST APIs. Some vendors think that XML is not the right way to go for describing RESTful web APIs because of the complexity involved in parsing XMLs, particularly when used in mobile clients or in JavaScript clients.

With this, we end our discussion on WADL. In the next section, we will discuss RESTful API Modeling Language, which is a YAML-based language for describing RESTful APIs.

RESTful API Modeling Language

RESTful API Modeling Language (RAML) provides human-readable and machine-processable documentation for your RESTful web services. It helps you to clearly document resources, methods, parameters, responses, media types, and other HTTP constructs that form the basis for a RESTful web service. RAML was first proposed in 2013 by the RAML Workgroup. Today, the RAML Workgroup includes technology leaders from various software vendors, such as MuleSoft Inc., PayPal Inc., Intuit Inc., and Cisco.

RAML is built on standards such as **Yaml Ain't Markup Language (YAML)**. YAML is a human-friendly data serialization standard that works with any programming language. If you are not familiar with YAML, go through the wiki page available at `http://en.wikipedia.org/wiki/YAML`.

Overview of the RAML structure

Let's take a quick look at the RAML file structure, which describes the RESTful web services. An RAML file is a text file with the recommended extension of `.raml`. It uses spaces as indentation; you can use two or four spaces for indentation. The details of the content that you will find in a typical RAML file are as follows. We are grouping the contents into different logical sections to keep this discussion simple and easy to follow:

- **Basic information**: An `RAML` file starts with the basic information of the RESTful web APIs that you want to describe. This information is listed in the root portion of the document. The basic information includes information about REST APIs, such as the API title, version, base URI, base URI parameters, and the data type definition for resources, protocols, and default media types. Optionally, the root portion can also include a variety of user documentation that serve as a user guide and reference documentation for the API. Such documentation details how the API works.

- **Data types**: `RAML 1.0` adds the capability to define the data types that can be used to describe a base or resource URI parameter, a query parameter, a request or response header, or a request or response body. The type definitions are not constrained with built-in data types; it allows custom data type definition as well. Also the `!include` tag can be used to import the external type definitions.

- **Security**: Mostly, the REST APIs that you see today are secure. You can have security scheme definitions for accessing APIs in the RAML file towards the beginning of the content, alongside the basic information.

- **Resources and nested resources**: The next step is to outline the resources and nested resources exposed via the REST APIs. Resources are identified by their relative URI. A nested resource (child resource) is a resource defined as the child of a parent resource. Nested resources are useful if you want to access a subset from a collection of resources (which is identified as the parent resource). The uriParameters property is used for describing the path parameter used for accessing the child resources.
- **HTTP methods**: Once you have all the RESTful resources defined in RAML, the next step is to define the HTTP methods, such as GET, POST, PUT, and DELETE, which a client can perform on resources:
    - **Query parameters**: If the REST resource method takes the query parameters, RAML lets you specify them along with HTTP methods via the queryParameters attribute, typically used with the HTTP GET method.
    - **Request data**: The request payload definition is also allowed in RAML. The request payload specifies the media type and form parameters present in the request, typically used with the HTTP PUT and POST methods.
    - **Response**: The definitions of the REST resource and the HTTP operations on them give a high-level overview of the REST APIs. However, to really consume these APIs in real life, the client application must be aware of the response codes and content type returned by the REST calls. RAML defines the response types for each resource method. This includes the HTTP status codes, descriptions, examples, or schemas.

Here is a simple RAML example. See the following JAX-RS resource method, which returns a Department object. Let's see how this JAX-RS resource can be represented in RAML:

```
@GET
@Path("{id}")
@Produces("application/json")
public Department findDepartment(@PathParam("id") Short id){
    //Method body is omitted for brevity...
}
```

The RAML file describing the preceding resource method will look like the following:

```
#%RAML 1.0
title: department resource
version: 1.0
```

```
baseUri: "http://localhost:8080/hrapp/webresources"
types:
  department: !include schemas/department.xsd
  department-jsonschema: !include schemas/department-jsonschema.json
/departments:
  get:
  /{id}:
    uriParameters:
      id:
        type: integer
    get:
      responses:
        200:
          body:
            application/json:
              type: department-jsonschema
              example: !include examples/department.json
```

A detailed tutorial on RAML is available at `http://raml.org/docs.html`. Here is the link to complete the RAML specification: `https://github.com/raml-org/raml-spec`

Generating RAML from JAX-RS

In this section, you will learn how to generate the RAML file for your JAX-RS application. To generate the RAML file for JAX-RS, we use the `jaxrs-to-raml-maven-plugin` Maven plugin that comes as a part of RAML for the JAX-RS project (from MuleSoft Inc.). The source for RAML for JAX-RS is available at `https://github.com/mulesoft/raml-for-jax-rs`.

The `jaxrs-to-raml-maven-plugin` Maven plugin is capable of identifying the JAX-RS annotation, which you can set on the resource class, resource methods, and fields, and uses this metadata to generate the RAML file while building the source. The `jaxrs-to-raml-maven-plugin` Maven plugin supports the following set of JAX-RS annotations: `@Path`, `@Consumes`, `@Produces`, `@QueryParam`, `@FormParam`, `@PathParam`, `@HeaderParam`, `@DELETE`, `@GET`, `@HEAD`, `@OPTIONS`, `@POST`, `@PUT`, and `@DefaultValue`. The JAXB annotated (`@XmlRootElement`) classes that appear in the `resource` method signature will be represented using JSON or XML schemas (depending upon the media type set for the method) in the RAML file.

The steps that you will perform for using JAX-RS to RAML Maven plugin in a JAX-RS application are as follows:

1. The `jaxrs-to-raml-maven-plugin` Maven plugin is available in the `https://repository-master.mulesoft.org/releases/`.

2. Go to the project where you have all JAX-RS resource classes defined, and include `jaxrs-raml-maven-plugin` in the project's `pom.xml` file. The `<plugin>` entry in the `pom.xml` file will look like the following with the required dependencies:

```
<build>
<plugins>
        <plugin>
                <groupId>org.raml.jaxrs</groupId>
                <artifactId>jaxrs-to-raml-maven-plugin</artifactId>
                <version>2.1.0</version>
                <dependencies>
                    <dependency>
                        <groupId>org.raml.jaxrs</groupId>
                        <artifactId>jaxrs-to-raml-methods</artifactId>
                        <version>2.1.0</version>
                    </dependency>
                    <dependency>
                        <groupId>org.eclipse.persistence</groupId>
                        <artifactId>javax.persistence</artifactId>
                        <version>2.1.0</version>
                    </dependency>
                </dependencies>
                <executions>
                    <execution>
                        <phase>package</phase>
                        <goals>
                            <goal>jaxrstoraml</goal>
                        </goals>
                        <configuration>
<baseUrl>http://localhost:28080/rest-chapter7-jaxrs2raml/webresources</baseUrl>
                            <title>department resource</title>
                            <version>1.0</version>
<sourceDirectory>${basedir}/src/main/java</sourceDirectory>
<outputFile>${project.build.directory}/generated-sources/jaxrs-raml/department-resource.raml</outputFile>
                            <removeOldOutput>true</removeOldOutput>
                        </configuration>
                    </execution>
                </executions>
```

```
            </plugin>
    <!-- Other plugin entries go here -->
</plugins>
</build>
```

You are now done with the setup. When you run `mvn compile` or `mvn package`, the `jaxrs-raml-maven-plugin` plugin that you added in the previous step will generate the RAML file in the Maven's generated-sources folder for all the JAX-RS resource classes found in the Maven source folder.

 The complete source code for this example is available at the Packt website. You can download the example from the Packt website link that we mentioned at the beginning of this book, in the *Preface* section. In the downloaded source code, see the `rest-chapter7-service-doctools/rest-chapter7-jaxrs2raml` project.

It is now time for us to see `jaxrs-to-raml-maven-plugin` in action. The RAML file generated for the `DepartmentResource` class, which we discussed a while ago in the *Generating WADL from JAX-RS* section, is shown here. You will also see an `annotations` folder in the generated source with the `Department` type object in it. The `Department` object represents the message entity used in this example:

```
#%RAML 1.0
title: Raml API generated from rest-chapter7-jaxrs2raml
version: 1.0
baseUri: "http://www.packtpub.com"
mediaType: "*/*"
types:
/departments:
    get:
        responses:
            200:
                body:
                    application/json:
                        type: List
        queryParameters:
            from:
                type: integer
                default: 1
                required: false
            to:
                type: integer
                default: 100
                required: false
    post:
        body:
```

```
                type: Department
    /{id}:
        put:
            body:
                type: Department
        get:
            responses:
                200:
                    body:
                        application/json:
                            type: Department
```

Generating RAML from JAX-RS via CLI

In addition to the maven plugin, RAML for the JAX-RS project also has a **command-line interface (CLI)** tool for generating RAML from the JAX-RS resources. Its usage is as follows:

1. Clone the `https://github.com/mulesoft-labs/raml-for-jax-rs` project and build it locally.
2. To generate the RAML code, run the `jaxrstoraml` command with the following arguments:

```
jaxrstoraml -a <arg> -o <arg> [-s <arg>] [-t <arg>]
 -a,--applicationDirectory <arg>     application path
 -o,--output <arg>                   RAML output file
 -s,--sourceRoot <arg>               JaxRs source root
 -t,--translatedAnnotations <arg>    translated annotation list
(comma separated)
```

From the `jaxrs-to-raml-cli` project folder, execute the `jaxrstoraml` program to generate the `test.raml` file, as shown ahead:

```
java -jar ./target/jaxrs-to-raml-cli-2.1.0-jar-with-dependencies.jar -a
../jaxrs-test-resources/target/classes -o /tmp/test.raml
```

Generating JAX-RS from RAML

In the previous section, we have seen how to generate the RAML documentation for the REST resource classes present in a JAX-RS application. In this section, you will learn how to generate the JAX-RS resources classes from an RAML documentation file. This feature is enabled via the `raml-to-jaxrs-maven-plugin` Maven plugin.

Perform the following steps for using RAML to the JAX-RS Maven plugin in a Maven project:

1. The `raml-to-jaxrs-maven-plugin` Maven plugin is available in the Maven central repository. If you do not see the latest release here, clone the Git repository available at `https://github.com/mulesoft/raml-for-jax-rs` and build the `raml-for-jax-rs/raml-to-jaxrs` project by executing `mvn install`.

2. Go to the maven project where you want to generate the JAX-RS resource classes from the RAML file. Include `raml-to-jaxrs-maven-plugin` in the project's `pom.xml` file. The `<plugin>` entry in the `pom.xml` file will look like the following:

```
<plugins>
        <plugin>
                <groupId>org.raml.jaxrs</groupId>
                <artifactId>raml-to-jaxrs-maven-plugin</artifactId>
                <version>2.1.0</version>
                <configuration>
<ramlFile>${basedir}/src/main/resources/raml/department-
resource.raml</ramlFile>
<resourcePackage>com.packtpub.rest.ch7.service</resourcePackage>
<modelPackage>com.packtpub.rest.ch7.model</modelPackage>
                        <jsonMapper>jackson2</jsonMapper>
                        <jsonMapperConfiguration>
<includeHashcodeAndEquals>true</includeHashcodeAndEquals>
                        </jsonMapperConfiguration>
                </configuration>
                <executions>
                        <execution>
                                <goals>
                                        <goal>generate</goal>
                                </goals>
                                <phase>generate-sources</phase>
                        </execution>
                </executions>
        </plugin>
  <!-- other plugins go here -->
  </plugins>
```

3. Keep the RAML file that you want to convert into JAX-RS in the `resources` folder of the maven project. The plugin configuration lets you specify the RAML file via the `<ramlFile>` element.

4. Run `mvn compile` or `mvn package`, which will result in the generation of the JAX-RS resource classes for the RAML file present in the source folder. You can find the newly generated source files in the `generated-sources` folder under Maven's target folder.

 Note that all the generated JAX-RS resource classes that you see here are just template classes derived from the RAML file. It is your responsibility to add the appropriate business logic to each `resource` method and make the necessary changes to make it production-ready.

Generating JAX-RS from RAML via CLI

In addition to the maven plugin, RAML for the JAX-RS project has a CLI tool for generating the JAX-RS resource classes from RAML. Its usage is as follows:

1. Clone the `https://github.com/mulesoft-labs/raml-for-jax-rs` project and build it locally.
2. To generate the JAX-RS code, run the `ramltojaxs` command with the following arguments:

```
ramltojaxrs -d <arg> [-g <arg>] [-m <arg>] [-r <arg>] [-s <arg>]
 -d,--directory <arg> generation directory
 -g,--generate-types-with <arg> generate types with plugins (jackson,
                                gson, jaxb, javadoc, jsr303)
 -m,--model-package <arg> model package
 -r,--resource-package <arg> resource package
 -s,--support-package <arg> support package
```

From the `jaxrs-to-raml-cli` project folder, execute the `ramltojaxrs` program to generate the JAX-RS resources from the `department-resource.raml` file, as shown ahead:

```
java -jar ./target/raml-to-jaxrs-cli-2.1.0-jar-with-dependencies.jar -d
/tmp -r com.packtpub.rest.ch7.service -m com.packtpub.rest.ch7.model -g
jsr303 ../../../rest-chapter7-service-doctools/rest-chapter7-
raml2jaxrs/src/main/resources/raml/department-resource.raml
```

A glance at the market adoption of RAML

RAML is simple and easy to use for describing the RESTful web APIs. It comes with advanced language constructs and good online design tool support, which eases the job of describing the APIs. You can build RAML even during the design phase of the application describing the APIs. Later, during the development phase, you can use the RAML definitions of APIs to generate high-level resource class dentitions.

During development, RAML allows you to develop and test the API client independent of the actual RESTful web service implementation.

Although RAML has many good features, its market adoption is less than that of the other competing products. This is mainly because it came late in the game. However, this tool looks promising in the long run because the community is quite active and there is a wide range of tools available today to support RAML.

In the next section, we will discuss Swagger. Swagger is not just yet another REST API documentation tool; rather, it offers many features in addition to the API documentation.

Swagger

Swagger offers a specification and a complete framework implementation for describing, producing, consuming, and visualizing RESTful web services. The Swagger framework works with many popular programming languages, such as Java, Scala, Clojure, Groovy, JavaScript, and .NET.

Swagger was initially developed by Wordnik (a property of Reverb) for meeting their in-house requirements, and the first version was released in 2011. The current release is Swagger 3.0. The Open API specification and public tools are open source, supported by many vendors, such as PayPal, Apigee, and 3scale.

The Swagger framework has the following three major components:

- **Server**: This component hosts the RESTful web API descriptions for the services that the clients want to use
- **Client**: This component uses the RESTful web API descriptions from the server to provide an automated interfacing mechanism to invoke the REST APIs
- **User interface**: This part of the framework reads a description of the APIs from the server, renders it as a web page, and provides an interactive sandbox to test the APIs

A quick overview of the Swagger structure

Let's take a quick look at the Swagger file structure before moving further. The Swagger 1.x file contents that describe the RESTful APIs are represented as the JSON objects. With Swagger 2.0 release onwards, you can also use the YAML format to describe the RESTful web APIs.

This section discusses the Swagger file contents represented as JSON. The basic constructs that we'll discuss in this section for JSON are also applicable for the YAML representation of APIs, although the syntax differs.

When using the JSON structure for describing the REST APIs, the Swagger file uses a Swagger object as the root document object for describing the APIs. Here is a quick overview of the various properties that you will find in a Swagger object:

- The following properties describe the basic information about the RESTful web application:
  - `swagger`: This property specifies the Swagger version.
  - `info`: This property provides metadata about the API.
  - `host`: This property locates the server where the APIs are hosted.
  - `basePath`: This property is the base path for the API. It is relative to the value set for the `host` field.
  - `schemes`: This property transfers the protocol for a RESTful web API, such as HTTP and HTTPS.

- The following properties allow you to specify the default values at the application level, which can be optionally overridden for each operation:
  - `consumes`: This property specifies the default internet media types that the APIs consume. It can be overridden at the API level.
  - `produces`: This property specifies the default internet media types that the APIs produce. It can be overridden at the API level.
  - `securityDefinitions`: This property globally defines the security schemes for the document. These definitions can be referred to from the security schemes specified for each API.

- The following properties describe the operations (REST APIs):
    - `paths`: This property specifies the path to the API or the resources. The path must be appended to the `basePath` property in order to get the full URI.
    - `definitions`: This property specifies the input and output entity types for operations on REST resources (APIs).
    - `parameters`: This property specifies the parameter details for an operation.
    - `responses`: This property specifies the response type for an operation.
    - `security`: This property specifies the security schemes in order to execute this operation.
    - `externalDocs`: This property links to the external documentation.

> **TIP**
>
> A complete Swagger 2.0 specification is available at `https://github.com/OAI/OpenAPI-Specification/blob/master/versions/2.0.md`.
> The Swagger specification was donated to the Open API initiative, which aims to standardize the format of the API specification and bring uniformity in usage. Swagger 2.0 was enhanced as part of the Open API initiative, and a new specification OAS 3.0 (Open API specification 3.0) was released in July 2017. The tools are still being worked on to support OAS3.0. I encourage you to explore the Open API Specification 3.0 available at `https://github.com/OAI/OpenAPI-Specification/blob/master/versions/3.0.0.md`.

An overview of Swagger APIs

The Swagger framework consists of many sub projects in the Git repository (`https://github.com/swagger-api`), each built with a specific purpose. Here is a quick summary of the key projects:

- `swagger-spec`: This repository contains the Swagger specification and the project in general.
- `swagger-ui`: This project is an interactive tool to display and execute the Swagger specification files. It is based on `swagger-js` (the JavaScript library).
- `swagger-editor`: This project allows you to edit the YAML files. It is released as a part of Swagger 2.0.

- `swagger-core`: This project provides the `scala` and `java` library to generate the Swagger specifications directly from code. It supports JAX-RS, the Servlet APIs, and the Play framework.
- `swagger-codegen`: This project provides a tool that can read the Swagger specification files and generate the client and server code that consumes and produces the specifications.

In the next section, you will learn how to use the `swagger-core` project offerings to generate the Swagger file for a JAX-RS application.

Generating Swagger from JAX-RS

Both the WADL and RAML tools that we discussed in the previous sections use the JAX-RS annotations metadata to generate the documentation for the APIs. The Swagger framework does not fully rely on the JAX-RS annotations but offers a set of proprietary annotations for describing the resources. This helps in the following scenarios:

- The Swagger core annotations provide more flexibility for generating documentations compliant with the Swagger specifications
- It allows you to use Swagger for generating documentations for web components that do not use the JAX-RS annotations, such as servlet and the servlet filter

The Swagger annotations are designed to work with JAX-RS, improving the quality of the API documentation generated by the framework. Note that the `swagger-core` project is currently supported on the Jersey and Restlet implementations. If you are considering any other runtime for your JAX-RS application, check the respective product manual and ensure the support before you start using Swagger for describing APIs.

Some of the commonly used Swagger annotations are as follows:

- The `@com.wordnik.swagger.annotations.Api` annotation marks a class as a Swagger resource. Note that only classes that are annotated with `@Api` will be considered for generating the documentation. The `@Api` annotation is used along with class-level JAX-RS annotations such as `@Produces` and `@Path`.

- Annotations that declare an operation are as follows:
    - `@com.wordnik.swagger.annotations.ApiOperation`: This annotation describes a `resource` method (operation) that is designated to respond to HTTP action methods, such as `GET`, `PUT`, `POST`, and `DELETE`.
    - `@com.wordnik.swagger.annotations.ApiParam`: This annotation is used for describing parameters used in an operation. This is designed for use in conjunction with the JAX-RS parameters, such as `@Path`, `@PathParam`, `@QueryParam`, `@HeaderParam`, `@FormParam`, and `@BeanParam`.
    - `@com.wordnik.swagger.annotations.ApiImplicitParam`: This annotation allows you to define the operation parameters manually. You can use this to override the `@PathParam` or `@QueryParam` values specified on a `resource` method with custom values. If you have multiple `ImplicitParam` for an operation, wrap them with `@ApiImplicitParams`.
    - `@com.wordnik.swagger.annotations.ApiResponse`: This annotation describes the status codes returned by an operation. If you have multiple responses, wrap them by using `@ApiResponses`.
    - `@com.wordnik.swagger.annotations.ResponseHeader`: This annotation describes a header that can be provided as part of the response.
    - `@com.wordnik.swagger.annotations.Authorization`: This annotation is used within either `Api` or `ApiOperation` to describe the authorization scheme used on a resource or an operation.

- Annotations that declare API models are as follows:
    - `@com.wordnik.swagger.annotations.ApiModel`: This annotation describes the model objects used in the application.
    - `@com.wordnik.swagger.annotations.ApiModelProperty`: This annotation describes the properties present in the `ApiModel` object.

A complete list of the Swagger core annotations is available at `https://github.com/swagger-api/swagger-core/wiki/Annotations-1.5.X`.

Having learned the basics of Swagger, it is time for us to move on and build a simple example to get a feel of the real-life use of Swagger in a JAX-RS application. As always, this example uses the Jersey implementation of JAX-RS.

Specifying dependency to Swagger

To use Swagger in your Jersey 2 application, specify the dependency to `swagger-jersey2-jaxrs jar`. If you use Maven for building the source, the dependency to the `swagger-core` library will look as follows:

```
<dependency>
    <groupId>com.wordnik</groupId>
    <artifactId>swagger-jersey2-jaxrs</artifactId>
    <version>1.5.1-M1</version>
    <!-use the appropriate version here,
    1.5.x supports Swagger 2.0 spec -->
</dependency>
```

You should be careful while choosing the `swagger-core` version for your product. Note that `swagger-core` `1.3` produces the Swagger 1.2 definitions, whereas `swagger-core` `1.5` produces the Swagger 2.0 definitions.

The next step is to hook the Swagger provider components into your Jersey application. This is done by configuring the Jersey servlet (`org.glassfish.jersey.servlet.ServletContainer`) in `web.xml`, as shown here:

```
<servlet>
    <servlet-name>jersey</servlet-name>
    <servlet-class>
        org.glassfish.jersey.servlet.ServletContainer
    </servlet-class>
    <init-param>
        <param-name>jersey.config.server.provider.packages
        </param-name>
        <param-value>
            com.wordnik.swagger.jaxrs.json,
            com.packtpub.rest.ch7.swagger
        </param-value>
```

```
        </init-param>
        <load-on-startup>1</load-on-startup>
    </servlet>
        <servlet-mapping>
            <servlet-name>jersey</servlet-name>
            <url-pattern>/webresources/*</url-pattern>
        </servlet-mapping>
```

To enable the Swagger documentation features, it is necessary to load the Swagger framework provider classes from the `com.wordnik.swagger.jaxrs.listing` package. The package names of the JAX-RS resource classes and provider components are configured as the value for the `jersey.config.server.provider.packages` init parameter. The Jersey framework scans through the configured packages for identifying the resource classes and provider components during the deployment of the application. Map the Jersey servlet to a request URI so that it responds to the REST resource calls that match the URI.

If you prefer not to use `web.xml`, you can also use the custom application subclass for (programmatically) specifying all the configuration entries discussed here. To try this option, refer to `https://github.com/swagger-api/swagger-core/wiki/Swagger-Core-JAX-RS-Project-Setup`.

Configuring the Swagger definition

After specifying the Swagger provider components, the next step is to configure and initialize the Swagger definition. This is done by configuring the `com.wordnik.swagger.jersey.config.JerseyJaxrsConfig` servlet in `web.xml`, as follows:

```
<servlet>
    <servlet-name>Jersey2Config</servlet-name>
    <servlet-class>
        com.wordnik.swagger.jersey.config.JerseyJaxrsConfig
    </servlet-class>
    <init-param>
        <param-name>api.version</param-name>
        <param-value>1.0.0</param-value>
    </init-param>
    <init-param>
        <param-name>swagger.api.basepath</param-name>
        <param-value>
            http://localhost:8080/hrapp/webresources
        </param-value>
```

```
      </init-param>
      <load-on-startup>1</load-on-startup>
   </servlet>
```

Here is a brief overview of the initialization parameters used for `JerseyJaxrsConfig`:

- `api.version`: This parameter specifies the API version for your application
- `swagger.api.basepath`: This parameter specifies the base path for your application

With this step, we have finished all the configuration entries for using Swagger in a JAX-RS (Jersey 2 implementation) application. In the next section, we will see how to use the Swagger metadata annotation on a JAX-RS resource class for describing the resources and operations.

Adding a Swagger annotation on a JAX-RS resource class

Let's revisit the `DepartmentResource` class used in the previous sections. In this example, we will enhance the `DepartmentResource` class by adding the Swagger annotations discussed earlier. We use `@Api` to mark `DepartmentResource` as the Swagger resource. The `@ApiOperation` annotation describes the operation exposed by the `DepartmentResource` class:

```java
import com.wordnik.swagger.annotations.Api;
import com.wordnik.swagger.annotations.ApiOperation;
import com.wordnik.swagger.annotations.ApiParam;
import com.wordnik.swagger.annotations.ApiResponse;
import com.wordnik.swagger.annotations.ApiResponses;
//Other imports are removed for brevity

@Stateless
@Path("departments")
@Api(value = "/departments", description = "Get departments
      details")
public class DepartmentResource  {

    @ApiOperation(value = "Find department by id",
        notes = "Specify a valid department id",
        response = Department.class)
    @ApiResponses(value = {
        @ApiResponse(code = 400, message =
        "Invalid department id supplied"),
        @ApiResponse(code = 404, message = "Department not found")
```

```
    })
    @GET
    @Path("{id}")
    @Produces("application/json")
    public Department findDepartment(
        @ApiParam(value = "The department id", required = true)
        @PathParam("id") Integer id){
            return findDepartmentEntity(id);
    }

    //Rest of the codes are removed for brevity


}
```

To view the Swagger documentation, build the source and deploy it to the server. Once the application is deployed, you can navigate to `http://<host>:<port>/<application-name>/<application-path>/swagger.json` to view the Swagger resource listing in the JSON format. The Swagger URL for this example will look like the following:
`http://localhost:8080/hrapp/webresource/swagger.json`

The following sample Swagger representation is for the `DepartmentResource` class discussed in this section:

```
{
  "swagger": "2.0",
  "info": {
    "version": "1.0.0",
    "title": ""
  },
  "host": "localhost:8080",
  "basePath": "/hrapp/webresources",
  "tags": [
    {
      "name": "user"
    }
  ],
  "schemes": [
    "http"
  ],
  "paths": {
    "/departments/{id}": {
      "get": {
        "tags": [
          "user"
        ],
        "summary": "Find department by id",
```

```
            "description": "",
            "operationId": "loginUser",
            "produces": [
              "application/json"
            ],
            "parameters": [
              {
                "name": "id",
                "in": "path",
                "description": "The department id",
                "required": true,
                "type": "integer",
                "format": "int32"
              }
            ],
            "responses": {
              "200": {
                "description": "successful operation",
                "schema": {
                  "$ref": "#/definitions/Department"
                }
              },
              "400": {
                "description": "Invalid department id supplied"
              },
              "404": {
                "description": "Department not found"
              }
            }
          }
        }
      }
    },
    "definitions": {
      "Department": {
        "properties": {
          "departmentId": {
            "type": "integer",
            "format": "int32"
          },
          "departmentName": {
            "type": "string"
          },
          "_persistence_shouldRefreshFetchGroup": {
            "type": "boolean"
          }
        }
      }
    }
  }
```

```
}
```

As mentioned at the beginning of this section, from the Swagger 2.0 release onward it supports the YAML representation of APIs. You can access the YAML representation by navigating to `swagger.yaml`. For instance, in the preceding example, the following URI gives you the YAML file:

`http://<host>:<port>/<application-name>/<application-path>/swagger.yaml`

The complete source code for this example is available at the Packt website. You can download the example from the Packt website link that we mentioned at the beginning of this book, in the *Preface* section. In the downloaded source code, see the `rest-chapter7-service-doctools/rest-chapter7-jaxrs2swagger` project.

Generating a Java client from Swagger

The Swagger framework is packaged with the Swagger code generation tool as well (`swagger-codegen-cli`), which allows you to generate client libraries by parsing the Swagger documentation file. You can download the `swagger-codegen-cli.jar` file from the Maven central repository by searching for `swagger-codegen-cli` in `http://search.maven.org`. Alternatively, you can clone the `https://github.com/swagger-api/swagger-codegen` Git repository and build the source locally by executing `mvn install`.

Once you have `swagger-codegen-cli.jar` locally available, run the following command to generate the Java client for the REST API described in Swagger:

```
java -jar swagger-codegen-cli.jar generate
-i <Input-URI-or-File-location-for-swagger.json>
-l <client-language-to-generate>
-o <output-directory>
```

The following example illustrates the use of this tool:

```
java -jar swagger-codegen-cli-2.1.0-M2.jar generate
-i http://localhost:8080/hrapp/webresources/swagger.json
-l java
-o generated-sources/java
```

When you run this tool, it scans through the RESTful web API description available at `http://localhost:8080/hrapp/webresources/swagger.json` and generates a Java client source in the `generated-sources/java` folder.

Note that the Swagger code generation process uses the mustache templates for generating the client source. If you are not happy with the generated source, Swagger lets you specify your own mustache template files. Use the -t flag to specify your template folder. To learn more, refer to the README.md file at https://github.com/swagger-api/swagger-codegen.

A glance at the market adoption of Swagger

The greatest strength of Swagger is its powerful API platform, which satisfies the client, documentation, and server needs. The Swagger UI framework serves as the documentation and testing utility. Its support for different languages and its matured tooling support have really grabbed the attention of many API vendors, and it seems to be the one with the most traction in the community today.

Swagger is built using Scala. This means that when you package your application, you need to have the entire Scala runtime into your build, which may considerably increase the size of your deployable artifact (the EAR or WAR file). That said, Swagger is however improving with each release. For example, the Swagger 2.0 release allows you to use YAML for describing APIs. So, keep a watch on this framework.

Revisiting the features offered in WADL, RAML, and Swagger

The following table summarizes the discussion that we have had so far on the WADL, RAML, and Swagger tools:

Features	WADL	RAML	Swagger
Release date	2009	2013	2011
File format	XML	RAML	JSON/YAML
Open source	Yes	Yes	Yes
Commercial offering	No	Yes	Yes
Language support	Java	JS, Java, Node, PHP, Python, and Ruby	Clojure, Go, JS, Java, .Net, Node, PHP, Python, Ruby, and Scala

Authentication	No	Basic, Digest, OAuth 1, and OAuth 2	Basic, API Key, and OAuth 2
API console	No	Yes	Yes
Code generation for server (Java)	No	Yes	Yes
Code generation for client (Java)	Yes	Yes	Yes

Summary

A number of RESTful web API metadata standards have emerged in the recent past. The objective of this chapter is to introduce you to some of the most popular RESTful web API documentation tools, namely WADL, RAML, and Swagger. This chapter is not meant for making any recommendations on choosing a documentation solution for your RESTful web application, but to help you understand the API documentation tools and their offerings in general. To choose the right solution for your organization, you should start by looking at the client applications that access the APIs and their usage pattern, and then choose a tool that makes the API consumption easier, which may eventually improve the adoption of APIs by the customers.

The next chapter summarizes the best practices and coding guidelines that developers will find useful when building RESTful web service applications. This chapter is very important for you as a developer, and it is worth spending time on each item that we discussed.

8
RESTful API Design Guidelines

REST is a software architectural style, not a specification, for building scalable web services. Since RESTful web services do not have any strict specifications for designing and building APIs, you may find many interpretations for how a RESTful web API should work.

In this chapter, you will learn standards, best practices, conventions, and tips and tricks that you can apply to your RESTful web service applications today. Some of the important topics discussed in this chapter are as follows:

- Designing RESTful APIs
- Implementing partial response
- Paging a resource collection
- Versioning RESTful web APIs
- Caching RESTful web API results
- Microservice architecture style for RESTful web applications

Designing RESTful web APIs

Over decades, SOAP web services have become the de facto standard for developing web services. Making a mind shift to adhere to REST architectural constraints is quite essential for the design of RESTful web APIs. Let's break down the design considerations of a RESTful web APIs, focusing on the core elements of the REST architecture style:

- Resources and their identifiers
- Interaction semantics for RESTful APIs (HTTP methods)
- Representation of resources
- Hypermedia controls

Let's start by discussing the guidelines for identifying resources in a problem domain.

 Richardson Maturity Model—Leonardo Richardson has developed a model to help with assessing the compliance of a service to REST architecture style. The model defines four levels of maturity, starting from level-0 to level-3 as the highest maturity level. The maturity levels are decided considering the aforementioned principle elements of the REST architecture.

Identifying resources in a problem domain

The basic steps that you may need to take while building a RESTful web API for a specific problem domain are as follows:

1. Identify all possible objects in the problem domain. This can be done by identifying all nouns in the problem domain. For example, if you are building an application to manage employees in a department, the obvious nouns are department and employee.

2. The next step is to identify the objects that can be manipulated using the CRUD operations. These objects can be classified as resources. Note that you should be careful while choosing resources. Based on the usage pattern, you can classify resources as top-level and nested resources (which are the children of a top-level resource). Also, there is no need to expose all resources for use by the client; expose only those resources that are required for implementing the business use case.

Transforming operations to HTTP methods

Once you have identified all the resources, as the next step, you may want to map the operations defined on the resources to the appropriate HTTP methods.

The most commonly used HTTP methods (verbs) in RESTful web APIs are POST, GET, PUT, and DELETE. Note that there is no one-to-one mapping between the CRUD operations defined on the resources and the HTTP methods. Understanding of idempotent and safe operation concepts will help with using the correct HTTP method.

An operation is called **idempotent** if multiple identical requests produce the same result. Similarly, an idempotent RESTful web API will always produce the same result on the server irrespective of how many times the request is executed with the same parameters; however, the response may change between requests.

An operation is called **safe** if it does not modify the state of the resources.

Check out the following table:

Method	Idempotent	Safe
GET	YES	YES
OPTIONS	YES	YES
HEAD	YES	YES
POST	NO	NO
PATCH	NO	NO
PUT	YES	NO
DELETE	YES	NO

Here are some tips for identifying the most appropriate HTTP method for the operations that you want to perform on the resources:

- GET: You can use this method for reading a representation of a resource from the server. According to the HTTP specification, GET is a safe operation, which means that it is only intended for retrieving data, not for making any state changes. As this is an idempotent operation, multiple identical GET requests will behave in the same manner.

  A GET method can return the 200 OK HTTP response code on the successful retrieval of resources. If there is any error, it can return an appropriate status code such as 404 NOT FOUND or 400 BAD REQUEST.

- DELETE: You can use this method for deleting resources. On successful deletion, DELETE can return the 200 OK status code. According to the HTTP specification, DELETE is an idempotent operation. Note that when you call DELETE on the same resource for the second time, the server may return the 404 NOT FOUND status code since it was already deleted, which is different from the response for the first request. The change in response for the second call is perfectly valid here. However, multiple DELETE calls on the same resource produce the same result (state) on the server.

- PUT: According to the HTTP specification, this method is idempotent. When a client invokes the PUT method on a resource, the resource available at the given URL is completely replaced with the resource representation sent by the client. When a client uses the PUT request on a resource, it has to send all the available properties of the resource to the server, not just the partial data that was modified within the request.

> You can use PUT to create or update a resource if all attributes of the resource are available with the client. This makes sure that the server state does not change with multiple PUT requests. On the other hand, if you send partial resource content in a PUT request multiple times, there is a chance that some other clients might have updated some attributes that are not present in your request. In such cases, the server cannot guarantee that the state of the resource on the server will remain identical when the same request is repeated, which breaks the idempotency rule.

- POST: This method is not idempotent. This method enables you to use the POST method to create or update resources when you do not know all the available attributes of a resource. For example, consider a scenario where the identifier field for an entity resource is generated at the server when the entity is persisted in the data store. You can use the POST method for creating such resources as the client does not have an identifier attribute while issuing the request. Here is a simplified example that illustrates this scenario. In this example, the employeeID attribute is generated on the server:

```
POST hrapp/api/employees HTTP/1.1
Host: packtpub.com
{employee entity resource in JSON}
```

- On the successful creation of a resource, it is recommended to return the status of 201 Created and the location of the newly created resource. This allows the client to access the newly created resource later (with server-generated attributes). The sample response for the preceding example will look as follows:

```
201 Created
Location: hrapp/api/employees/1001
```

Best practice

Use caching only for idempotent and safe HTTP methods, as others have an impact on the state of the resources.

Understanding the difference between PUT and POST

A common question that you will encounter while designing a RESTful web API is when to use the PUT and POST methods? Here is the simplified answer:

You can use PUT for creating or updating a resource, when the client has the full resource content available. In this case, all values are with the client and the server does not generate a value for any of the fields.

You will use POST for creating or updating a resource if the client has only partial resource content available. Note that you are losing the idempotency support with POST. An idempotent method means that you can call the same API multiple times without changing the state. This is not true for the POST method; each POST method call may result in a server state change. PUT is idempotent, and POST is not. If you have strong customer demands, you can support both methods and let the client choose the suitable one on the basis of the use case.

Naming RESTful web resources

Resources are a very fundamental concept in a RESTful web service. A resource represents an entity that is accessible via the URI that you provide. The URI, which refers to a resource (which is known as a RESTful web API), should have a logically meaningful name. Having meaningful names improves the intuitiveness of the APIs and, thereby, their usability. Some of the widely followed recommendations for naming resources are shown here:

- It is recommended to use nouns to name both resources and path segments that will appear in the resource URI. You should avoid using verbs for naming resources and resource path segments. Using nouns to name a resource improves the readability of the corresponding RESTful web API, particularly when you are planning to release the API over the internet for the general public.
- You should always use plural nouns to refer to a collection of resources. Make sure that you are not mixing up singular and plural nouns while forming the REST URIs. For instance, to get all departments, the resource URI must look like /departments.
- If you want to read a specific department from the collection, the URI becomes /departments/{id}. Following the convention, the URI for reading the details of the HR department identified by id=10 should look like /departments/10.
- The following table illustrates how you can map the HTTP methods (verbs) to the operations defined for the departments' resources:

Resource	GET	POST	PUT	DELETE
/departments	Get all departments	Create a new department	Bulk update on departments	Delete all departments
/departments/10	Get the HR department with id=10	Not allowed	Update the HR department	Delete the HR department

- While naming resources, prefer more concrete names over generic names. For instance, to read all programmers' details of a software firm, it is preferable to have a resource URI of the form /programmers (which tells about the type of resource), over the much generic form /employees. This improves the intuitiveness of the APIs by clearly communicating the type of resources that it deals with.
- Keep the resource names that appear in the URI in lowercase to improve the readability of the resulting resource URI.

- Resource names may include hyphens; avoid using underscores and other punctuation.
- If the entity resource is represented in the JSON format, field names used in the resource must conform to the following guidelines:
    - Use meaningful names for the properties
    - Follow the camel case naming convention: The first letter of the name is in lowercase, for example, `departmentName`
    - The first character must be a letter, an underscore (_), or a dollar sign ($), and the subsequent characters can be letters, digits, underscores, and/or dollar signs
    - Avoid using the reserved JavaScript keywords
- If a resource is related to another resource(s), use a subresource to refer to the child resource. You can use the path parameter in the URI to connect a subresource to its base resource. For instance, the resource URI path to get all employees belonging to the HR department (with `id=10`) will look like `/departments/10/employees`. To get the details of `employee` with `id=200` in the HR department, you can use the following URI: `/departments/10/employees/200`. To learn how to implement subresources using JAX-RS, refer back to the *Understanding subresources and subresource locators in JAX-RS* section in `Chapter 4`, *Advanced Features in the JAX-RS APIs*.

> The resource path URI may contain plural nouns representing a collection of resources, followed by a singular resource identifier to return a specific resource item from the collection. This pattern can repeat in the URI, allowing you to drill down a collection for reading a specific item. For instance, the following URI represents an employee resource identified by `id=200` within the HR department: `/departments/hr/employees/200`.
>
> Although the HTTP protocol does not place any limit on the length of the resource URI, it is recommended not to exceed 2,000 characters because of the restriction set by many popular browsers.
>
> Best practice: Avoid using actions or verbs in the URI as it refers to a resource.

Using HATEOAS in response representation

Hypertext as the Engine of Application State (HATEOAS) refers to the use of hypermedia links in the resource representations. This architectural style lets the clients dynamically navigate to the desired resource by traversing the hypermedia links present in the response body. There is no universally accepted single format for representing links between two resources in JSON. This section shows some of the popular standards for defining links between resources.

Hypertext Application Language

The **Hypertext API Language (HAL)** is a promising proposal that sets the conventions for expressing hypermedia controls (such as links) with JSON or XML. Currently, this proposal is in the draft stage. It mainly describes two concepts for linking resources:

- **Embedded resources**: This concept provides a way to embed another resource within the current one. In the JSON format, you will use the `_embedded` attribute to indicate the embedded resource.
- **Links**: This concept provides links to associated resources. In the JSON format, you will use the `_links` attribute to link resources.

Here is the link to this proposal: `http://tools.ietf.org/html/draft-kelly-json-hal-06`. It defines the following properties for each resource link:

- `href`: This property indicates the URI to the target resource representation
- `template`: This property would be true if the URI value for `href` has any PATH variable inside it (template)
- `title`: This property is used for labeling the URI
- `hreflang`: This property specifies the language for the target resource
- `title`: This property is used for documentation purposes
- `name`: This property is used for uniquely identifying a link

The following example demonstrates how you can use the HAL format for describing the department resource containing hyperlinks to the associated employee resources. This example uses the JSON HAL for representing resources, which is represented using the `application/hal+json` media type:

```
GET /departments/10 HTTP/1.1
Host: packtpub.com
Accept: application/hal+json
```

```
HTTP/1.1 200 OK
Content-Type: application/hal+json

{
  "_links": {
    "self": { "href": "/departments/10" },
    "employees": { "href": "/departments/10/employees" },
    "employee": { "href": "/employees/{id}", "templated": true  }
  },
  "_embedded": {
    "manager": {
      "_links": { "self": { "href": "/employees/1700" } },
      "firstName": "Chinmay",
      "lastName": "Jobinesh",
      "employeeId": "1700",

    }
  },
  "departmentId": 10,
  "departmentName": "Administration"
}
```

RFC 5988 - web linking

RFC 5988 offers a framework for building links that define the relation between resources on the web. Although this specification defines the properties for the links, it does not define how the links as a whole should be represented in an HTTP message. However, it defines the guidelines for specifying the `Link` HTTP header. The syntax set for links in the HTTP headers in this specification may supplement the JSON resources as well. Each link in RFC 5988 may contain the following properties:

- **Target URI**: Each link should contain a target **Internationalized Resource Identifier (IRI)**. This property is represented by the `href` attribute. In case you are not familiar with IRIs, they are not the same as URIs in a function. However, IRIs extend upon URIs by using the universal character set, whereas URIs are limited to ASCII characters.
- **Link relation type**: The link relation type describes how the current context (source) is related to the target resource. This is represented by the `rel` attribute.
- **Attributes for target IRI**: The attributes for a link include `hreflang`, `media`, `title`, `title*`, and `type`, as well as any extension link parameters.

You can learn more about RFC 5988 (web linking)
at http://tools.ietf.org/html/rfc5988.

The following example demonstrates how you can use the `Link` entity-header fields for
describing a relationship between two resources. This example defines the relation between
the department (identified by `id=10`) and the employee resources:

```
GET /departments/10 HTTP/1.1
Host: packtpub.com
Accept: application/json

HTTP/1.1 200 OK
Content-Type: application/json
Link: <http://www.packtpub.com/departments/10>; rel="self";
   type="application/json"; title="Self Link"Link:
<http://www.packtpub.com/departments/10/employees>;
   rel="employees"; type="application/json"; title="Employees"Link:
<http://www.packtpub.com/employees/1700>; rel="manager";
   type="application/json"; title="Manager"
{"departmentId": 10, "departmentName": "Administration",
  "locationId": 1700}
```

Note that the syntax set for links in the HTTP headers can also be leveraged for adding the
entity links within the resource body. For example, the department response entity in the
preceding example can be modified to include the entity links as follows:

```
{
  "departmentId": 10,
  "departmentName": "Administration",
  "locationId": 1700
  "links": {
    { "rel"="self", "href": "/departments/10",
      type="application/json" },
    { "rel"="employees", "href": "/departments/10/employees",
      type="application/json" },
    { "rel"="manager","href": "/employees/1700",
      type="application/json" }
  }
}
```

A detailed discussion on resource link formats falls outside the scope of this book. However, the short but fruitful discussion that we had on HAL and RFC 5988 will definitely help you quickly learn any other resource linking schemes. Here is a quick summary of a few other formats available today for formatting resource links:

- **Collection + JSON**: This format is a JSON-based hypermedia type for describing a collection of resources represented in JSON. You can learn more about this type at `http://amundsen.com/media-types/collection/format`.
- **JSON Schema**: This format is a JSON-based format for defining the structure of the JSON data. As part of this definition, it provides a method for extracting the link relations from one resource to another. To learn more about JSON Schema, go to `http://tools.ietf.org/html/draft-zyp-json-schema-04`.
- **JSON for Linking Data (JSON-LD)**: This format is a lightweight linked data format. To learn more about JSON-LD, go to `http://json-ld.org/`.

Although RFC 5988 standardizes the syntax for the `Link` headers to link web resources, many API vendors do not prefer using the `Link` headers for linking resources. One of the reasons for not using the `Link` header is because this approach does not really work when the API returns the collection of resources. This is due to the fact that it is not easy for a client to accurately identify the `Link` header for a specific resource item present in the collection. Many API vendors prefer to place the links in the entity body as it is more convenient for a client to process. Note that there is no clear consensus among various resource linking schemes that we have today on how the links should be formatted within resource representations. You can choose a format that meets your requirements and stick to it. Also, you may want to document all the APIs clearly, indicating the type of format used for generating the resource links, which will help your API consumers.

Once you decide on the format for representing hypermedia links, the next step is to choose the right tool for implementing it in the application. Here is a quick summary of the JAX-RS and Jersey framework offerings for generating the HTTP links for your REST resource representations:

- `javax.ws.rs.core.Link`: You can use the `Link` utility class offered by JAX-RS for generating the HTTP links (based on RFC 5988)
- `@org.glassfish.jersey.linking.InjectLink`:
  The `@InjectLink` annotation can be applied on the resource entity class fields to declaratively generate the HTTP links linking the web resources

To learn how to use the
`javax.ws.rs.core.Link` and `org.glassfish.jersey.linking.InjectLink` APIs for
generating resource links, refer to the *Building Hypermedia as the Engine of Application State
(HATEOAS) APIs* section in `Chapter 5`, *Introducing JAX-RS Implementation Framework
Extensions.*

Fine-grained and coarse-grained resource APIs

While building a RESTful web API, you should try avoiding the chattiness of APIs. On the
other hand, APIs should not be very coarse-grained as well. Highly coarse-grained APIs
become too complex to use because the response representation may contain a lot of
information, all of which may not be used by a majority of your API clients.

Let's take an example to understand the difference between fine-grained and coarse-grained
approaches for building APIs. Suppose that you are building a very fine-grained API to
read the employee details as follows:

- **API to read employee name**: `GET /employees/10/name`
- **API to read employee address1**: `GET /employees/10/address1`
- **API to read employee address2**: `GET /employees/10/address2`
- **API to read employee email**: `GET /employees/10/email`

It is obvious that a majority of your clients may need all the preceding details to work on an
employee resource. As a result, clients may end up making four different remote API calls
to get all the required details of an employee resource. This is very expensive in terms of the
network (resource) usage and CPU cycles. A possible solution to this scenario of converting
all these fine-grained APIs into a coarse-grained API that returns all the required details as
part of a single API call is `GET /employees/10`.

On the other hand, highly coarse-grained APIs may not fit all use cases. Suppose that you
built a very coarse-grained API that returns an employee resource along with the associated
department, `/employees/{id}`. If not many consumers use the department details present
in the employee resource, it simply makes the API complex to use and does not add any
value for the consumers.

A better solution to this scenario is to build two separate fine-grained APIs, one for reading employee details and the other for reading the department details as shown here:

- **API to read individual employee details**: GET /employees/10
- **API to read department of an employee**: GET /employees/10/departments

To summarize this discussion, always look at the usage pattern of the APIs and the consumer requirements before deciding on the granularity of the APIs. Although very fine-grained APIs may not be an efficient solution for many use cases, it is perfectly valid to have fine-grained inner interfaces (not exposed for public) if this improves the modularity of the application.

Using header parameters for content negotiation

It is recommended to have an appropriate header parameter in the client request and in the server response to indicate how the entity body is serialized when transmitted over a wire:

- Accept: This request header field defines a list of acceptable response formats for the response, for example, Accept: application/json, application/xml.

  The javax.ws.rs.client.WebTarget class allows you to specify the Accept header via the request() method for a JAX-RS client application.

- Content-Type: This header field defines the type of the request or response message body content, for example, Content-Type: text/plain; charset=UTF-8.

 Note that when you use the @javax.ws.rs.Produces annotation, the JAX-RS runtime sets the content type automatically.

Multilingual RESTful web API resources

If your RESTful web API needs to return the resource representations in different languages depending upon the client locale, use the content negotiation offering in HTTP:

- Clients can use the `Accept-Language` request header to specify language preferences.
- While generating a response, the server is expected to translate the messages into the language supported by the client. The server can use the `Content-Language` entity-header field to describe the natural language(s) of the intended audience.

Representing date and time in RESTful web resources

Here is a list of recommendations when you have the date (and time) fields in the RESTful web API resources:

- ISO 8601 is the International Standard for the representation of dates and times. It is recommended to use the **ISO-8601** format for representing the date and time in your RESTful web APIs. Here is an example for the ISO-8601 date and time: `YYYY-MM-DDThh:mm:ss.sTZD` (for example, `2015-06-16T11:20:30.45+01:00`).
- The API that you build must be capable of accepting any time zone set by the client.
- While storing the date and time fields present in the resource representation in the database, use **Coordinated Universal Time (UTC)**. UTC is guaranteed to be consistent.
- While retuning the date and time fields in response to an API call, use the UTC time zone. The client can easily convert the date field present in the resource into the desired local time by using an appropriate UTC offset.

Implementing partial response

Partial response refers to an optimization technique offered by the RESTful web APIs to return only the information (fields) required by the client. In this mechanism, the client sends the required field names as the query parameters for an API to the server, and the server trims down the default response content by removing the fields that are not required by the client. In the following example, the `select` query parameter is used for selecting fields that would be transferred over the wire:

```
/employees/1234?select=firstName,lastName,email
```

The Jersey framework supports the partial response feature via `org.glassfish.jersey.message.filtering.SelectableEntityFilteringFeature`. To enable this feature, you just need to register `SelectableEntityFilteringFeature` in the application. The client can use the `select` query parameter to select the fields that would be transferred over the wire, as illustrated in the following example:

```
GET employees/1234?select=email,department.departmentName HTTP/1.1
```

To learn more about this feature, see the Jersey example available at `https://github.com/jersey/jersey/tree/2.18/examples/entity-filtering-selectable`.

Implementing partial update

When a client changes only one part of the resource, you can optimize the entire update process by allowing the client to send only the modified part to the server, thereby saving the bandwidth and server resources. **RFC 5789** proposes a solution for this use case via a new HTTP method called `PATCH`. To learn more about this RFC, visit `https://tools.ietf.org/html/rfc5789`. Note that `PATCH` is not yet officially a part of HTTP/1.1. However, the HTTP protocol allows both the client and the server to implement any new method. Leveraging this flexibility, many vendors have started supporting the HTTP `PATCH` method.

The `PATCH` method takes the following form:

```
PATCH /departments/10 HTTP/1.1
[Description of changes]
```

The [Description of changes] section, in the preceding PATCH method, contains instructions describing how a resource currently residing on the origin server should be modified in order to reflect the changes performed by the client. **RFC 6902** defines a JSON document structure for expressing the sequence of changes performed on the resource by the client. Note that you can also have the XML structure for describing the changes performed on the XML representation of the resource. We are not covering the XML-based description in this book, because most of the RESTful web APIs currently use the JSON format for representing resources. You can learn more about RFC 6902 at https://tools.ietf.org/html/rfc6902. The PATCH operations supported by JSON PATCH are add, remove, replace, move, copy, and test.

The following example illustrates how you can use JSON PATCH for describing changes performed by a client on a department resource.

As the first step, the client retrieves the department resource from the server that looks like the following:

```
{"departmentId":10, "departmentName":"Administration",
    "managerId":200, "comments":"Administrative works" }
```

The client then performs the following modifications on the department resource:

- Modifies the manager by setting managerId to 300
- Adds a new locationId=1200 value to the department resource
- Removes the comments attribute

The JSON PATCH request body containing the preceding changes will look like the following:

```
PATCH /departments/10 HTTP/1.1
[
  { "op": "replace", "path": "/managerId", "value": 300 },
  { "op": "add", "path": "/locationId", "value": 1200 },
  { "op": "remove", "path": "/comments" }
]
```

The server applies the data manipulation instructions present in the incoming JSON PATCH document and modifies the original resource to reflect the changes performed by the client. After applying the modifications, the department resource on the server will look like the following:

```
{"departmentId":10, "departmentName":"Administration",
    "managerId":300, locationId=1200}
```

Currently, neither JAX-RS 2 nor Jersey support PATCH out of the box. However, JAX-RS allows you to add support for the new HTTP methods via the `javax.ws.rs.HttpMethod` annotation. To learn how to enable the complete support for the HTTP PATCH method in your JAX-RS application, refer to the *Appendix* of this book.

Returning modified resources to the caller

In a typical REST request-response model, an API client reads a resource from the server, makes some modifications, and sends the modified resource back to the server to save the changes via the PUT, POST, or PATCH operations as appropriate. While persisting changes, there are chances that the server may modify some of the fields, such as the version field and the modification date. In such cases, it makes sense to return the modified resource representation back to the client in order to keep both the client and the server in sync. The following example returns the modified Department entity back to the caller:

```
@POST
@Path("{id}")
public Department editDepartment(@PathParam("id") Short id,
    Department entity) {
  Department modifiedEntity=editDepartmentEntity(entity);
  return modifiedEntity;
}
```

If you are using the POST operation for creating a resource, you can use the HTTP 201 status code in the response, indicating the status of operation, and include a Location header that points to the URL of the new resource. Here is an example:

```
import javax.ws.rs.core.Response;
import javax.ws.rs.core.UriInfo;
import javax.ws.rs.core.Context;

@POST
public Response createDepartment(Department entity,
    @Context UriInfo uriInfo) {
    Integer deptId=createDepartmentEntity(entity);
    //Builds a URI for the newly created resource
    UriBuilder builder = uriInfo.getAbsolutePathBuilder();
    builder.path(deptId.toString());
    return Response.created(builder.build()).build();
}
```

Paging a resource collection

It is not considered good practice to return all resources that you may have in the database (or in any other data source) to a client in response to a GET API call. A very common approach for limiting the resource collection returned by an API is to allow the client to specify the offset and the page size for the collection. For example, the API that allows the client to specify the offset and the limit for the resource collection as the query parameters is /departments?offset=1&limit=20.

The following code snippet demonstrates how you can build a JAX-RS resource method that takes the offset and the page size (limit) sent by the client via query parameters:

```
@GET
@Produces("application/json")
public List<Department> findDepartments(@QueryParam("offset")
@DefaultValue("0") Integer offset, @QueryParam("limit")
    @DefaultValue("20") Integer limit) {
    //Complete method implementation is not shown for brevity
    return findDepartmentEntitiesInRange(offset, limit);
}
```

The preceding example is the simplest solution for paging a resource collection. You can improve this solution by including additional attributes in the collection resource representation as follows:

- hasMore: This attribute indicates whether the collection has more elements to be retrieved
- limit: This attribute indicates the limit used by the server while querying the collection; this scenario arises if the limit is missing in the client request
- count: This attribute indicates the total number of elements in the collection
- totalSize: This attribute indicates the number of elements on the server that match the criteria used for reading the collection
- links: This attribute contains links to the next and the previous sets

The following example illustrates the resource collection returned by the server with the additional pagination attribute that we discussed:

```
{
    "departments": [{
        "departmentId": "11",
        "departmentName": "HR"
    },{
        "departmentId": "12",
        "departmentName": "IT"
```

```
},...
],
"hasMore": true,
"count": 10,
"totalSize": 25,
"links": [
    {"rel":"self",
    "href":"/hrapp/api/departments?offset=10&limit=10"},
    {"rel":"prev",
    "href":"/hrapp/api/departments?offset=0&limit=10"},
    {"rel":"next",
    "href":"/hrapp/api/departments?offset=20&limit=10"}
]
}
```

Implementing search and sort operations

Allowing a client to perform the search and sort operations on a resource collection is very essential to improve the market adoption of your APIs. As there is no existing standard for passing sort criteria or search conditions, various API vendors follow different patterns. A very common approach is to pass the search and sort criteria as the query parameters to the server.

The following example illustrates how you can pass the search criteria as the query parameters to the server:

```
/employees?departmentName=hr&salary>500000
```

The query parameters present in the preceding resource request URI can be used by the RESTful API implementation to find out the employee resources belonging to the HR department whose annual salary is greater than 500000.

Similarly, to read the collection of resources in a sorted order, you can pass the sort criteria as the query parameter to the API. The following example uses the sort keyword as the query parameter to indicate the beginning of fields in the URI for sorting, followed by the asc or desc keyword, indicating the sort order:

```
/employees?sort=firstName:asc,lastName:asc
```

If you have complex search conditions that cannot be easily represented as the request parameter in the URI, you can consider moving the search conditions into the request body and use the POST method for issuing the search. Here is an example:

```
POST  employees/searches HTTP/1.1
Host: packtpub.com
Accept: application/json
Content-Type: application/json
{
  "criteria": [{
    "firstName": "A";
    "operator": "startswith"
  }],
  "sort": [{"firstName":"asc","lastName":"asc" }
}
```

Versioning RESTful web APIs

You should always version the RESTful web APIs. Versioning of APIs helps you to roll out new releases without affecting the existing customer base as you can continue to offer the old API versions for a certain period of time. Later, a customer can move on to a new version if he/she prefers to do so.

You can version RESTful web APIs in many ways. Three popular techniques for versioning RESTful web APIs are given in this section.

Including the version in the resource URI – URI versioning

In the URI versioning approach, the version is appended along with the URI. An example is as follows:

```
GET /api/v1/departments HTTP/1.1
```

A sample RESTful web API implementation that takes a version identifier as part of the resource URI will look like the following:

```
//Imports are removed for brevity
@Path("v1/departments")
public class DepartmentResourceV1{
    @GET
    @Produces("application/json")
    public List<Department> findDepartmentsInRange(
        @QueryParam("offset") @DefaultValue("1") Integer offset,
        @QueryParam("limit") @DefaultValue("20") Integer limit) {

        return findAllDepartmentEntities(offset, limit);
    }
    //Other methods are removed for brevity
}
```

With this approach, if you want to upgrade the version for a resource, you will have to build a new resource class that takes the latest API version as the Path parameter. To avoid code duplication, you can subclass the existing resource class and override only the modified resource methods as shown here:

```
//Imports are removed for brevity
@Path("v2/departments")
public class DepartmentResourceV2 extends DepartmentResourceV1{
    @GET
    @Produces("application/json")
    @Override
    public List<Department> findDepartmentsInRange(
        @QueryParam("offset") @DefaultValue("1") Integer offset,
        @QueryParam("limit") @DefaultValue("20") Integer limit) {

        return findAllDepartmentEntities(offset, limit);
    }
    //Other methods are removed for brevity
}
```

Many big players (Twitter, Facebook, and so on) use the URI versioning approach for versioning the APIs.

Conceptually, this is the simplest solution for API versioning. However, there are certain drawbacks associated with this approach:

- As the resource URI changes with each release, client applications may have to change all the existing URI references in order to migrate to a new release. The impact may be minimal if all the resource URIs are localized and stored in a configuration file.
- This approach may disrupt the concept of HATEOAS.
- Since the URI path for an API gets updated for each change in the REST resource class, you may experience a large URI footprint over a period of time. This may result in a code maintenance issue for both the client and the server.
- If the URI is versioned, the cache may contain multiple copies of each resource, one for every version of the API.

Including the version in a custom HTTP request header – HTTP header versioning

The HTTP header versioning approach uses a custom header field to hold the API version. While requesting for a resource, the client sets the version in the header along with other information (if any). The server can be built to use the version information sent by the client in order to identify the correct version of the resource.

The following example uses a custom header to specify the API version that the client is looking for:

```
GET /api/departments HTTP/1.1
api-version: 1.0
```

The API implementation can read the request header via @javax.ws.rs.HeaderParam:

```
//Other imports are omitted for brevity
import javax.ws.rs.HeaderParam;
@GET
@Produces("application/json")
public List<Department> findAllDepartments(
    @HeaderParam("api-version") String version){
    //Method body is omitted for brevity
}
```

Including the version in the HTTP Accept header – media type versioning

The media type versioning approach adds the version information to the media content type. You can do this by introducing custom vendor media types that hold the version information along with the media type details. The version information in the Accept header takes the following form:

```
Accept: application/vnd.{app_name}.{version}+{response_type}
```

The vnd part that you see in the Accept header is based on **RFC 6838**. The vnd keyword indicates the custom vendor-specific media types. More details are available at https://tools.ietf.org/html/rfc6838.

When you use this approach for versioning APIs, the client has to specify the version in the HTTP Accept header, as shown in the following example:

```
GET /api/v1/departments
Accept: application/vnd.packtpubapi.v1+json
```

A sample RESTful web API implementation that uses the media type versioning approach is shown here for your reference:

```java
@Path("departments")
@Produces({"application/json", "application/vnd.packtpub.v1+json"})
@Consumes({"application/json", "application/vnd.packtpub.v1+json"})
public class DepartmentResource{
    //The following method is a modified implementation
    //to read the list of employees, so the version number has been
incremented
    @GET
    @Produces({"application/vnd.packtpub.v2+json"})
    public List<Department> findDepartmentsInRangeV2(
        @QueryParam("offset") @DefaultValue("1") Integer offset,
        @QueryParam("limit") @DefaultValue("20") Integer limit) {
        return findDepartmentEntitiesWithDetails(offset, limit);
    }

    @GET
    public List<Department> findDepartmentsInRangeV1(
        @QueryParam("offset") @DefaultValue("1") Integer offset,
        @QueryParam("limit") @DefaultValue("20") Integer limit){
        return findDepartmentEntities(offset, limit);
    }

}
```

The preceding implementation has two methods annotated with different media type versions. At runtime, the Jersey framework automatically picks up a method to serve a request on the basis of the media type version information present in the `Accept` header parameter.

Many new API vendors have started supporting this approach. For example, GitHub uses the `Accept` header approach for versioning its APIs.

 Although this approach works for many of the common use cases, there are challenges associated with the caching of results returned by these kinds of APIs. Many user agents do not consider the `Accept` header while reading the cached contents. For instance, when using the same URI for multiple versions of APIs, there are chances of caching proxies to return wrong representations from the cache. Although you can configure caching proxies to consider the `Accept` headers along with the URI, doing so may add complexity to your network configuration.

Hybrid approach for versioning APIs

Some API vendors choose a combination of URI versioning and HTTP header versioning approaches, where the major version information is kept along with the URI and the minor version information for subresources is stored in the custom header field. In this case, the major version information indicates the structural stability of the API as a whole, while the minor versions indicate smaller changes at the implementation level.

To summarize the discussion, there is no wrong and right approach for versioning APIs. You can choose one of the options that we have discussed here for your application as long as it meets your application's needs.

Caching RESTful web API results

The ability to cache and reuse previously retrieved resources is very essential for improving the performance of a REST application. The HTTP/1.1 protocol specification provides a number of features to facilitate the caching of network resources. These offerings can be leveraged for improving the performance of the RESTful web APIs accessed over the HTTP protocol.

HTTP Cache-Control directive

The HTTP `Cache-Control` directive defines the HTTP response caching policies. You can use it for enabling the caching of the RESTful web API results for a specified interval. Here is a quick summary of the important HTTP `Cache-Control` directives:

HTTP Cache-Control directive	Description
`public`	In this directive, public resources can be cached by the client and all intermediate public proxies.
`private`	In this directive, private resources can be cached only by the client.
`max-age`	This directive specifies how long a resource cached on the client is valid (measured in seconds).
`smax-age`	This property specifies the maximum age for a shared cache such as proxy cache (for example, content delivery network).
`no-cache`	This directive indicates that the resource should not be cached.
`no-store`	This directive indicates that the cached resource should not be stored on disk; however, it can be cached in-memory.
`must-revalidate`	This directive indicates that once the cache expires, the cache must revalidate the resource with the origin server even if the client is willing to work on the stale resource.

JAX-RS allows you to specify the `Cache-Control` directives on the `javax.ws.rs.core.Response` object via the `javax.ws.rs.core.CacheControl` class. To learn how to use the `CacheControl` class in your JAX-RS resource class, refer to the *Using Cache-Control directives to manage the HTTP cache* section in `Chapter 4`, *Advanced Features in the JAX-RS APIs*.

HTTP conditional requests

The conditional requests feature offered by HTTP allows clients to ask the server whether it has an updated copy of the resource by including some extra header parameters in the request. The server will return the resource back to the client only if the resource that the client has is not up to date.

Conditional requests can be implemented either by comparing the hash value of resource contents (via the ETag header) or by checking the time at which the resource is modified (via the Last-Modified header). Here is the quick summary of the request and response header parameters used in conditional requests:

- ETag: When requesting for a resource, the client adds an ETag header, containing a hash or checksum of the resource that the client has received from the server for the last request. This hash value should change whenever the resource representation changes on the server. This allows the server to identify whether the client-cached contents of the resource are different from the actual content at the server.

- Last-Modified: This header works similar to ETag, except that it uses the timestamp for validating the cache. While generating a response, the server generates the Last-Modified header for the resource and passes it to the client. Subsequent requests from the client can send this timestamp information to the server via the If-Modified-Since request header, which tells the server not to send the resource again if it has not been changed.

You can use the mentioned conditional approach while modifying a resource as well. This will help you ensure that the update is not happening against a stale instance of the resource. Your RESTful web API can be designed to throw 412 Precondition Failed if the ETag header sent by the client does not match the ETag header generated on the server using the latest contents.

To enable conditional requests, JAX-RS offers APIs such as `javax.ws.rs.core.EntityTag` and `javax.ws.rs.core.Request::evaluatePreconditions()`, the former to generate `ETag` and the latter to evaluate the preconditions present in the request, such as `If-Modified-Since` and `If-None-Match`. To learn the usage of the `ETag` and `Last-Modified` headers in a JAX-RS application, you can refer to the *Conditional request processing with the Last-Modified HTTP response header* and *Conditional request processing with the ETag HTTP response header* sections in `Chapter 4`, *Advanced Features in the JAX-RS APIs*.

Using HTTP status codes in RESTful web APIs

Currently, there are over 75 status codes to report the statuses of various operations. The HTTP status codes are classified into the following five categories:

- `1xx Informational`: This code indicates informational messages
- `2xx Successful`: This code indicates successful processing of the requests
- `3xx Redirection`: This code indicates that an action needs to be taken by the client to complete the request
- `4xx Client error`: This code indicates a client error
- `5xx Server error`: This code indicates a server failure in fulfilling the request

It is always recommended to return the appropriate status codes in response to a RESTful web API call. The status code present in the response helps the client take an appropriate action, depending upon the status of the operation. The following table summarizes the commonly used HTTP status codes to describe the status of a RESTful web API call:

Commonly used HTTP status codes	Description
200 OK	This status indicates a successful GET, PUT, PATCH, or DELETE operation. This status can be used for POST if an existing resource has been updated.
201 Created	This status is generated in response to a POST operation that creates a new resource.

204 No Content	This code tells that the server has processed the request but not returned any content. For example, this can be used with the PUT, POST, GET, or DELETE operations if they do not result in any result body.
304 Not Modified	This code tells the client that it can use the cached resource that was retrieved in the previous call. This code is typically used with the GET operation.
400 Bad Request	This code indicates that the request sent by the client was invalid (client error) and could not be served. The exact error should be explained in the response entity body payload.
401 Unauthorized	This code indicates that the REST API call requires user authentication. The client can take the necessary steps for authentication based on this response status.
403 Forbidden	This code indicates that the caller (even after authentication) does not have an access to the requested resource.
404 Not Found	This code indicates that the requested resource is not found at this moment but may be available again in the future.
405 Method Not Allowed	This code indicates that the HTTP method requested by the caller is not supported by the resource.
406 Not Acceptable	This code indicates that the server does not support the required representation. For example, this can be used in response to the GET, PUT, or POST operations if the underlying REST API does not support the representation of the resource that the client is asking for.
409 Conflict	This code indicates that the request could not be completed due to some general conflict with the current state of the resource. This response code makes sense where the caller is capable of resolving the conflict by looking at the error details present in the response body and resubmitting the request. For example, this code can be used in response to PUT, POST, and DELETE if the client sends an outdated resource object to the server or if the operation results in the duplication of resources.
410 Gone	This code indicates that the resource identified by this URI is no longer available. Upon receiving a 410 status code, the caller should not request the resource again in the future.

415 Unsupported Media Type	This code indicates that the entity media type present in the request (PUT or POST) is not supported by the server.
422 Unprocessable Entity	This code indicates that the server cannot process the entity present in the request body. Typically, this happens due to semantic errors such as validation errors.
429 Too Many Requests	This code indicates that the client has sent too many requests in a given time, which results in the rejection of requests due to rate limiting. Note that rate limiting is used for controlling the rate of traffic sent or received by a network interface controller.
500 Internal Server Error	This code indicates that the server encountered an unexpected error scenario while processing the request.

When an operation fails on a resource, the RESTful web API should provide a useful error message to the caller. As a best practice, it is recommended to copy the detailed exception messages into the response body so that the client can take appropriate actions. By default, all JAX-RS containers intercept all exceptions thrown during the processing of the REST APIs and process them in their own way. However, you can provide your own javax.ws.rs.ext.ExceptionMapper to override the default exception handling offered by the JAX-RS runtime. We have discussed this topic in detail under the *Mapping exceptions to the response message using ExceptionMapper* section in Chapter 4, *Advanced Features in the JAX-RS APIs*. The following code snippet illustrates how you can build an ExceptionMapper provider for handling javax.validation.ValidationException. The ValidationException errors are typically thrown by the framework when the bean validation rules that you set on the model class fail:

```
//Imports are removed for brevity
@Provider
// A provider that maps Java exceptions to a Response
public class ValidationExceptionMapper implements
ExceptionMapper<ValidationException> {

    // Map validation exception to a Response
    @Override
    public Response toResponse(ValidationException exception) {
        //Set 400 Bad Request status and error message entity
        if (exception instanceof ConstraintViolationException) {
            return buildResponse(unwrapException((
                ConstraintViolationException) exception),
                MediaType.TEXT_PLAIN, Status.BAD_REQUEST);
        }else{
        return buildResponse(unwrapException(exception),
            MediaType.TEXT_PLAIN, Status.BAD_REQUEST);
```

```
            }
        }
        //Build response obj containing error message as entity
        protected Response buildResponse(Object entity,
            String mediaType,
            Status status) {
            ResponseBuilder builder = Response.status(status).
                entity(entity);
            builder.type(MediaType.TEXT_PLAIN);
            builder.header("validation-Error", "true");
            return builder.build();
        }
    //unwrapException() method definition is removed for brevity
}
```

The complete source code for this example is available at the Packt
website. You can download the example from the Packt website link
mentioned at the beginning of this book in the *Preface* section. In the
downloaded source code, see the Java source file called
`com.packtpub.rest.ch8.service.exception.ValidationExcepti`
`onMapper`, available in the `rest-chapter8-jaxrs/rest-chapter8-`
`service` project.

Overriding HTTP methods

Due to security reasons, some corporate firewalls (HTTP proxies) support only the POST
and GET methods. This restriction forces a REST API client to use only those HTTP methods
that are allowed through the firewall. RESTful web API implementations can work around
this restriction by letting the client override the HTTP method via the custom X-HTTP-
Method-Override HTTP header. The REST API client can specify an X-HTTP-Method-
Override request header with a string value containing either PUT, PATCH, or DELETE.
When the server gets the request, the server replaces the POST method call with the method
string value set for X-HTTP-Method-Override.

JAX-RS allows you to implement this behavior via prematching
`javax.ws.rs.container.ContainerRequestFilter`. To learn more about
ContainerRequestFilter, refer to the *Understanding the filters and interceptors in JAX-RS*
section in Chapter 4, *Advanced Features in the JAX-RS APIs*:

```
//Other imports are omitted for brevity
import javax.ws.rs.container.PreMatching;
@Provider
@PreMatching
```

```
// A provider impl for handling the X-Http-Method-Override header
public class HttpOverride implements ContainerRequestFilter {

    public void filter(ContainerRequestContext ctx) {
        String method = ctx.getHeaderString
            ("X-Http-Method-Override");
        //override header should only be accepted on POST
        if (method != null
            && ctx.getMethod().equals("POST"))
        //Set the method to the X-HTTP-Method-Override header value
            ctx.setMethod(method);
    }
}
```

Documenting RESTful web APIs

Good API documentation improves the market adoption of APIs. The API documentation should be both human and machine readable. There are many tools available today for documenting RESTful web APIs. Some of the popular RESTful web API documentation tools are listed here for your quick reference:

- **WADL**: This tool is an XML description of HTTP-based web applications such as RESTful web services. Not many vendors use WADL nowadays due to the emergence of more developer-friendly API documentation tools such as Swagger, RAML, and API Blueprint. To learn more about the WADL specification, visit http://www.w3.org/Submission/wadl.
- **RAML**: This tool provides both human- and machine-readable formats (YAML) for describing APIs. This is relatively new in the market and is well supported by the active open source community. To learn more about RAML, visit the official site at http://raml.org.
- **Swagger**: This tool allows you to define APIs either in YAML or JSON and is backed up by a large open source community. More details can be found at http://swagger.io.
- **API Blueprint**: This tool provides a documentation-oriented web API description language that uses the markdown format for describing the APIs. It is backed by Apiary and a large open source community. To learn more, visit the official site at https://apiblueprint.org.

We discussed WADL, RAML, and Swagger in detail in Chapter 7, *Description and Discovery of RESTful Web Services*.

Asynchronous execution of RESTful web APIs

If your RESTful web API takes a considerable amount of time to finish the job and the users cannot wait for the API to finish, you may want to consider using the asynchronous mode of execution.

The asynchronous RESTful web API works as explained here. The client calls the asynchronous RESTful API as any other API:

```
POST /employees HTTP/1.1
[{"departmentId": 10, "departmentName": "IT"},
{"departmentId": 20, "departmentName": "HR"},...]
```

The asynchronous API that is responsible for handling the preceding request accepts the request and returns the `202 Accepted` status to the caller without keeping the caller waiting for the request to finish. The response also can have a temporary resource inside the `Location` header, which can be used by the client to query the status of the process. Here is an example of the response generated by the server:

```
HTTP/1.1 202 Accepted
Location: /queue/job1234
```

The JAX-RS 2.x specification allows you to build asynchronous APIs via the following two classes:

- `javax.ws.rs.container.AsyncResponse`: This interface gives you a means for asynchronous server-side response processing
- `@javax.ws.rs.container.Suspended`: This annotation is used for injecting a suspended `AsyncResponse` object into a parameter of an invoked JAX-RS resource

To learn how to build an asynchronous RESTful web API with the JAX-RS APIs, refer to the *Asynchronous RESTful web services* section in `Chapter 4`, *Advanced Features in the JAX-RS APIs*.

Microservice architecture style for RESTful web application

Microservice is an architectural style for implementing a single application as a suite of small services. Each service can be deployed and managed separately. This is an emerging software architectural style adopted by many enterprises today in order to meet the rapidly evolving business needs. To follow this pattern for your JAX-RS application, you may want to break down the top-level monolithic JAX-RS resources into separate modules, where each module contains the logically related JAX-RS resource classes. Each module is deployed as a self-contained WAR file. Services communicate with each other via synchronous protocols such as REST over HTTP or asynchronous protocols such as messaging queue. If the performance is really a concern, you can consider using binary protocols, such as Thrift or Avro, for enabling the communication between services. The following diagram demonstrates how you can break down the human resource services application of an organization into multiple microservices. It also illustrates the interaction between various microservices:

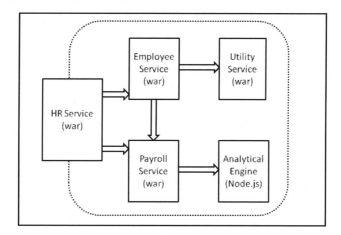

Some of the advantages of the microservice architecture are as follows:

- Small, modular, and easily manageable code base
- Each service can be deployed, managed, and tuned separately
- Ability to use the most appropriate technology stack (polyglot programming model) for individual services
- Improved resilience for the entire application
- Individual module can be redeployed without affecting the entire application

A quick recap

Having gone through in detail of various design guidelines in preceding sections, let's do a quick recap of the best practices as applicable to each of the key focus areas:

Focus area	Best practices
Resource	• Expose only those resources that are required for implementing the business use case • Naming of resource must be nouns; avoid using verbs • Avoid using generic name for resources, rather be specific • Resource names may include hyphens; avoid using underscores and other punctuation • Limit the length of the resource URI not to exceed 2,000 characters • Child resource must limit the scope to respective parent
Resource representation	• Specify the content type supported by consumers of the API • Avoid using multiple content type for a resource representation, JSON is becoming the de facto standard for content type, so avoid using XML • Include `Content-Type` header in the response • If the API supports multiple content types, recommend client to specify their preferred content type in the Accept Request Header • If the API supports multiple languages, recommend client to specify their preferred language in the Accept-Language Request Header • It is recommended to use the ISO-8601 format for representing the date and time in your RESTful APIs • Use pagination to avoid returning all the records in response when the result set is of large size and connect the paginated results using Link Header • When large datasets are requested, use relevant encoding such as GZIP compression for efficient usage of the available bandwidth

HTTP method	• Avoid using idempotent HTTP methods for non-idempotent operation • Avoid using safe HTTP methods for non-safe operation • Use each HTTP method for its defined purpose • To modify the state of a resource, use the widely supported HTTP POST method • Restrict the DELETE operation on a collection of resources, if the result is expected to perform hard delete and unrecoverable • Use caching only for idempotent and safe HTTP methods • Use the relevant HTTP status code in the response to qualify the correct response status • Faults must be qualified with correct HTTP error status code • Avoid sending OK Status(200) in case of faults • Enforce clients to use X-RateLimit-Limit and X-RateLimit-Remaining headers to avoid overloading the service
Security	• Whitelist allowable actions on an entity. • Mention only allowable action verbs such as GET/POST, so other actions even if triggered by client are denied. • Validate the input data against the interface contract specification and reject bad request. • Validate URL to protect from injection attacks. • Avoid encoding sensitive information in the URL. If the request/response involves sensitive data/personal identification information as classified by enterprise data security guidelines, use HTTPs for encrypting the communication. For APIs exposed outside the enterprise for third-party clients, implement robust authentication and authorization such as JWT or OAuth 2.0.
Documentation of API	• The interface must be documented clearly, qualifying the request, response, errors, and metadata as relevant • Specify example of request and response for applicable business scenarios • Mentio the backward and forward compatibility of newer version of APIs

Summary

This chapter summarized the design guidelines, best practices, and coding tips that developers will find useful when building RESTful web services. You can freely refer to this chapter while working with the JAX-RS and Jersey frameworks.

This chapter started with tips for designing and developing scalable RESTful web APIs and moved from the design guidelines to REST API optimization techniques such as caching, partial representation, partial update, and asynchronous API calls. It then moved on to discuss the microservice architectural style and its relevance. By now, you should have learned how to build scalable and well-performing RESTful applications by using the JAX-RS and Jersey APIs.

9
The Role of RESTful APIs in Emerging Technologies

Two decades ago, the IT industry saw tremendous opportunities with the dot-com boom. Similar to the dot-com bubble, the IT industry is transitioning through another period of innovation disrupting all lines of business with recent technology trends such as the cloud, the **Internet of Things (IOT)**, single-page applications, and Open Data Protocol. What these trends are, what benefits it offers, and how RESTFul APIs play a role in each of these emerging areas will be covered in this chapter. We will be covering the following topics in this chapter; let's begin our exploration:

- Cloud services
- Internet of Things
- Single-page applications
- Social media
- Open Data Protocol

Cloud services

We are in an era where business and IT are married together. For enterprises, thinking of a business model without an IT strategy is becoming out of the equation. Keeping the interest on the core business, often the challenge that lies ahead of the executive team is optimizing the IT budget. Cloud computing has come to the rescue of the executive team in bringing savings to the IT spending incurred for running a business.

Cloud computing is an IT model for enabling anytime, anywhere, convenient, on-demand network access to a shared pool of configurable computing resources. In simple terms, cloud computing refers to the delivery of hosted services over the internet that can be quickly provisioned and decommissioned with minimal management effort and less intervention from the service provider.

Cloud characteristics

Five key characteristics deemed essential for cloud computing are as follows:

- **On-demand Self-service:** Ability to automatically provision cloud-based IT resources as and when required by the cloud service consumer
- **Broad Network Access:** Ability to support seamless network access for cloud-based IT resources via different network elements such as devices, network protocols, security layers, and so on
- **Resource Pooling:** Ability to share IT resources for cloud service consumers using the multi-tenant model
- **Rapid Elasticity:** Ability to dynamically scale IT resources at runtime and also release IT resources based on the demand
- **Measured Service:** Ability to meter the service usage to ensure cloud service consumers are charged only for the services utilized

Cloud offering models

Cloud offerings can be broadly grouped into three major categories, IaaS, PaaS, and SaaS, based on their usage in the technology stack:

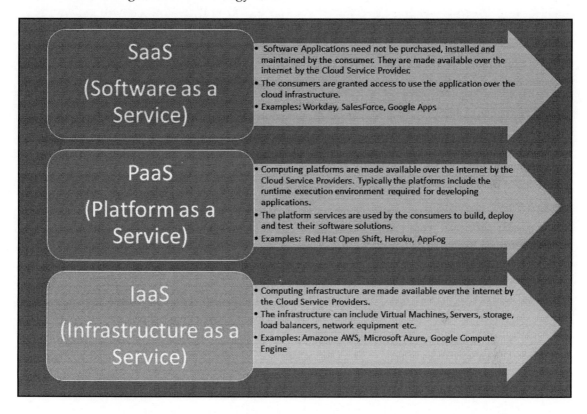

- **Software as a Service (SaaS)** delivers the application required by an enterprise, saving the costs an enterprise needs to procure, install, and maintain these applications, which will now be offered by a cloud service provider at competitive pricing
- **Platform as a Service (PaaS)** delivers the platforms required by an enterprise for building their applications, saving the cost the enterprise needs to set up and maintain these platforms, which will now be offered by a cloud service provider at competitive pricing
- **Infrastructure as a Service (IaaS)** delivers the infrastructure required by an enterprise for running their platforms or applications, saving the cost the enterprise needs to set up and maintain the infrastructure components, which will now be offered by a cloud service provider at competitive pricing

RESTful API Role in cloud services

RESTful APIs can be looked on as the glue that connects the cloud service providers and cloud service consumers. For example, application developers requiring to display a weather forecast can consume the Google Weather API. In this section, we will look at the applicability of RESTful APIs for provisioning resources in the cloud.

 For an illustration of RESTful APIs, we will be using the Oracle Cloud service platform. Users can set up a free trial account via `https://Cloud.oracle.com/home` and try out the examples discussed in the following sections.

Provisioning IT resources using RESTful APIs

Oracle provides various REST APIs for creating and managing IT resources in the cloud infrastructure.

 Refer to `http://docs.oracle.com/en/Cloud/iaas/compute-iaas-Cloud/stcsa/index.html` for details of REST APIs available for the Oracle IaaS cloud offering.

For example, we will try to set up a test virtual machine instance using the REST APIs. The high-level steps required to be performed are as follows:

1. Locate REST API endpoint
2. Generate authentication cookie
3. Provision virtual machine instance

Locating the REST API endpoint

Once users have signed up for an Oracle Cloud account, they can locate the REST API endpoint to be used by navigating via the following steps:

1. Login screen: Choose the relevant **Cloud Account** details and click the **My Services** button as shown in the screenshot ahead:

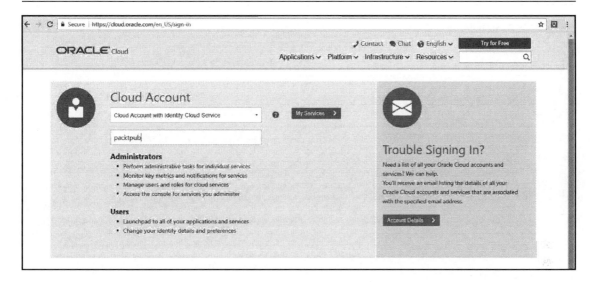

2. Home page: Displays the cloud services **Dashboard** for the user. Click the **Dashboard** icon as shown in the following screenshot:

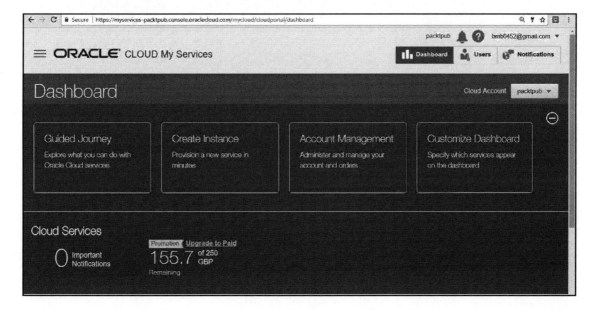

3. **Dashboard** screen: Lists the various cloud offerings. Click the **Compute Classic** offering:

4. **Compute Classic** screen: Displays the details of infrastructure resources utilized by the user:

5. **Site Selector** screen: Displays the REST endpoint:

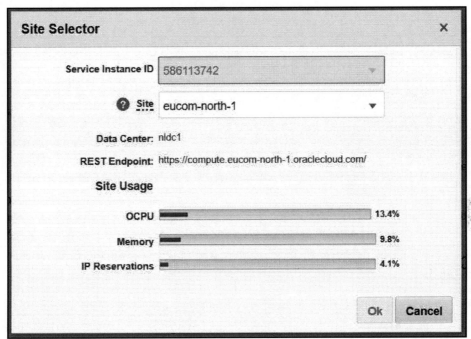

Generating an authentication cookie

Authentication is required for provisioning the IT resources. For this purpose, we will be required to generate an authentication cookie using the Authenticate User REST API. The details of the API are as follows:

API details	Description
API function	Authenticate supplied user credential and generate authentication cookie for use in the subsequent API calls.
Endpoint	`<RESTEndpoint captured in previous section>/authenticate/` **Example:** `https://compute.eucom-north-1.oracleCloud.com/ authenticate/`
HTTP method	`POST`

Request header properties	`Content-Type:application/oracle-compute-v3+jsonAccept: application/oracle-compute-v3+json`

Request body	• **user**: Two-part name of the user in the `format/Computeidentity_domain/user`
	• **password**: Password for the specified `userSample`
	• **request**:{
	`"password": "xxxxx",`
	`"user": "/Compute-586113456/test@gmail.com"`
	`}`

Response header properties	**set-cookie**: Authentication cookie value

The following screenshot shows the authentication cookie generated by invoking the Authenticate User REST API via the Postman tool:

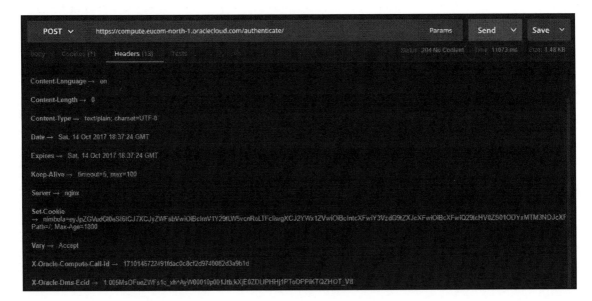

Provisioning a virtual machine instance

Consumer are allowed to provision IT resources on the Oracle Compute Cloud infrastructure service, using the LaunchPlans or Orchestration REST API. For this demonstration, we will use the LaunchPlans REST API. The details of the API are as follows:

API function	Launch plan used to provision infra resources in Oracle Compute Cloud Service.
Endpoint	`<RESTEndpoint captured in above section>/launchplan/` **Example:** `https://compute.eucom-north-1.oracleCloud.com/launchplan/`
HTTP method	`POST`
Request header properties	Content-Type:application/oracle-compute-v3+json Accept: application/oracle-compute-v3+json Cookie: <Authentication cookie>

Request body	• **instances**: Array of instances to be provisioned. For details of properties required by each instance, refer to `http://docs.oracle.com/en/Cloud/iaas/` `compute-iaas-Cloud/stcsa/op-launchplan--post.html`.
	• **relationships**: Mention if any relationship with other instances.
	• **Sample Request**:
	<pre>{
	    "instances": [
	        {
	            "shape": "oc3",
	            "imagelist": "/oracle/public/oel_6.4_2GB_v1",
	            "name": "/Compute-586113742/test@gmail.com/test-vm-1",
	            "label": "test-vm-1",
	            "sshkeys":[]
	        }
	    ]
	}</pre>

Response body	Provisioned list of instances and their relationships

The following screenshot shows the creation of a test virtual machine instance by invoking the LaunchPlan REST API via the Postman tool:

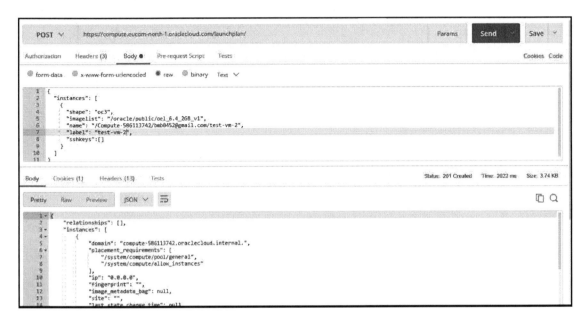

HTTP Response Status 201 confirms the request for provisioning was successful. Check the provisioned instance status via the cloud service instances page as shown here:

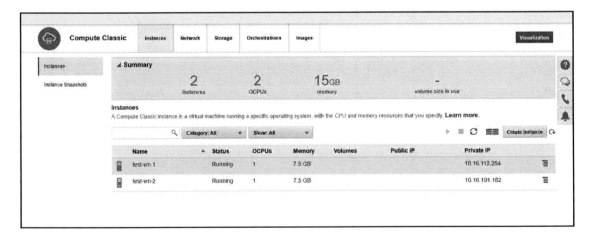

Internet of things

The **Internet of Things (IoT)**, as the name says, can be considered as a technology enabler for things (which includes people as well) to connect or disconnect from the internet. The term IoT was first coined by Kelvin Ashton in 1999. With broadband Wi-Fi becoming widely available, it is becoming a lot easier to connect things to the internet. This a has lot of potential to enable a smart way of living and already there are many projects being spoken about smart homes, smart cities, and so on. A simple use case can be predicting the arrival time of a bus so that commuters can get a benefit, if there are any delays and plan accordingly. In many developing countries, the transport system is enabled with smart devices which help commuters predict the arrival or departure time for a bus or train precisely. Gartner analysts firm has predicted that more than 26 billion devices will be connected to the internet by 2020. The following diagram from Wikipedia shows the technology roadmap depicting the applicability of the IoT by 2020 across different areas:

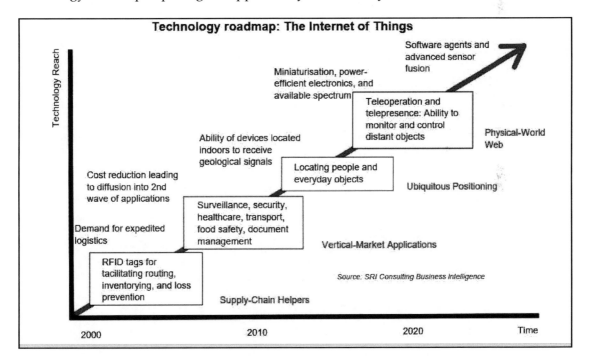

IoT platform

The IoT platform consists of four functional layers—the device, data, integration, and service layers. For each functional layer, let us understand the capabilities required for the IoT platform:

Device	Device management capabilities supporting device registration, provisioning, and controlling access to devices. Seamless connectivity to devices to send and receive data.
Data	Management of huge volume of data transmitted between devices. Derive intelligence from data collected and trigger actions.
Integration	Collaboration of information between devices.
Service	API gateways exposing the APIs.

IoT benefits

The IoT platform is seen as the latest evolution of the internet, offering various benefits as shown here:

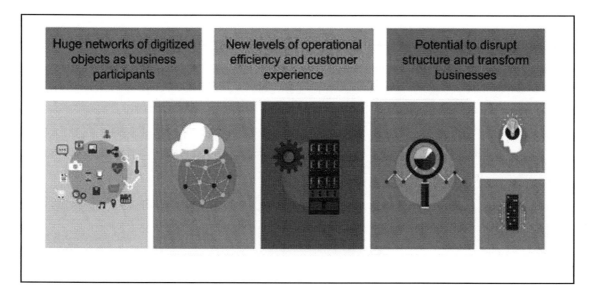

The IoT is becoming widely used due to lowering cost of technologies such as cheap sensors, cheap hardware, and low cost of high bandwidth network.

The connected human is the most visible outcome of the IoT revolution. People are connected to the IoT through various means such as Wearables, Hearables, Nearables, and so on, which can be used to improve the lifestyle, health, and wellbeing of human beings:

- **Wearables:** Wearables are any form of sophisticated, computer- like technology which can be worn or carried by a person, such as smart watches, fitness devices, and so on.
- **Hearables:** Hearables are wireless computing earpieces, such as headphones.
- **Nearables:** Nearables are smart objects with computing devices attached to them, such as door locks, car locks, and so on. Unlike Wearables or Hearables, Nearables are static.

Also, in the healthcare industry, the IoT-enabled devices can be used to monitor patients' heart rate or diabetes. Smart pills and nanobots could eventually replace surgery and reduce the risk of complications.

RESTful API role in the IoT

The architectural pattern used for the realization of the majority of the IoT use cases follows the event-driven architecture pattern. The event-driven architecture software pattern deals with the creation, consumption, and identification of events. An event can be generalized to refer the change in state of an entity.

For example, a printer device connected to the internet may emit an event when the printer cartridge is low on ink so that the user can order a new cartridge. The following diagram shows the same with different devices connected to the internet:

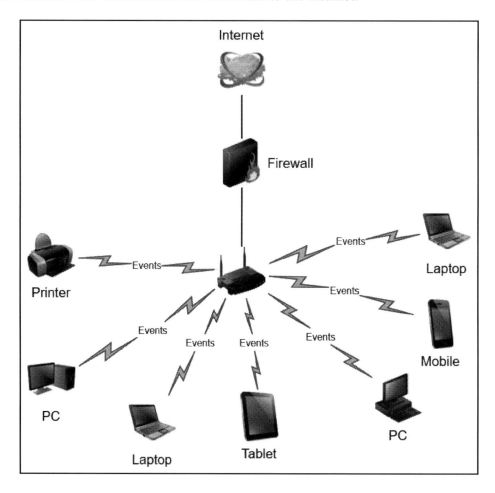

The common capability required for devices connected to the internet is the ability to send and receive event data. This can be easily accomplished with RESTful APIs. The following are some of the IoT APIs available on the market:

- **Hayo API**: The Hayo API is used by developers to build virtual remote controls for the IoT devices in a home. The API senses and transmits events between virtual remote controls and devices, making it easier for users to achieve desired actions on applications by simply manipulating a virtual remote control.
- **Mozilla Battery Status API**: The Mozilla Battery Status API is used to monitor system battery levels of mobile devices and streams notification events for changes in the battery levels and charging progress. Its integration allows users to retrieve real-time updates of device battery levels and status.
- **Caret API**: The Caret API allows status sharing across devices. The status can be customized as well.

Modern web applications

Web-based applications have seen drastic evolution from Web 1.0 to Web 2.0. Web 1.0 sites were designed mostly with static pages; Web 2.0 has added more dynamism to it. Let us take a quick snapshot of the evolution of web technologies over the years.

1993-1995	Static HTML Websites with embedded images and minimal JavaScript
1995-2000	Dynamic web pages driven by JSP, ASP, CSS for styling, JavaScript for client side validations.
2000-2008	Content Management Systems like Word Press, Joomla, Drupal, and so on.
2009-2013	Rich Internet Applications, Portals, Animations, Ajax, Mobile Web applications
2014 Onwards	Singe Page App, Mashup, Social Web

Single-page applications

Single-page applications are web applications designed to load the application in a single HTML page. Unlike traditional web applications, rather than refreshing the whole page for displaying content change, it enhances the user experience by dynamically updating the current page, similar to a desktop application. The following are some of the key features or benefits of single-page applications:

- Load contents in single page
- No refresh of page
- Responsive design
- Better user experience
- Capability to fetch data asynchronously using Ajax
- Capability for dynamic data binding

RESTFul API role in single-page applications

In a traditional web application, the client requests a URI and the requested page is displayed in the browser. Subsequent to that, if the user wants to submit a form then the submitted form data is sent to the server and the response is displayed by reloading the whole page as follows:

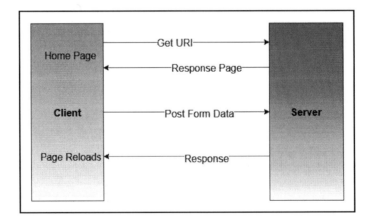

Unlike traditional web applications, the overhead of refreshing the page is reduced by single-page applications leveraging a REST API to load the page data as follows:

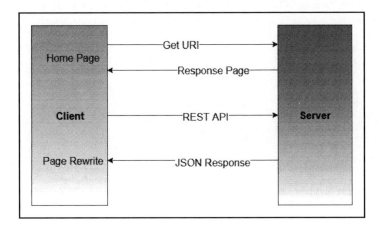

Social media

Social media is the future of communication that not only lets one interact but also enables the transfer of different content formats such as audio, video, and image between users. In Web 2.0 terms, social media is a channel that interacts with you along with providing information. While regular media is a one-way communication, social media is a two-way communication that asks for one's comments and lets one vote. Social media has seen tremendous usage via networking sites such as Facebook, LinkedIn, and so on.

Social media platforms

Social media platforms are based on Web 2.0 technology which serves as the interactive medium for collaboration, communication, and sharing among users. We can classify social media platforms broadly based on their usage as follows:

Social networking services	Platforms where people manage their social circles and interact with each other, such as Facebook.
Social bookmarking services	Allows one to save, organize, and manage links to various resource over the internet, such as StumbleUpon.
Social media news	Platform that allows people to post news or articles, such as reddit.

Blogging services	Platform where users can exchange their comments on views, such as Twitter.
Document sharing services	Platform that lets you share your documents, such as SlideShare.
Media sharing services	Platform that lets you share media contents, such as YouTube.
Crowd sourcing services	Obtaining needed services, ideas, or content by soliciting contributions from a large group of people or an online community, such as Ushahidi.

Social media benefits

User engagement through social media has seen tremendous growth and many companies use social media channels for campaigns and branding. Let us look at various benefits social media offers:

Customer relationship management	A company can use social media to campaigns their brand and potentially benefit with positive feedback from customer review.
Customer retention and expansion	Customer reviews can become a valuable source of information for retention and also help to add new customers.
Market research	Social media conversations can become useful insight for market research and planning.
Gain competitive advantage	Ability to get a view of competitors' messages which enables a company to build strategies to handle their peers in the market.
Public relations	Corporate news can be conveyed to audience in real time.
Cost control	Compared to traditional methods of campaigning, social media offers better advertising at cheaper cost.

RESTful API role in social media

Many of the social networks provides RESTful APIs to expose their capabilities. Let us look at the RESTful APIs of popular social media services:

Social media services	RESTful API	Reference
YouTube	Add YouTube features to your application, including the ability to upload videos, create and manage playlists, and more.	`https://developers.google.com/youtube/v3/`
Facebook	The Graph API is the primary way to get data out of, and put data into, Facebook's platform. It's a low-level HTTP-based API that you can use to programmatically query data, post new stories, manage ads, upload photos, and perform a variety of other tasks that an app might implement.	`https://developers.facebook.com/docs/graph-api/overview`
Twitter	Twitter provides APIs to search, filter, and create an ads campaign.	`https://developer.twitter.com/en/docs`

Using Open Data Protocol with RESTful web APIs

REST is an architecture style for sending messages back and forth from the client to the server over HTTP. The REST architectural style does not define any standard for querying and updating data. **Open Data Protocol (OData)** defines a web protocol for querying and updating data via RESTful web APIs uniformly. Many companies, including Microsoft, IBM, and SAP, support OData today, and it is governed by **Organization for the Advancement of Structured Information Standards (OASIS)**. Currently, the latest release of OData is Version 4.0.

A quick look at OData

OData provides you with a uniform way of describing the data and the data model. This helps you to consume the REST APIs from various vendors uniformly. Let's take a quick look at some of the core features offered in OData with some examples.

URI convention for OData-based REST APIs

The OData specification defines a set of recommendations for forming the URIs that identify OData-based REST APIs. The URI for an OData service may take up to three parts as follows:

- **Service root**: This part identifies the root of an OData service
- **Resource path**: This part identifies the resources exposed by an OData service
- **Query string options**: This part identifies the query options (built-in or custom) for the resource

Here is an example:

Reading resources

Resources from OData RESTful APIs are accessible via the HTTP GET request. For instance, the following GET request retrieves the `Departments` entity collection from the OData REST API server as follows:

```
GET http://localhost:8080/hrapp/odata/Departments HTTP/1.1
```

The result that you may get from the OData REST API server in response to the preceding call will be structured in accordance with the OData protocol specification. This keeps the client code simple and reusable.

To read the individual resource element, you can pass the unique identifier for the resource, as shown in the following code snippet. This example reads the details of the department with the given ID:

```
GET http://localhost:8080/hrapp/odata/Departments(10) HTTP/1.1.
```

Querying data

OData supports various kinds of query options as query parameters. For instance, $orderby can be used for sorting the query results. Here is an example:

```
GET http://localhost:8080/hrapp/odata/Departments?$orderby=
    DepartmentName HTTP/1.1
```

Similarly, you can use the $select option for limiting the attributes on the entity resources returned by a REST API. Here is an example:

```
GET http://localhost:8080/hrapp/odata/Departments?
$orderby=DepartmentName&$select=DepartmentName,ManagerId HTTP/1.1
```

Some of the frequently used query options are listed in the following table:

Query Option	Description	Example
$filter	This option allows the client to filter a collection of resources.	/Employees? $filter=FirstName eq 'Jobinesh'
$expand	This option includes the specified (child) resource in line with the retrieved resources.	/Departments(10)?$expand= Employees
$select	This option includes the supplied attributes alone in the resulting entity.	/Departments?$select=Name, LocationId
$orderby	This option sorts the query result by one or more attributes.	Departments?$orderby= DepartmentName desc
$top	This option returns only the specified number of items (from the top) in the result collection.	Departments?$top=10
$skip	This option indicates how many items need to be skipped from the top while returning the result.	Departments?$skip=10
$count	This option indicates the total number of items in the result.	Departments/$count

Modifying data

The updatable OData services provide a standardized interface for performing the following operations on entities exposed via the OData services:

- `Create`: This operation is performed via HTTP POST
- `Update`: This operation is performed via HTTP PUT or HTTP PATCH
- `Delete`: This operation is performed via HTTP DELETE

Relationship operations

OData supports the linking of related resources. Relationships from one entity to another are represented as navigation properties. The following API reads employees in the HR department:

```
http://localhost:8080/hrapp/odata/Departments("HR")/
    EmployeeDetails
```

The OData service even allows you to add, update, and remove a relation via navigation properties. The following example shows how you can use the navigation properties to link the employee with the id value of 1700 to the IT department:

```
POST odata/Departments('IT')/Employees/$ref
OData-Version: 4.0
Content-Type: application/json;odata.metadata=minimal
Accept: application/json
{
  "@odata.id": "odata/Employees(1700)"
}
```

Many API vendors have started considering OData for standardizing their REST APIs, particularly with the release of OData Version 4.0. A detailed discussion of OData is beyond the scope of this book. To learn more about OData, visit the official documentation page available at http://www.odata.org/documentation.

To learn how to transform the **Java Persistence API (JPA)** entities into OData REST APIs, refer to the *Transforming the JPA model into OData-enabled RESTful web services* section in the Appendix, *Useful Features and Techniques*, of this book.

Summary

This chapter discussed modern technology trends and the role of RESTful APIs in each of these areas. Starting with the cloud, we discussed the different offering models and saw an example of provisioning a virtual machine in the Oracle Cloud platform using a RESTful API. Then we touched upon the IoT and how RESTful APIs are used in connecting devices following the event-driven architecture pattern. Also, we briefly discussed social media and single-page applications and its benefits of improved user experience with RESTful API usage. The chapter concluded by discussing OData in short and its usage. With this chapter, we finish our journey through *RESTful Java Web Services, Third Edition*. We began with the theory of REST, continued with the JAX-RS APIs and the Jersey framework, and completed our study with topics on security, API documentation, design guidelines, and emerging technology trends. We hope that you enjoyed reading this book.

We strongly recommend the reader of this book to practice different recipes covered in the book for designing and implementing RESTful APIs. We also suggest further reading of the following books from Packt covering related topics on RESTful web services:

- *RESTful Web API Design*
- *RESTful Java Patterns And Best Practices*
- *RESTful Java Web Services Security*

Useful Features and Techniques

This appendix discusses various useful features and techniques that we deferred while discussing specific topics in this book. Make sure that you read the first three chapters of this book before you start reading this appendix. The following topics are discussed in this appendix:

- Tools for building a JAX-RS application
- The integration testing of JAX-RS resources with Arquillian
- Using third-party entity provider frameworks with Jersey
- Transforming a JPA model into OData-enabled RESTful web services
- The packaging and deploying of JAX-RS applications

Tools for building a JAX-RS application

The JAX-RS examples discussed in this book are built using the following software and tools:

- **Java SE Development Kit 8 (JDK 8) or newer**: You can download the latest JDK from
  `http://www.oracle.com/technetwork/java/javase/downloads/index.html`.
  After downloading the appropriate release of JDK, you can navigate to the **Installation Instructions** section on the download page for detailed instructions on how to install JDK on your computer.

- **NetBeans IDE 8.2 (with Java EE bundle) or newer**: The NetBeans IDE helps you to quickly develop JAX-RS web applications. You can download the latest NetBeans IDE from `https://netbeans.org/downloads`. In the download page, choose either the **Java EE** or **All** download bundles because many of the examples discussed in this book are based on Java EE features. Detailed instructions for setting up the NetBeans IDE are available at `https://netbeans.org/community/releases/82/install.html`.

- **GlassFish server 4.1 or newer**: GlassFish is an open source application server project for the Java EE platform. The NetBeans Java EE download bundle comes with an integrated GlassFish server, which is good enough for you to run all the examples discussed in this book. Alternatively, you can download the latest release of the GlassFish server from `https://glassfish.java.net/download.html` and wire it with NetBeans. The `README.txt` file in the downloaded ZIP file contains instructions for installing the GlassFish server.

- **Apache Maven 3.2.3 or newer**: Apache Maven is a build tool used in Java applications to compile source files, execute unit tests, and generate deployable artifacts. The NetBeans IDE standard installation comes with an integrated Maven installation by default. Alternatively, you can configure NetBeans to use an external Maven installation to build the source. To download Maven, visit `https://maven.apache.org` and navigate to the **Download** section. You will find the installation instructions under the **Installation Instructions** section on the download page itself. To point the NetBeans IDE to use an external Maven installation, choose the **Tools | Options** menu item, and in the **Java** tab, choose the **Maven** tab. In the Maven page, make sure that **External Maven Home** points to your Maven installation folder.

- **Oracle Database Express Edition 11g release 2 or newer**: Oracle Database Express Edition is a lightweight RDBMS, based on the Oracle database. We use this database to build the examples discussed in this book. To directly download Oracle Database Express Edition 11g Release 2, go to `http://www.oracle.com/technetwork/database/database-technologies/express-edition/downloads/index.html`. Alternatively, you can visit the Oracle Technology Network site at `http://www.oracle.com/technetwork/index.html` and, then, navigate to the **Downloads and Trails | Database | Oracle Database 11g Express Edition** menu options to reach the download page.

If you want, you can use any lightweight database, such as Apache Derby or db4o, instead of the Oracle database to try out the examples that we discussed in this book. However, in such a case, all the examples that you will download from the Packt website need to be reconfigured to fit into the database that you choose.

- **Oracle Database JDBC Driver (ojdbc7.jar or newer)**: The JDBC driver is a software library that lets Java applications interact with a database. You can download the latest JDBC driver from `http://www.oracle.com/technetwork/database/features/jdbc/jdbc-drivers-12c-download-1958347.html`.

To learn how to use the NetBeans IDE for building JAX-RS web applications, refer to the *Building a simple RESTful web service application using NetBeans IDE* section in `Chapter 3`, *Introducing the JAX-RS API*.

Integration testing of JAX-RS resources with Arquillian

Integration testing tests the interactions between the individual software components in a system. It helps you uncover faults with the integrated components of a system earlier in the lifecycle. In this section, you will learn how to develop and run integration tests for a JAX-RS web application.

A typical JAX-RS web application is comprised of various software components, such as databases, the persistence layer, business service implementation, and the client interface layer. The integration tests that you write for a JAX-RS application should test the interaction between all these components when putting them together to build the complete application.

Unit testing versus integration testing

A unit test is typically a test written by developers to verify a relatively small piece of code, and it should not depend upon any other components or external resources, such as the database. They are narrow in scope.

An integration test verifies that the different pieces of the system are in sync when they are put together to build a complete system. These tests typically require external resources, such as database instances or third-party APIs.

JBoss Arquillian is a powerful tool for the integration testing of Java EE applications. With Arquillian, you do not need to take care of setting up the environment, including the container for running integration tests. Arquillian lets you set up the container in three modes, as follows:

- **Remote**: This container runs in a separate JVM
- **Managed**: This container is functionally the same as the remote container, except that its lifecycle (starting and stopping) is managed by Arquillian
- **Embedded**: This container resides in the same JVM as your test case

A container can be of any of the following types:

- **Servlet container**: Examples of a servlet container are Tomcat and Jetty
- **Full-fledged Java EE application server**: Examples of a full-fledged Java EE application server are JBoss AS, GlassFish, and WebLogic
- **Java SE contexts and Dependency Injection(CDI) environment**: Examples of Java SE contexts and dependency injection (CDI) environment are OpenEJB and Weld SE

Let's learn how to use Arquillian for building integration tests for a JAX-RS application. The following diagram illustrates the high-level architecture of the application that we'll use in this example:

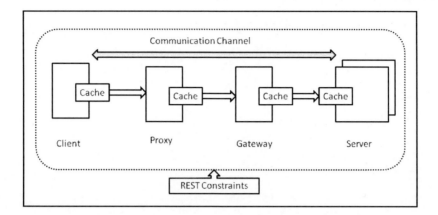

This example exposes the stateless session beans as RESTful web resources, and it uses the **Java Persistence API (JPA)** for database access. We will use Maven to build this example. In reality, you can use Arquillian with your favorite build tools, such as Ant, Maven, or Gradle.

The following discussion assumes that you have already created a Maven-based JAX-RS application. The source structure may look as follows:

```
-src/
    -main/
      -java/ [Contains all application Java source files]
      -resources/ [Contains all application configuration files]
      -webapp/ [Contains all web files]
    -test/
      -java/ [Contains all test Java source files]
      -resources/ [Contains all test configuration files here]
-pom.xml [The Maven build file]
```

If you are not sure how to build Maven-based JAX-RS applications, refer to the *Building a simple RESTful web service application using NetBeans IDE* section, in Chapter 3, *Introducing the JAX-RS API*.

Now, we will look at the steps for adding Aquillian to a Maven-based JAX-RS application.

Adding Arquillian dependencies to the Maven-based project

The Arquillian dependency entries in your `pom.xml` file may look like the following:

```xml
<dependency>
  <groupId>junit</groupId>
  <artifactId>junit</artifactId>
  <version>4.11</version>
  <scope>test</scope>
</dependency>
<dependency>
  <groupId>org.jboss.arquillian.junit</groupId>
  <artifactId>arquillian-junit-container</artifactId>
  <scope>test</scope>
</dependency>
<dependency>
  <groupId>org.jboss.arquillian.container</groupId>
  <artifactId>arquillian-glassfish-managed-3.1</artifactId>
  <version>1.0.0.Final-SNAPSHOT</version>
  <scope>test</scope>
</dependency>
<dependency>
  <groupId>org.glassfish.jersey.containers</groupId>
  <artifactId>jersey-container-servlet-core</artifactId>
  <version>2.0</version>
  <type>jar</type>
  <scope>provided</scope>
</dependency>
```

To use the latest release of Arquillian, point your Maven to use a repository hosted on `repository.jboss.org`. A quick summary of the dependencies set for Arquillian are as follows:

- The `junit` and `arquillian-junit-container` dependency: These are the dependencies for the JUnit and Arquillian JUnit extensions, respectively
- The `arquillian-glassfish-managed` dependency: This represents the managed GlassFish server instance for running the integrations tests
- The `jersey-container-servlet-core` dependency: This dependency is used for Jersey implementation of the JAX-RS API

The minimum recommended versions of Java and JUnit for using Arquillian are Java 1.6 and JUnit 4.8, respectively.

Configuring the container for running the tests

Arquillian uses `arquillian.xml` to locate and communicate with the container. Typically, this file is placed in the `src/test/resources` folder. The following `arquillian.xml` file demonstrates the entries for connecting to a locally installed GlassFish server, which we use in this example:

```xml
<?xml version="1.0"?>
<arquillian xmlns:xsi="http://www.w3.org/2001/XMLSchema-instance"
            xmlns="http://jboss.org/schema/arquillian"
            xsi:schemaLocation="http://jboss.org/schema/arquillian
                http://jboss.org/schema/arquillian/
arquillian_1_0.xsd">
    <container qualifier="glassfish" default="true">
        <configuration>
            <property name="glassFishHome">
             D:\glassfish-4.1
            </property>
            <property name="adminHost">localhost</property>
            <property name="adminPort">4848</property>
            <property name="adminUser">admin</property>
            <property name="adminPassword">admin</property>
        </configuration>
    </container>
</arquillian>
```

Adding Arquillian test classes to the project

Once you have the basic infrastructure ready for running the tests, you can start building the test cases. Add your test classes to the `src/test` folder in the Maven project structure. The following annotations will help you avail the Arquillian features in your test classes:

- Annotate the class with the `@org.junit.runner.RunWith(Arquillian.class)` annotation. This tells JUnit to invoke Arquillian for running the tests.

- Designate a `public static` method to return a deployable archive by annotating it with `@org.jboss.arquillian.container.test.api.Deployment`. This method should return an `org.jboss.shrinkwrap.api.ShrinkWrap.ShrinkWrap` archive. `ShrinkWrap` is an easy way to create deployable archives in Java, and Arquillian uses this API to build minimal deployable artifacts for running tests. You can learn more about `ShrinkWrap` at `http://arquillian.org/guides/shrinkwrap_introduction`.
- Annotate all the methods that need to be tested with `@org.junit.Test`.

The following is an Arquillian test class example for your quick reference. This class performs integration tests on the department resource:

```
//Other imports are removed for brevity
import org.junit.Test;
import org.jboss.arquillian.container.test.api.Deployment;
import org.jboss.arquillian.junit.Arquillian;
import org.jboss.arquillian.junit.InSequence;
import org.jboss.shrinkwrap.api.ShrinkWrap;
import org.jboss.shrinkwrap.api.spec.WebArchive;

@RunWith(Arquillian.class)
public class DepartmentResourceTest {

    public DepartmentResourceTest() {
    }

    //This method return minimal files that needs to be deployed
    //for running integration test
    //@Deployment(testable=true) : Runs within container(default)
    //@Deployment(testable=false) : Runs outside of container
    @Deployment(testable=true)
    public static WebArchive createDeployment() {
        return ShrinkWrap
                .create(WebArchive.class, "arquilian-demo-test.war")
                .addClasses(Department.class,ApplicationConfig.class,
                        JPAResource.class,
                        DepartmentResource.class)
                .addAsWebInfResource("test-web.xml",
                                    "web.xml")
                .addAsResource("test-persistence.xml",
                            "META-INF/persistence.xml");
    }

    //Method to be tested
```

```
@Test
@InSequence(1)
public void testAddDeptResource() {
    WebTarget target = ClientBuilder.newClient()
            .target(
    "http://localhost:8080/arquilian-demo-test/api/departments");
    // Crate a new dept.
    Department dept = new Department();
    dept.setDepartmentId(new Short((short) 10));
    dept.setDepartmentName("HR");
    Department  deptResult = target.request("application/json").
                post(Entity.json(dept), Department.class);
    assertEquals("HR", deptResult.getDepartmentName());
}

//Rest of the methods are removed for brevity
}
```

If you have used JUnit before the preceding test class implementation, it may look familiar to you, except for a couple of methods and APIs:

- The `createDeployment()` method used in this example generates a web archive and deploys it to the container. You do not need to build and deploy an entire application for testing a specific API. The `ShrinkWrap` class exposes APIs to create a WebArchive. You can use the `addClasses()` method on the WebArchive to add only the required classes in the web archive file.

- Use the `WebArchive::addAsWebInfResource()` API to specify different configuration files for testing. For instance, in the preceding example's API, calling `WebArchive::addAsWebInfResource("test-web.xml", "web.xml")` adds `test-web.xml` to the web archive in the place of `web.xml`. This feature allows you to specify a different set of deployment descriptors and configuration files for the purpose of testing. All the test-related resources, such as deployment descriptors and configuration files, are stored in the `src/test/resources` folder.

The complete source code for this example is available on the Packt website. You can download the example from the Packt website link that we mentioned at the beginning of this book, in the *Preface*. In the downloaded source code, see the `rest-appendix-arquillian` project to a get a feel for the end-to-end implementation.

Running Arquillian tests

Once all the necessary settings and test classes are ready, you can run the Arquillian tests. This process is just like running any unit tests in your project. For example, with Maven, you can use the following command:

```
mvn test
```

Arquillian takes the following steps to run the tests:

1. When the test is run, the `@org.junit.runner.RunWith(Arquillian.class)` annotation present on the test class tells JUnit to invoke Arquillian for running the tests instead of the default runner built into JUnit.
2. Arquillian then looks for a `public static` method annotated with the `@org.jboss.arquillian.container.test.api.Deployment` annotation in the test class to retrieve the deployable archive.
3. In the next step, Arquillian contacts the container configured in `arquillian.xml` and deploys the archive to the container.
4. All methods annotated with `@org.junit.Test` are run now.

> An in-depth coverage of Arquillian is beyond the scope of this book. To learn more about Arquillian, visit `http://arquillian.org`.
> The Jersey framework comes with built-in support for unit testing the JAX-RS server-side components. However, this lacks many features as compared to Arquillian and is not an ideal tool for performing full-fledged integration tests on Java EE components. You can learn more about the Jersey test framework at `https://jersey.java.net/documentation/latest/test-framework.html`.

Using third-party entity provider frameworks with Jersey

We discussed the various frameworks for JSON processing (and binding) in Chapter 2, *Java APIs for JSON Processing*. In this section, we will see how to tell the JAX-RS runtime to use a different entity provider framework (also known as the binding framework) instead of the default one provided by the container.

When you deploy the JAX-RS 2.0 application on the WebLogic or GlassFish server, the runtime automatically adds MOXy as the JSON binding framework for your application. Note that MOXy is EclipseLink's object-to-XML and object-to-JSON mapping provider. However, you can override the default JSON processor framework offered by the Jersey runtime with one that you may prefer for your application.

The following example overrides the default JSON framework used in the Jersey implementation with Jackson (`https://github.com/FasterXML/jackson`):

1. The first step is to add a dependency to the JSON processor framework that you want to use. For instance, to use Jackson, you need to add the `jackson-jaxrs-json-provider` and `jackson-databind` JAR files to the application.

2. Jersey allows you to disable the MOXy JSON framework by setting the `jersey.config.disableMoxyJson` configuration property to `true`. You can do this by overriding `javax.ws.rs.core.Application::getProperties()`. This is shown in the code snippet given towards the end of this section.

3. The next step is to register the `Provider` class. You can register the `provider` class as a singleton, as this provider does not hold any state.

The following code snippet shows a configuration that you will need to make in the `Application` subclass to use `JacksonJsonProvider` as the JSON binding framework:

```
//Other imports are omitted for brevity
import javax.ws.rs.core.Application;
import javax.ws.rs.ext.Provider;
import com.fasterxml.jackson.jaxrs.json.JacksonJsonProvider;

@javax.ws.rs.ApplicationPath("webresources")
public class HRApplication extends Application {

    @Override
    public Set<Class<?>> getClasses() {
        Set<Class<?>> resources = new java.util.HashSet<>();
        resources.add(HRService.class);
        return resources;
    }

    @Override
    public Set<Object> getSingletons() {
        Set<Object> set = new HashSet<>();
        // Register JacksonJsonProvider as a singleton
        // to allow reuse of ObjectMapper:
        set.add(
            new com.fasterxml.jackson.jaxrs.json.
            JacksonJsonProvider());
```

```
        return set;
    }

    @Override
    public Map<String, Object> getProperties() {
        Map<String, Object> map = new HashMap<>();
        //Disables configuration of MOXy Json feature.
        map.put("jersey.config.disableMoxyJson.server", true);
        return map;
    }
}
```

Transforming the JPA model into OData-enabled RESTful web services

Open Data Protocol (OData) is an open protocol for the web. We discussed the advantages of using OData with RESTful web APIs in the *Using Open Data Protocol (OData) with RESTful web APIs* section in Chapter 9, *The Role of RESTful APIs in Emerging Technologies*. In this section, we will see how to build the OData services for the **Java Persistence API (JPA)** model.

Apache Olingo is an open source Java library that implements the OData protocol. You can use the Apache Olingo framework to enable OData services for your JPA model.

With the Olingo framework, you can easily transform your JPA models into OData services using the OData JPA Processor Library.

The high-level steps for enabling the OData 2 services for your JPA model are listed as follows:

1. Build a web project to hold the RESTful web API components.
2. Generate the JPA entities as appropriate.
3. The next step is to configure the application to use the Apache Olingo framework for generating the OData services for the JPA model.
4. Add a dependency to the Olingo OData Library (Java) and the OData JPA Processor Library. The complete list of the JAR files is listed at http://olingo.apache.org/doc/odata2/tutorials/CreateWebApp.html.

5. Add a service factory implementation, which provides the means for initializing the OData JPA Processors and the data model provider (JPA entity). You can do this by adding a class that extends `org.apache.olingo.odata2.jpa.processor.api.ODataJPAServiceFactory`, as shown in the following:

```
//Imports are removed for brevity
public class ODataJPAServiceFactoryImpl extends
    ODataJPAServiceFactory {
  //HR-PU is the persistence unit
  //configured in persistence.xml for the JPA model
    final String PUNIT_NAME = "HR-PU";
  @Override
  public ODataJPAContext initializeODataJPAContext()
    throws ODataJPARuntimeException {
    ODataJPAContext oDataJPAContext =
        getODataJPAContext();
    oDataJPAContext.setEntityManagerFactory(
    JPAEntityManagerFactory
    .getEntityManagerFactory(PUNIT_NAME));
      oDataJPAContext.setPersistenceUnitName(PUNIT_NAME);
  return oDataJPAContext;
  }
  //Other methods are removed for brevity
}
```

6. Configure the web application by adding `CXFNonSpringJaxrsServlet` to `web.xml`. This servlet manages the OData features for your JPA model. Specify the service factory implementation class that you created in the last step as one of the `init` parameters for this servlet. The `web.xml` configuration may look like the following lines:

```
<servlet>
    <servlet-name>ODataEnabledJPAServlet</servlet-name>
    <servlet-class>
      org.apache.cxf.jaxrs.servlet.CXFNonSpringJaxrsServlet
    </servlet-class>
    <init-param>
      <param-name>javax.ws.rs.Application</param-name>
      <param-value>
        org.apache.olingo.odata2.core.rest.app.ODataApplication
      </param-value>
    </init-param>
    <init-param>
      <param-name>org.apache.olingo.odata2.service.factory</param-
name>
```

```
        <param-
value>com.packtpub.odata.ODataJPAServiceFactoryImpl</param-value>
        </init-param>
        <load-on-startup>1</load-on-startup>
    </servlet>
    <servlet-mapping>
      <servlet-name>ODataEnabledJPAServlet</servlet-name>
      <url-pattern>/odata/*</url-pattern>
    </servlet-mapping>
```

Now you can build the application and deploy it to a JAX-RS container, such as the GlassFish server. The Olingo framework will automatically convert all the JPA entities into the OData services. You can access the APIs via standard OData clients.

To test the deployment, try accessing the OData service as follows:
`http://localhost:8080/<appname>/odata`

You can go through the tutorial to learn how to build a Java client for OData services at `https://olingo.apache.org/doc/odata2/tutorials/OlingoV2BasicClientSample.html`.

> The complete source code for this example is available on the Packt website. You can download the example from the Packt website link that we mentioned at the beginning of this book, in the *Preface*. In the downloaded source code, see the `rest-chapter9-odata/rest-chapter9-odata-service` project.

Packaging and deploying JAX-RS applications

There are multiple ways to configure, package, and deploy a JAX-RS application. While configuring an application, you can use an annotation-based approach (for the Servlet 3.x-based container) and thereby avoid deployment descriptors such as `web.xml`. Alternatively, you can use a mix of both approaches, which uses both annotations and `web.xml`. This section describes the various configurations and packaging models followed for a JAX-RS web service application.

The JAX-RS specification states that a RESTful web service must be packaged as part of a web application if you want to run it in a container (web server or application server). Following this rule, any JAX-RS application that you want to deploy on a server must be packaged in a **Web Application Archive (WAR)** file. If the web service is implemented using an EJB, it must be packaged and deployed within a WAR file. The application classes are packaged in WEB-INF/classes or WEB-INF/lib and all the dependent library JARs are packaged in WEB-INF/lib. You can configure a JAX-RS application in the following ways:

- Using the javax.ws.rs.core.Application subclass without web.xml
- Using the Application subclass and web.xml
- Using web.xml without the Application subclass

Let's take a closer look at all these packaging models. The following discussion presumes the Jersey framework as the JAX-RS implementation. Though the basic packaging model is the same across all JAX-RS implementations, the exact value for certain metadata fields used in the deployment descriptors, such as the servlet class, may change with each implementation. Please refer to the product documentation if you are using a different JAX-RS implementation.

Packaging JAX-RS applications with an Application subclass

The servlet 3.0 specification allows you to build a web application without web.xml. You will annotate the component as appropriate without describing them in web.xml. JAX-RS also follows the same model and allows you to annotate components for supplying the metadata required by the runtime, thereby avoiding deployment descriptors, such as web.xml, for holding the metadata.

In this packaging model, you will define a class that extends javax.ws.rs.core.Application. Your subclass will have entries for all the root resources and providers, such as filters, interceptors, message body readers/writers, and feature classes, that are used in the application. Additionally, this class can return a map of custom application-wide properties. You can use the @javax.ws.rs.ApplicationPath annotation on the subclass to configure the context path for the RESTful web service.

The following is an example of a class that extends `javax.ws.rs.core.Application`. This class configures all the REST resources, message body reader and writer, filters, and interceptors that are used in the application:

```
//Other imports are removed for brevity
import javax.ws.rs.core.Application;

@javax.ws.rs.ApplicationPath("webresources")
public class HRApplication extends Application {
    //Get a set of root resource, provider and feature classes.
    @Override
    public Set<Class<?>> getClasses() {
        Set<Class<?>> resources = new java.util.HashSet<>();
        //Configure resource classes
        resources.add(HRResource.class);
        //Message body writer
        resources.add(CSVMessageBodyWriter.class);
        //Filters and interceptors
        resources.add(CORSResponseFilter.class);
        resources.add(ZippedWriterInterceptor.class);
        return resources;
    }
    //Get a map of custom application-wide properties
    @Override
    public Map<String, Object> getProperties() {
        return super.getProperties();
    }
    //Get Singletons instances of set of root resource,
    //provider and feature classes
    @Override
    public Set<Object> getSingletons() {
        return super.getSingletons();
    }
}
```

The default implementations of `getClasses()` and `getSingletons()` return empty sets, which tells the runtime to add all the resource and provider classes that are identified via annotations. While deploying the application, the JAX-RS runtime scans the deployed artifacts for the REST resource classes (identified by the `@Path` annotation) and providers (identified by the `@Provider` annotation), and automatically discovers and registers all the components before the activation of the application.

This packaging model assumes that the application is not bundled with any `web.xml` file. This model leverages the pluggability mechanism offered by the servlet 3.x framework to enable portability between containers. You cannot follow this model if you are deploying the application into servlet 2.x-based containers.

If you would like to have a `web.xml` file for the application, then follow the steps given in the next section to configure the applications with a servlet, which will show you how to update a `web.xml` file with entries for the JAX-RS servlet.

Packaging the JAX-RS applications with web.xml and an Application subclass

Sometimes, you may want to use both `Application` and `web.xml` for your JAX-RS application. This deployment model will be the best fit for the following scenarios, where you will use `web.xml`:

- To configure security for the application
- To specify some context parameters for the application
- To configure some container-specific parameters for the application

Depending on the capabilities of the target server, configuration entries in `web.xml` vary. This will be explained in the following sections.

Configuring web.xml for a servlet 2.x container

The following example illustrates the `web.xml` entries that you make for packaging a JAX-RS application, which contains both `Application` and `web.xml`. This example uses `com.packtpub.rest.ch4.service.HRApplication` as the application subclass. The following `web.xml` file shows the configuration entries that you may need to add for deploying into a servlet 2.x container. If there are multiple application subclasses, then you will need to configure them separately:

```
<web-app ... >
    <servlet>
        <servlet-name>jaxrs.servlet</servlet-name>

        <!-- Set this to fully qualified name of the
        Servlet offered by the JAX-RS runtime -->
        <servlet-class>
        org.glassfish.jersey.servlet.ServletContainer
        </servlet-class>

        <!-- Set this element to define the class that
        extends the javax.ws.rs.core.Application -->
        <init-param>
            <param-name>javax.ws.rs.Application</param-name>
```

```
                    <param-value>
                     com.packtpub.rest.ch4.service.HRApplication
                    </param-value>
            </init-param>
            <!--Use init params as appropriate-->
            <load-on-startup>1</load-on-startup>
        </servlet>
        <servlet-mapping>
            <servlet-name>jaxrs.servlet</servlet-name>
            <url-pattern>/webresources/*</url-pattern>
        </servlet-mapping>
    </web-app>
```

Configuring web.xml for a servlet 3.x container

If you are deploying the application on a servlet 3.x container, then the configuration entries are much simpler. In this case, you just need to mention the servlet name and servlet mapping, as follows (for each application subclass bundled in the application). The runtime will automatically add the servlet class and assign it to the name that you'd specified:

```
<web-app ...
    <servlet>
        <!-- Set this element to the fully qualified
        name of the class that extends javax.ws.rs.core.Application
        -->
         <servlet-name>
          com.packtpub.rest.ch4.service.HRApplication
         </servlet-name>
        <!-- servlet-class and init-param are not needed -->
    </servlet>
    <servlet-mapping>
        <servlet-name>
         com.packtpub.rest.ch4.service.HRApplication
        </servlet-name>
        <url-pattern>/webresources/*</url-pattern>
    </servlet-mapping>
</web-app>
```

Packaging the JAX-RS applications with web.xml and without an Application subclass

In some cases, your JAX-RS application will not have any `Application` subclass apart from `web.xml`. Though this scenario is rare, the framework supports such a packaging model.

Configuring web.xml for the servlet 2.x container

If the JAX-RS application does not have an `Application` subclass in the project, then you need to specify a fully qualified servlet class that is used by the JAX-RS runtime and a servlet-mapping entry in `web.xml`. You can also specify the package where the runtime should scan though to find the JAX-RS components, such as class resources, filters, interceptors, and so on.

The following example shows the configuration entries that you may need to make in `web.xml` to deploy a JAX-RS application without the `Application` subclass on the servlet 2.0 based container:

```xml
<web-app>
    <servlet>
        <servlet-name>jaxrs.servlet</servlet-name>
        <servlet-class>
         org.glassfish.jersey.servlet.ServletContainer
        </servlet-class>
        <!-- Register resources and providers
         under com.packtpub.rest -->
        <init-param>
            <param-name>
             jersey.config.server.provider.packages</param-name>
            <param-value>com.packtpub.rest</param-value>
        </init-param>

        <!-
         Register custom providers
         (not needed if they are in com.packtpub.rest)   -->
        <init-param>
            <param-name>
             jersey.config.server.provider.classnames</param-name>
            <param-value>
             com.packtpub.rest.filetr.SecurityRequestFilter;
             com.packtpub.rest.filetr.Logger
           </param-value>
        </init-param>
    </servlet>
```

```
    <servlet-mapping>
        <servlet-name>jaxrs.servlet</servlet-name>
        <url-pattern>/webresources/*</url-pattern>
    </servlet-mapping>

</web-app>
```

Configuring web.xml for the servlet 3.x container

The following web.xml shows the configurations to deploy a JAX-RS application on the servlet 3.0 container. In this case, we will add only the mapping entry and not the corresponding servlet class. The container is responsible for adding the corresponding servlet class automatically for the javax.ws.rs.core.Application servlet name. The following web.xml demonstrates this configuration:

```
<web-app ...>
    <servlet>
        <servlet-name>javax.ws.rs.core.Application</servlet-name>
    </servlet>
    <servlet-mapping>
        <servlet-name>javax.ws.rs.core.Application</servlet-name>
        <url-pattern>/webresources/*</url-pattern>
    </servlet-mapping>
</web-app>
```

Note that in the preceding case, the runtime will automatically detect and register JAX-RS components (by scanning through the annotations).

Summary

In this appendix, we discussed the tools needed for building a JAX-RS application and the integration testing of JAX-RS applications with Arquillian. We also discussed an example showing how to convert JPA models into OData-enabled RESTful web services. We ended our discussions by taking a look at the various packaging and deployment models for JAX-RS applications.

Index

HATEOAS p34-35

Printed in Poland
by Amazon Fulfillment
Poland Sp. z o.o., Wrocław